HOW EDUCATORS DECIDE
WHO IS
LEARNING DISABLED

HOW EDUCATORS DECIDE WHO IS LEARNING DISABLED

Challenge to Psychology and Public Policy in the Schools

By

MARY LEE SMITH

Laboratory of Educational Research
University of Colorado
Boulder, Colorado

CHARLES C THOMAS • PUBLISHER
Springfield • Illinois • U.S.A.

Published and Distributed Throughout the World by

CHARLES C THOMAS • PUBLISHER

2600 South First Street

Springfield, Illinois, 62717, U.S.A.

© *1982 by* CHARLES C THOMAS • PUBLISHER

ISBN 0-398-04733-2

Library of Congress Catalog Card Number: 82-50684

With **THOMAS BOOKS** *careful attention is given to all details of manufacturing and
design. It is the Publisher's desire to present books that are satisfactory as to their physical
qualities and artistic possibilities and appropriate for their particular use.* THOMAS
BOOKS *will be true to those laws of quality that assure a good name and good will.*

Printed in the United States of America

RX-1

PREFACE

Because its title may be misleading, let me first state what this book is not. It is not a survey of the field of learning disabilities. Nor is it a manual of methods for identifying the learning disabled. Instead this book presents evidence and analysis from research on a significant educational problem.

Educators are now faced with the need to determine whether certain children qualify for the rights of the handicapped and the services of special education. They must do this, in the case of learning disabilities, without an unequivocal definition or means of detecting the disorder. The purposes of this book are to document the process by which educators determine whether a child is learning disabled and to sketch the antecedents and implications of this process.

I offer this explanation of the subtitle. Psychology is the discipline that dominates the process by which educators decide who is learning disabled. Surely, physicians, teachers, occupational therapists, and others are involved. Yet the realm of discourse they use is psychological. The limits of this discipline are fully tested in the identification of learning disabilities. Public policy is likewise tested. Although their intentions were honorable, government's efforts to protect the rights of the handicapped have imposed legalistic and onerous regulations on educator's decision-making. The actual effects of the policy may prove inimical to its intentions.

ACKNOWLEDGMENTS

The people of Belleview endured my intrusions with grace. I wish to express my respect and gratitude to them. Thanks are also due to the following people for the following reasons:

Dr. Lorrie Shepard, for allowing me use of data from the study she directed (Part III);

Dean Richard Turner, for making clerical support available;

Sue Reissig, Jo Kearney, Barbara Pazier, and Sheri Harms, for typing the manuscript;

Marilyn Averill, Alan Davis, Cathy George, Nancy George, Jean Rice, Lorrie Shepard, Joan Smokoski, and Elaine Worrell, for reading the manuscript.

I owe special thanks to Gene V Glass who painstakingly edited and made suggestions about the manuscript. No writer could ask for a better model or editor. If only his pupil were more able. Although I can, with his advice, remove the glitches, I can never match the sound his words make on the page.

TABLE OF CONTENTS

TABLE OF CONTENTS
(continued)

Page

HOW EDUCATORS DECIDE
WHO IS
LEARNING DISABLED

PART I

DESCRIBING HOW EDUCATORS DECIDE WHO IS LEARNING DISABLED: THE STAFFING PROCESS

Part I is a portrayal of the process by which educators decide whether the particular children referred to them are learning disabled. The series of activities--referral, assessment, staffing conference, and placement decision--is collectively referred to as the staffing process. The staffing process is governed by very detailed Federal and State laws and regulations. Despite the legally imposed commonalities of the explicit, formal features of the staffing process, variations from school district to school district exist. Therefore the first step in understanding how educators decide who is learning disabled must be a naturalistic study of a single district. The case chosen was Belleview, Colorado.

CHAPTER ONE

INTRODUCTION TO THE STAFFING PROCESS

Ten years ago a teacher who suspected that a child had a handicap went first to the principal. The principal might have some tests run by the psychologist and might talk to the child's parents. Whether or not he asked for this advice, he alone decided if the child should be placed in a special education class. The decision was his. It was local. It was not systematic. And undoubtedly mistakes were made and injustices were perpetrated. Perhaps a child who needed special education was denied it if, say, the school district could not afford to run a program for chidren with his sort of handicap. Sometimes the opposite error was made; when, for example, a principal assigned a child who was not handicapped to special education, responding, perhaps to pressure from a frustrated teacher or parent. This error was particularly severe and poignant when the child was a member of a minority group.

Now there exist laws that were designed to prevent these errors. These laws govern the procedures for deciding who is handicapped and who, therefore, deserves the rights of the handicapped for special education. The laws were intended to make the decision-making process--the "staffing process"--as it is called, standard throughout the nation. They have taken the powers of decision out of the hands of teachers and principals and turned these powers over to staffing committees.

At a national meeting in 1978, a federal official said that there was hardly a school district in the country that would not be affected by these laws. She was right. But does the staffing process work in the manner she thinks? Has it eliminated the errors and injustices of the old ways? What are the costs to schools and to society of the new system? Are there side-effects that its advocates did not anticipate?

Unlike most subjects of case studies, the "staffing process" is not an event or place. It is an abstraction that stands for all the activities people in a school district carry out in deciding whether a child is to be declared handicapped and placed in special education. Yet, collectively, these activities can be regarded as a case because they are highly interdependent, they are regulated by a set of laws and rules, and thus have assumed a uniform shape. Clear patterns of action of educators have emerged.

The events that shaped the staffing process into a system can be briefly described as follows. Parents and special interest groups representing the handicapped brought suits against school districts. This litigation was aimed at forcing the public schools to assume responsibility for handicapped children's special education. The cases were generally settled in favor of the plaintiffs and established the principle that the handicapped were a "class" with special legal status. As a member of this class, children had a "right" to education at public expense, that the local public school system must provide it, that it must be "appropriate" (i.e., tailored to his individual needs), that, as much as possible, it must be delivered in the same building or classroom with age-mates who were not handicapped (the idea called "mainstreaming"). The court cases established the rights and responsibilities of this new class--the handicapped. It remained for state and federal laws to specify procedures for determining whether or not a particular individual was to be

3

defined as handicapped and thus assume the rights of the class. The other primary function of the legislation was to distribute the rights to all handicapped persons, not just the ones involved directly in litigation. Powerful lobbies made up of parents and other advocates of handicapped children worked hard to shape the provision of the legislation and to encourage its passage by Congress. Professional associations of special educators, school psychologists and others joined the movement. The resulting federal law, Public Law 94-142, the Education for All Handicapped Children Act of 1975, reflected the interests of the lobbying groups as well as the principles established in the legal cases. Besides reaffirming the rights of the handicapped to a "free, appropriate education," the law and its accompanying Rules and Regulations laid down procedures that a school system must follow in determining whether a child is handicapped. These procedures included the use of valid tests, administered by trained clinicians, in the child's dominant language; the condition that several clinicians representing different specialites be involved in assessment, that the parents have the right to review all assessment data and ask for another evaluation by a professional not employed by the school district; that the parents and several professionals be involved in the decision about whether the child is handicapped and about what his program should be; that parents can challenge the decision in impartial hearings; that "due process" procedures must be employed throughout.

The federal law also provided large sums of money to school districts (funneled through state departments of education) to help discharge these new responsibilities. A bureaucracy has grown up since the passage of the legislation for providing "technical assistance" to states and local school districts as well as monitoring their compliance with prescribed procedures. Meanwhile most state legislatures have passed state laws on education for the handicapped. These laws have been even more specific on staffing procedures, providing clearer definitions for the various handicapping conditions, thereby apparently standardizing further the districts' decision-making practices. These laws have provided additional funds to local school districts to cope with these new responsibilities. More special education bureaucracy has developed in the state departments of education.

With moderate success, schools have struggled to comply with regulations from Washington and their state capitols. Despite the apparent standardization of the staffing process, however, a local school district has considerable latitude in deciding who is handicapped. There are definitions and criteria for selection of each handicapping condition written in both state and federal rules. Yet even for the best understood of these diagnostic categories, the definitions are vague enough for errors to be made and to allow variations in interpretation from staffing committee to staffing committee. This is evident in the dramatic variation from state to state and from district to district in the rates of handicapped children served. Of course it is possible to hypothesize alternatively that there is a true difference in prevalence of say, mental retardation in different states. But there exists no independent evidence or logical justification for the extreme variations that exist. The preferred hypothesis is that variations in decision-making processes and implicit eligibility criteria exist among individuals and schools involved in staffing. The variation in local criteria and decision-making processes produces the variation in numbers of handicapped children identified. Some of these local variations are portrayed in Chapter Two and explained in Part II of this book.

The handicap known as learning disability has always been controversial and difficult to define. Definitions of learning disabilities are myriad, ranging from medical-sounding terms such as "minimal brain dysfunction," to pop psychology terms such as "educationally out-of-step." There are no symptoms that unequivocally indicate whether an individual has a learning disability. Instead there is a welter of characteristics said to be clues that a learning disability exists. These vary from "mixed dominance" (where a child has not clearly established a preference for right or left handedness) to "high distractibility" to "reading below potential" (where a child's reading achievement score is well below his intellectual ability score). Definitions vary; yet they have one thing in common: signs of learning disabilities are never simply a behavior, a test score, or a reading from a device such as an electroencephalogram. Diagnosing a learning disability always requries an *inference*, a leap, based on several separate characteristics. What is troublesome is that these same characteristics are shared by many normal children. Twenty years of research have not removed this ambiguity. Diagnosis of a learning disability always involves some person--usually a parent or teacher--with some personal ideas about what a learning disability is, having recognized a problem and sounded the alarm.

Because the definitions of learning disabilities are so vague, schools have great latitude in deciding who belongs in this category. For any individual child examined for a learning disability, a staffing committee may uncover sufficient reliable evidence to support the inference that he is indeed disabled. But a committee might gather data on another child that are equivocal, yet still declare the child disabled because he is a boy or speaks only Spanish, or because he disturbs his teacher or has some other characteristics that ought to be irrevelant to the diagnosis. Because of the vague criteria and definitions, a district's staffing committee may be influenced by a variety of motives (also irrelevant to the child's characteristics) such as the need of the institution to protect itself, the needs of the parents to justify themselves, the needs of the teachers to deal with deviance by labeling and shifting responsibility for the deviant, the needs of the professional groups or individuals to establish their technical expertise and authority to deal with the handicapped, the needs of the local schools to maintain their traditional autonomy in the face of external demands for restructuring, the needs of the school to avoid litigation. All of these motives can be expressed in the course of the staffing process. Learning disabilities, with its problematic definitions and dubious scientific credentials, give room for these needs to be expressed, and thus are one good test for how the staffing process works.

Learning disabilities also attract the attention of laymen, professionals and scholars because of their prevalence. Of all the handicapped children identified by government surveys, almost one-third are said to be learning disabled. The adjacent and similarly vague categories of speech handicaps and emotional disturbance, added to the figures for learning disabilities constitute almost three-quarters of the handicapped.

These were reasons enough for me to study the staffing process. Doing so involved the use of multiple methods of research. The principal ones were naturalistic. I studied the staffing process in a single school district, first-hand and over a six month period. Based on extensive observations, interviews, and examination of the extensive documents typically produced in the staffing process, a case study was written. This product appears in Chapter Two of this book and the methods are explained in more detail in Appendix A.

The methods of scholarly analysis and review of professional literature were used to understand and explain the events and forces that were uncovered in the case study. The results of this analysis are contained in Part II, Chapters Three through Nine.

The question of whether the staffing process studied in Belleview School District was unique or typical was addressed in Part III of this book. Chapter 10 consists of a report of the methods and results of a study of the staffing of learning disabilities throughout Colorado. In Chapter 11, the national picture is considered.

The research reported in this book was pursued without assumptions about the correctness of requirements imposed on schools by federal or state laws or court rulings. All conditions, events, and consequences of the staffing process were judged to be subject to inspection and analysis. I invite the reader to adopt this same perspective.

CHAPTER TWO

THE STAFFING PROCESS IN BELLEVIEW SCHOOL DISTRICT: A CASE STUDY

BELLEVIEW: HOW THE SETTING INFLUENCES STAFFING

Belleview is a city of 100,00; a suburb of a large city in Colorado. Both Belleview the town and the school district are prosperous. The local economy is dominated by commerce, light and high technology industry, recreation and tourism. The population is predominantly middle and upper-middle class, white, and well-educated. The children served by the schools reflect the community. The average intelligence of the school population is well above the average for the nation as a whole. Consequently, one would expect fewer children categorized as mentally retarded, since that designation is usually defined according to the national distribution of intelligence quotients; and such is the case. The over-all percentage of handicapped children in Belleview is about the same as for the state of Colorado, however. This district has proportionately more children classified as having emotional disturbance, speech disorders, or learning disabilities. Parent's expectations for their children's educational performance tend to be high, and teachers' expectations match them. A child who is considered "educationally out of step" in Belleview might go unnoticed in a nearby city; he might even be a star.

Black and Chicano children are scarce in Belleview, so that the special problems related to the coincidence of ethnic background and special education placement are rarely encountered. Of course there are poor people and ethnic minorities in Belleview, but they tend to be concentrated in three or four small neighborhoods in less than half a dozen schools. An observer stated that it is always a surprise to encounter someone who isn't white, as if such a person did not really belong here.

This is a school district with sophisticated parents who know their rights and demand them, who volunteer frequently to help the schools, and come often into the classroom. They are, in general, the allies of the public schools. Teachers and adminstrators are sophisticated; they pick up quickly on most new trends in education and they are eager to experiment with them. There is a large budget for conducting in-service education, hiring guest speakers, and paying for curricular improvement. As in most districts striving to maintain personnel and programs while enrollment declines, Belleview administrators are trying to increase efficiency and centralize authority over decision-making.

Belleview has not succumbed to the general malaise in education nationally. A school bond issue was passed recently, in an era of tax revolt and contracting of budgets. In an era of increasing adversarial relations in education, Belleview has escaped any serious legal action against its schools, nor has it suffered a teacher strike. It is a good system in many ways.

Yet there have been rumblings about special education, generally concerned that the budget for general education has been

9

decreasing while, for the past three years, the budget for special education is increasing. From the same quarters comes the mild but growing complaint that too much time by too many highly-paid professionals is being spent in the special education staffing process.

Belleview's special education department is competently staffed and managed. Its members have made sure that nearly all the district teachers and principals have received in-service training to recognize handicapped children and to understand the provisions of laws and mandated procedures for staffing and educating handicapped pupils.

The director of special education reports to the assistant superintendent; yet for many of his duties he is responsible to the state special education bureaucracy as well. Several classes of the personnel (e.g., nurses, psychologists) involved in the staffing process report to administrators other than the director of special education.

HOW THE STAFFING PROCESS IS DESIGNED TO WORK IN BELLEVIEW SCHOOLS

The staff of the special education department has devised a standard set of procedures that each school is supposed to follow in its staffing process. This district model was constructed to ensure that the activities and resulting decisions would be both educationally sound and in accord with the regulations handed down from the state and federal authorities. Standard criteria for judging which children are handicapped and eligible for services have been developed for each category of handicap to insure that the staffing process results in decisions that are correct and uniform from one school to another. The following vignette about a hypothetical student suspected of having a learning disability illustrates the way the district model for the staffing process is designed to work in all Belleview schools. Joey is not a real person and these "events" did not occur.

10

THE CASE OF JOEY

Miss Jones is concerned about Joey's progress in her second grade class. She has discussed this concern with Joey's mother during two parent conferences and now takes this concern to the school principal. Together they look over Joey's classroom work and his achievement test results. Miss Jones says that Joey is doing very well in math but is reading only at the mid-first grade level. He seems to have trouble understanding spoken directions. The principal proposes filing a Form A* (Referral) and beginning a child study. Joey's parents sign this form providing their consent for a child study and signifying that they have been informed of their rights. The reading specialist is then asked to do an assessment of Joey's reading ability. The special education teacher in the resource room of the school is asked to consult with Miss Jones and observe Joey in class to get any ideas about Joey's difficulty. After these assessments are completed, an Educational Planning Conference takes place (school people refer to it as mini-staffing). At this conference the principal, parent, teacher, reading specialist, and resource room teacher hear the results of the asessments and decide what to do next. Since the results do not look serious enough to warrant immediate attention by special education, those attending the conference decide to try some remedial techniques suggested by the resource room teacher. These are to be carried out by Joey's classroom teacher who is to watch closely to see if Joey's difficulties are overcome. One month later, as prearranged, the same people get together again to evaluate the effect of these remedial techniques. Unfortunately, Joey has not responded as they had hoped, so they decide to file Form B, the Request for Special Education Staffing. Joey's mother agrees in writing, again having read detailed information about what the staffing process will entail and what the rights of the parents are in such

---

*See Appendix B for samples of forms used by Belleview Schools.

11

a situation (for example, Joey's parents have the right to request that some other qualified professionals not employed by the schools do an independent, separate assessment of Joey, at the school district's expense).

Up until this point the special education department has not been involved except to open a file on Joey in their central office. The school, not special education, has so far been responsible. Upon receiving Form B, however, the special education department is engaged. Its office personnel set a date for a staffing conference which will terminate the staffing process in about one month's time. Notices are sent to the various clinicians (specialists in evaluating various aspects of the functioning of children) who are assigned to Joey's school. Joey's name goes up on a large board where each clinician checks off when his or her assessments are complete. A person in the special eduation office entitled Staffing Chairman makes sure all the assessments get done and the proper forms are completed. She reviews all the results as they come in. The perspectives of many different professionals are used in staffing to provide a "wholistic assessment" of the child, provide many sources of information and prevent (as the laws forbid) any one person or any single instrument from having too much weight in the eventual staffing decision. This procedure prevents violations of civil rights that might occur from the use of a racially or ethnically biased test in the staffing of a child of a minority group.

Among the clinicians doing the assessment (likely to be a school psychologist, a social worker, nurse, speech-language specialist, and perhaps others) each one decides what tests and how many tests he will administer to do the best assessment job possible.

The staffing conference is the concluding event. There all the specialists who did any assessments on Joey meet with the parents, teacher, and principal. The Staffing Chairman represents the special education department, manages the meeting, records information, and guides the conferees to a decision. Test results are reviewed. As a group, the conferees decide whether Joey is handicapped according to the district criteria and what his particular deficits are. They judge from the data that his educational achievement is significantly lower than one would predict from his abilities. They rule out language and cultural differences as well as vision and hearing loss, any of which conditions might have accounted for the observed discrepancy between his ability and his achievement. Since these data correspond to the district's criteria for determining learning disabilities, those in attendance declare that Joey has a learning disability and qualifies for special education.* The people at the meeting discuss what services would be appropriate for

---

*The district defines a Learning Disability as having a "significant discrepancy between estimated intellectual potential and actual level of performance which is related to basic disorders in the learning process." To be eligible a child must:

"Exhibit a valid significant educational deficit, defined as a difference between achievement and anticipated achievement which is significant at or below the 10th percentile in areas of total reading, total language arts or total math.

This discrepancy must not be secondary to limited intellectual capacity, sensory impairment, emotional or motivational disorders and/or experiential or cultural information.

Processing and/or communicative disorders are assumed and may be identifiable but are not necessarily directly measurable. Professional judgment of the assessment team will be considered.

The staffing team agrees to, in writing, evidence which supports the conclusion that the student has a learning disability.

The staffing team will consider alternatives that would explain the discrepancy between the intellectual potential and the achievement level of the student. These alternatives may include low motivation, cultural differences, environmental deprivation, test idiosyncratic performance, etc. The staffing team will determine that these alternatives are not the primary reason for the discrepancy between the intellectual potential and the achievement of the child."

his needs and make a recommendation for his placement in a resource room. There he will meet individually with a special education teacher for one hour each day to work on his areas of difficulty. The rest of the day he will spend in his regular classroom. Joey's mother is asked for, and provides her signature indicating her consent to this decision. An Individual Educational Planning conference is then convened to set up goals and objectives for Joey's work. His mother is asked to participate in this activity and agree to the finished document. The system provides for a reevaluation, at the end of the year or sooner if the resource room teacher thinks it appropriate, to determine whether Joey has met his objectives and can return full-time to the regular classroom. Copies of the forms reviewed and signed in this meeting are then returned to the central office where they will be available only to the special education personnel directly dealing with Joey, to his parents, or to the personnel from the state department of special education in their periodic reviews of district procedures.

If Joey's parents had not agreed with the procedures or the decision, they would have had the right to appeal through prescribed channels. The final appeal would be decided at a hearing presided over by an "impartial hearing officer" as prescribed by federal law. Not given satisfaction at that hearing, the parents would have the right to sue the school district under the provisions of P.L. - 94-142 and Section 504 of the Rehabilitation Act of 1973. Although members of the special education staff are prepared for this, they make efforts to avoid it if possible.

The vignette about Joey is idealized, as policies are, representing the way the Belleview staffing process is supposed to work. But policies help or hurt depending on how they are translated into practice by fallible humans. What follows are the stories of two real children and their encounters with the staffing process.

HOW JENNY CAME TO BE CALLED HANDICAPPED

The date is the nineteenth of March, 1979 the day of Jenny Johnson's staffing conference at Aspen Elementary School. Today is the culmination of eight months in which Jenny has been involved in the special education staffing process. Now it will be decided whether Jenny is handicapped, whether, more specifically, she has a learning disability, and whether she will be taken from her regular second grade class and placed full-time in a special education class.

Kathy, who presides over the Remedial lab and coordinates all of Aspen's staffings, pulls metal chairs up to a long cafeteria table and points out the coffee pot to each person who comes in. The music teacher, whose room this is, remains seated for a while at her desk and so at first appears to preside over the meeting. Then she leaves us to her room, full of music-making gadgets and musical notes and symbols on the walls. The room is dazzling from the reflection of sun off the snow outside in the courtyard. It is eight in the morning and people struggle against the remains of sleep in their systems.

Aspen is fairly typical of elementary schools built in the late 1960's--sprawling one-story blond brick with lots of glass. The school is large; three self-contained classes for each grade, two special education classes. It seems to be a bustling, happy, well-run place. The community is a thin slice of middle-class America.

We find our places aroud the table. There are eleven of us, everyone but Jenny's mother is a professional person; all except she and I are employed by the district. Mrs. Johnson places herself in the chair between the psychologist and the social worker. Perhaps she does this instinctively, seeking allies. Yet there are no adversaries here, surely. Everyone has expressed the sincere wish to make the best decision for Jenny.

Looking back from the perspective of a year, I recognize that there were only three people there whose personalities absorbed my attention. I refer to them by name and describe them briefly. The other remain with me merely as occupants of positions or roles and are referred to as such--the principal, the teacher, the special education teacher into whose class Jenny was likely to be placed, the school psychologist, the social worker, the speech teacher, and the nurse. All are anonymous except Karen, Mrs. Johnson, and Kathy.

Karen was the Staffing Chairman, employed by and responsible to the district's central administration of special education. Her role was stressful. She not only had to keep the meeting going but record and integrate the reports of several clinicians. It was her job to impose standard criteria on school committees that have disparate populations and idiosyncratic ideas about what constitutes handicaps such as learning disabilities. She chaired almost 300 of these conferences in a year. She always performed with intelligence and poise on those difficult occasions when the school's preferences conflicted with the district. She blended professionalism with empathy; there is a severely handicapped child in her own family.

No one would think of Mrs. Johnson as a pushy mother. She looked little older than a child herself, with long straight hair and casual clothes. She spoke barely a word during the conference, yet watched intently as each person reported. She was not about to be overawed by technical jargon. I had gone some weeks before to her apartment to meet her. She said that perhaps Jenny needed some help but would "come out all right." She was more worried that some people at the school wanted Jenny in a special education class full-time. She has been shown the class and thought it was full of rough boys who might distract and be a bad influence on her daughter. She was glad that at least some people at school did not think Jenny was retarded or emotionally disturbed.

Kathy was trained as a learning disabilities specialist but managed the Remedial Lab--a place where children who were having difficulty with their academic skills could be sent for help. Not teaching herself, she tested, prescribed, and evaluated progress of Remedial Lab children tutored by volunteers. She held a prominent position in the school, and was deferred to on matters of which

16

children need help beyond what was available in class and Remedial Lab. She seemed to convey to teachers the idea that they should refer children with problems to someone or some program with greater expertise.

The group is settled and Karen begins by introducing the staff to Mrs. Johnson, who is already quite familiar with everyone. As I have come to expect with each staffing conference, Karen explains the purpose of the meeting to Mrs. Johnson.

Karen: "Each person here has worked with Jenny. What we are trying to do is find out what seems to be interfering with her classroom learning. What we're looking for is any significant discrepancies. We're looking for patterns. We want to come up with an explanation. Please feel free to add any information we might leave out or ask us any questions you might have as we go along. Marty, will you please start out by telling us how Jenny is doing in the classroom?"

The order of speakers in staffing conferences hardly varies. The staffing chairmen have worked out this arrangement as the most efficient. The classroom teacher always gave an account of the child first, then the nurse, followed by the social worker, special education diagnostician, speech-language specialist, the reading specialist, and last the school psychologist. Each presented a report of the assessment given, much like grand rounds in medicine and psychiatry. Each clinician, it seemed to me, settled into a carefully defined, professional, and ceremoniously official role. Each knew what part to play, what words to choose, what emotions to express. This was not difficult to understand; each one had gone through scores of these conferences.

Marty, the classroom teacher begins. "I had Jenny last year in my first grade class. She was distractible and seemed academically lower than the other kids so we had her tested and some problems showed up. She attended special education summer school and in the fall she seemed to be caught up with the others. Then the problems started again. Now her reading level is even lower."

Karen: "What are her skill levels specifically? How does she compare with your other kids?"

Teacher: "In individual reading she is in the lower third of my (second grade) class. She excells in math facts."

The principal breaks in to clarify a point the teacher has not made very well. "Marty, tell how your class is different from ordinary second grade classes."

Teacher: "I have a selected group of kids who were all low last year in first grade. They all were in Remedial Lab. They all have learning problems. In my class all the instruction is individual or small-group."

Karen: "Other than being distractible, are there any other behavioral problems?"

Teacher: "Her attention has improved, but there is a problem with bossiness. The other kids don't like it. She's easily frustrated. She almost comes to tears when she can't pass our mastery tests."

Karen: "What about her language skills?"

Teacher: "They seem adequate as far as being able to communicate and write stories. But spelling is a problem for her.

The teacher seemed a little frustrated at that point because the words of her oral report did not reflect what I knew to be her feelings about the seriousness of Jenny's problem. Karen's questions had brought out several strengths as well as weaknesses and did not make Jenny look deficient in comparison with other children. In an interview held two weeks earlier, the teacher had elaborated on Jenny's problems in a less ambiguous way.

"When she came into my first grade class in May last year she seemed to be low relative to the rest of my class. So automatically I had her tested by the reading specialist and recommended summer school."

The teacher then showed me the report of the summer school teacher, a learning disabilities specialist. It said that Jenny had made good progress over the summer but still had trouble "crossing the midline"* and this interfered with her writing. The teacher (Marty) continued her interview: "Jenny has always needed a lot of help. Her attention span is short even on a one-to-one basis. It's hard for her to work independently. She always needs me to repeat instructions. We found out that she was in resource room (special education) when she lived in Centennial, before the family moved here. They had seen auditory problems, related to following directions. She repeated kindegarten so she's a year older than the rest of the class. It's been hard for her to develop friendships, which don't seem to last long. She's better now."

To understand Marty's personal ideas and beliefs about learning disabilities I asked her if Jenny has a "perceptual problem?"

"She's not hearing what we think she's hearing. I'm using a reading program that's based on visual and oral activities--learning vocabulary from wall charts and making an oral response. In this program, which is an individualized, mastery-learning system, reading and langauge arts are learned together, so if you can't do one you may have problems all the way through. She also has vision problems. She just got a new prescription this week, so she may not have been seeing clearly."

"Is Jenny handicapped?"

No, but she needs some special help--some special attention."

"Does Jenny have an emotional problem?"

---

*See pages 61 and 120 for explanation of crossing the midline.

"Her behavior is distracting so much from her learning. It is difficult for her to stay on a task. She is easily distracted even one-to-one." She always has to have something in her hands. When she gets bored she bothers the other kids.

Marty reported continual consultations among herself and the reading specialist and Kathy the coordinator of the Remedial Room about Jenny's progress and about her performance on various reading and perceptual tests. "But all that is just not enough. She's still at the bottom of the class and needs more individual help than she gets from me." The best outcome of the staffing process, according to Marty, would be a full-time placement in a self-contained special education class where she could learn to control her behavior. Asked about the possibility of negative side-effects of such a decision, Marty said it was true that behavior problems can spread from four or five catalysts to other children, but at Aspen there was no negative labeling or negative connotation to special education. The teacher of the self-contained class is continuously reevaluating and aware of the need to get her kids back into the regular classroom.

Karen sees that Marty is finished and indicates it is the nurse's turn. She reads her written report, based on an inteview with Mrs. Johnson, in its entirety.

Nurse: "This was a normal pregnancy, labor, and delivery. Although the delivery was in the breech position, there were no breathing problems. She was a collicky baby. There were feeding problems. Mother indicated that it was an anxious and uneasy feeding situtation. She walked early (nine months old), talked without problems (at 18-24 months). She is left-handed. There were fine motor problems; she has a short attention span and is always fidgity. She had repeated throat or ear infections through age four. She had a myringotomy on both ears at age five. She had "T and A"in 1975; her tonsils were so large that she had to have some speech help to learn to form sounds again. She wears glasses and recently changed prescription. She passed her hearing screening. She is a small child for her age."

As the nurse pauses, **Nancy** the social worker who spends about a half day each week at Aspen, sees it is her turn and begins. "Jenny is the oldest of two children. She and her sister get along well except when Jenny gets too bossy. She has a good relationship with her mother. Her father spends a lot of time parenting especially when mother works. She can be kept track of; they always know where she is going to play. She often tests limits. She is *very* active and busy but not to the point of being a problem. She takes care of her things. She doesn't handle problem-solving all that well and needs help. She comes to her mother to talk when she has a problem. There's some indication of an early onset of puberty which might account for recent occasional moodiness. She's a happy child. She sings and has a good time. When she's unhappy she cries. Are there any questions?"

There were none. Nancy's written report outlined the methods she had used in her assessment: observation of Jenny in the classroom, discussion with her teacher and principal, review of records, and an interview with Mrs. Johnson. Information about the following was gathered: relationships with parents, siblings, peers and school staff; self-concept, emotional expression, acceptance of limit-setting, resolution of conflict, organization of time and life energy, use and care of material belongings, problem-solving capacity, independent functioning, and strengths. Nancy had spent about eight hours with this study. Her written report also carried the following recommendation--"Appropriate academic planning in least restrictive environment."

Because I had seen all the written reports, I already knew what was not then evident from the routine course of the conference: that there was a basic difference of opinion about what was wrong and what was to be done with Jenny.

Kathy recognizes that the social worker is finished and begins to given the results of her own clinical evaluation.

21

"When she came in (to the Remedial Lab) we were concerned because she was eight years old and reading at the pre-primer level. The Illinois Test of Psycholinguistic Abilities results show that there were not any significant problems except that all auditory areas were weaker than the visual, affecting decoding skills, being able to retain words. . . . I'm concerned about some of Jenny's behavior. She subvocalizes. She shows some impulsive responses. There's perseveration. On one test she chose the first picture 11 out of 13 times without thinking about making the correct response. The social worker reported that Jenny is very busy at home; she is awfully busy at school, too. She's very distractible even on a one-to-one basis. The volunteer only has her attention for about five minutes. She tries to see what's going on around her. Her behavior is affecting more than just reading. Her math scores are only at the 9th percentile.

Karen interrupts. "Is she understanding concepts or is it a problem with computation?"

The **teacher** interrrupts. "Is that percentile based on age or grade?" When Kathy says that age-norms were used, Marty says that Jenny is doing fine in math if one compares her with children of her own grade.

Kathy explains Jenny's poor performance on Kathy's tests. "The test deals a lot with math concepts and also is presented auditorially."

There the conversation died a little. The professionals were using their short-cut language and Mrs. Johnson looked confused and uncomprehending. Conflicting data about Jenny had been suggested and different pictures of her had begun to emerge. Was she having problems in arithmetic or not? Was it unfair to compare her with other eight-year-olds, most of whom are in the third grade? Or were second graders a better comparison group? And how should the group review the behavioral traits brought up by Kathy and associated by some experts as suspicious signs of learning disabilities?

Kathy had condensed a great deal of material from her written report. The test data themselves are reproduced in Table 1, page 35. Kathy summarized that Jenny's "ITPA profile shows intra-individual deficits in all auditory areas. . . inhibiting acquisition of both decoding skills and sight words. . . she is unable to start or attend to task on an individual basis and is making little if any progress academically. . . has great difficulty establishing and maintaining satisfactory peer relationships." Kathy recommended placement in a self-contained classroom for "Significant Identifiable Emotional or Behavioral Disorder." At Aspen elementary school there is such a class, but it holds not only children who are emotionally disturbed but several children classified as learning disabled as well. In an interview Kathy outlined the chronology of contact with Jenny, and this information was supplemented by a review of Jenny's file. According to Kathy, the teacher had referred Jenny to the Remedial Lab in May of 1978, based on Jenny's poor progress in first grade reading. She was tested by the reading specialist who found that she was reading at the primer level and was "highly distractible and fidgety" during testing. On that basis she was assigned to the Remedial Lab for the fall and to a "slow" second grade classroom, taught by Marty. Kathy wrote an "Individualized Educational Plan" for her then, setting an objective that Jenny would be reading at the grade equivalent of the fourth month of the third grade after a year in Remedial Lab; i.e., progress two years in one. To accomplish this objective, the tutors would work on academics and perceptual training.

Meanwhile, Jenny's parents enrolled her in summer school, where a special education teacher's report said she did well. In September (Jenny was then starting second grade), a Form A (Referral for Special Eduation) was filed indicating Jenny's poor academic progress. According to Kathy:

". . . we suspected problems when she was referred. . .
impulsive behavior, perseveration, poor peer relations.
She was given a tutor who is assigned to the worst cases.
. . still not making any progress reading-wise or socially.
. . going more and more inside herself."

An in-school conference was conducted in October with Kathy, Jenny's teacher, the principal, and the speech-language specialist. They discussed her lack of progress and even her

23

apparent regression since summer school. Because Jenny was showing needs greater than they could serve in the Remedial Lab, they
decided to step up the special education staffing process. Meanwhile they accelerated her involvement in Remedial Lab to one hour
each day, an extraordinary amount of time in that program. The
reading specialist did another assessment with results similar to
those he had found five months earlier. In other words, Jenny was
not making much progress. There were several conferences with
Mrs. Johnson, Kathy, teacher and principal, discussing what might
become a full-time special education placement for Jenny. At first
Mr. Johnson had been upset with the possibility that Jenny would be
in a class for "the retarded." She was asked to visit the class every
one felt Jenny needed. They explained to her that this program was
not for the retarded, but provided full-time monitoring of behavior
and one-to-one academic help. According to Kathy, Mrs. Johnson
was then relieved and had approved continuation of the staffing
process. During January and February Jenny was tested by the
psychologist, by Kathy and the Speech-language specialist, and again
by the reading specialist. The mini-staffing took place in March to
review the results of the assessments. The school psychologist
attended as well as the speech-language specialist, Kathy, and
Marty. Although there was a difference of opinion about the extent
of Jenny's needs (the psychologist did not see the problem in the
same way the others did), they decided to go on with the formal
staffing.

By the time Kathy finished her report, the atmosphere of
the staffing had changed. People were becoming aware that there
were discrepancies in information and differences in judgment about
Jenny's characteristics and needs. It was almost possible to see
alliances building as one person's eyes sought those of another.
There seemed to be a need for each side, not just to present data,
but to build a case and sell the others on it.

Karen calls on the **speech language specialist**, who
begins, "In the testing Jenny was cooperative but distracted visually by the windows and the bulletin board,
although this doesn't affect the test results. She seems
to be able to do both, but this may not apply to the

classroom. From Kathy and Marty I understand that her attention is not good in the classroom, but her attention *was* good for me. She had a lot of problems recalling a series of unrelated words. She exhibited subvocal speech--she would mouth my words as I said them. This would hurt auditory skills; but she may be doing this to give herself more input."

Sue, the teacher of the self-contained special education class, breaks in. "That behavior could be the result of the reading program that Marty uses. It asks the kids to say words as they read them."

Kathy: "But it also could be one more example of her need to always be doing something with her hands, with her mouth, with her pencil."

The attempt by the special education teacher to explain a child's problem in terms of the curriculum or teaching was almost unknown in staffing conferences. The clinicians have a vocabulary and implicit definitions about learning disabilities that invariably locate the problem in the child; but poor teaching or deficient materials are rarely considered. Her question dropped like a rock into a well, and Kathy preemptorily returned to psychological explanations. All the members of the staffing team were by then struggling more obviously with the discrepancies being presented.

The **speech-language specialist** continues, "If this (subvocalizing) is a compensatory thing with her, it's not going to be very effective in the classroom. She has no problems with auditory discrimination and sequencing. Her single word vocabularly was good. She doesn't seem to have established concept of left and right. She has problems with conceptual development. . . . Her expressive skills and articulation are adequate."

The **special education teacher** again interrupts to ask the classroom teacher if she has been aware of any problems Jenny has in discriminating left from right, or if she reverses letters or if there is a pattern to Jenny's spelling errors. Spelling is a problem, according to the classroom teacher, but not reversals or discriminating left and right. "It's her confidence, too. She's afraid to take the mastery tests."

When **Karen** asks, "Does she participate in oral discussions?" The teacher says, "Not much--usually she's talking to the people next to her." But the **social worker** adds, "When I observed her in class, she was reading by herself and whistling. She seemed very happy to me."

The report of the speech-language therapist was a lengthy one (See Table 1). She summarized her scores in her written report as follows:

". . . possible auditory perceptual deficits involving short-term auditory memory skills. Additional reports of other personnel suggest deficits in Jenny's auditory attention to tasks, which is negatively affecting class-room performance. Jenny exhibits receptive and ex-pressive language which are appropriate for a child her age. . . . no articulation errors. . . . inadequate auditory attention in classroom but tests showed no apparent dif-ficulties with auditory figure-ground perception. . . . Jenny has not seemed to clearly establish her knowledge of left and right, days of the week, seasonal concepts, and time relationships. This often suggests difficulties with cognitive-conceptual development which will affect other areas of academic functioning."

Before calling on the psychologist, Karen read the report of the reading specialist who was not in attendance. He had given the Silvaroli reading test and found that Jenny was reading at the primer level, showing weak decoding and sightword skills but good comprehension.

Psychologist: "People felt at different times that we should hold back (on staffing process), that she was a marginal case; until recently when the evaluation was stepped up. During testing there was some carelessness in response. She was fairly active, visually distracted. A couple of times we had to stop so she could explore a little, then we could get back. This didn't seem to interfere with production. She strikes me as being more curious than disruptive. In my opinion there is no significant emotional-behavior problem. She has average ability intellectually. Her achievement is not discrepant when you refer to her grade level but is discrepant when you refer to her age level. My recommendation is that we work to close the gap between what she can do and what she does. She needs resource room attention. She needs extra work in language areas. I'm not sure how severe that is or what time is necessary to correct it, but it's part-time, shorter than full-time--either continue in Remedial Lab and summer school or a resource room."

Mrs. Johnson asks, "What is a resource room?" Karen explains that it is a program for children with learning disabilities, which the children attend for an hour each day but spend the rest of the time in regular classroom.

The psychologist had integrated results from five tests, the Wechsler Intelligence Scale for Children, the Wide Range Achievement Test, the Bender-Gestalt perceptual tests, a human figure drawing test and a sentence completion test. He also observed Jenny in class and interviewed her teacher. He had spent nearly sixteen hours with this assessment. He found her verbal IQ to be in the expected range 91-99 and her performance IQ between 98 and 106. He found her social-emotional development "although variable," to be "within normal limits" (see test results in Table 1).

So ended the phase of the staffing conference devoted to reporting information. Over an hour had passed and only a half hour remained before other commitments would force the members to adjourn. Busy recording details of the exchange, I was only dimly

27

aware of the meaning of what had transpired. I wanted to give the benefit of the doubt to the information presented or perhaps I was snowed by the technical terminology or just lazy and too trusting to ask, "What of substance was conveyed? Had we really learned about Jenny?" Perhaps Jenny's mother felt the same. I have the vague impression, clarified later, that these pieces of information about Jenny did not really add up to anything, all thrown out and accepted without regard to their quality or coherence. Low on auditory for one examiner but not another; one report of appropriate achievement and another report that achievement was too low. Boehm this and Detroit that; whistling for one and crying for another--if you thought about it long enough (which nobody did because it happened so fast) it could be all chimerical. One longed for facts and there were no facts.

There was disagreement among the members with regard to the data. Yet the arguments seemed to involve personalities and professions and personal visions. Again the image of grand rounds presents itself-but either these people mimic the doctors or the doctors themselves engage in a similar ritual.

These people were required to be there, doing what they were doing so that the regulations of the law could be satisfied. It was the procedural due process that had to be ensured and the content of the staffing merely filled the time. The wiser ones there knew it; the rest thought they were engaging in differential diagnosis of a human personality.

During the presentations, Karen had been listening and filling out Form C, the report of the staffing conference. The reports finished, she must attempt to synthesize the information (seeing it for the first time in the staffing), reconcile conflicting data and guide the group to a decision. In addition she must apply the eligibility criteria to the data presented. The criteria act as an external standard so that all Belleview schools will define eligibility the same way--and to prevent the situation that a child might be judged handicaped if evaluated by School A but not handicapped if judged by School B.

Sensing the disagreement among the members, Karen asked for each person's separate conclusion and recommendations. Before everyone could be polled, the survey turned into a general debate.

Social worker: "I agree with the psychologist. Unless there was some support for intensive *academic* help, that she should be retained in the regular classroom plus receive resource room help."

Speech-language specialist: "I'm on the fence. Attention affects academics. I would support the self-contained class for learning how to attend. She needs a smaller class. She needs experience with what school requires. I know the academics aren't that low but what has happened since fall? She isn't doing well but still feels good about herself. We need to bring it to her attention that it's *not okay* to go along without keeping up."

The **special education teacher** again mentions the possiblity that the reading program used in Jenny's class may be at fault, not some psychological characteristic of Jenny. Again she is ignored.

Kathy: "We wouldn't see the tears of she didn't care."

Social worker: "She cares. She really likes coming to school here."

Teacher: "We've really worked on her self-confidence."

Kathy, now actively promoting: "But look at the reading specialist's evaluations. She was at the pre-primer level at all three testings. She's not making progress despite Reading Lab, despite Marty's reading program, and despite summer school."

Karen: "But look at the PIAT reading results: 2.0.*

Kathy: "You can get a 2.0 if you just can read 'go, run, jump.'"

---

*Peabody Individual Achievement Tests scores presented are grade equivalents. A score of 2.0 would be the average score obtained by a child beginning second grade.

Teacher: "She is not making steady progress. She is still where she was last May."

The tone of the meeting had become contentious, the once business-like atmoshere slightly emotional. Each person was genuinely concerned for Jenny but saw different solutions as most justified. Karen attempted to steer the committee in the direction of the criteria.

Karen: "Do we see a *significant* learning disability here. There is a discrepancy. It is mild and borderline. The problem seems to be distraction, not perception."

Speech-language specialist: "But what is causing the frustration?"

Karen: "Maybe we should be looking at her as 'emotional-behavioral.'"

Social worker, with emphasis: "I have a lot of trouble seeing her as an emotional-behavioral problem."

Psychologist: "Mrs. Johnson, do you see her as a behavior problem at home?"

Mrs. Johnson: "No, you have to be stern with her, but no."

The principal, is called out of the meeting to respond to an emergency and the general discussion continues.

Psychologist: "That's my impression too. She's active, she's curious, she jumps around. Where do you draw the line between curiosity and disruptiveness? She's not over the line."

Karen: "That's what I think too. There are so many questions about this--these are borderline problems--so we need to go with the least restrictive environment before we could recommend a self-contained placement. The least restrictive environment would be a resource room."

There is a general consternation that no resource room exists at Aspen, although almost every other elementary school in Belleview district has one. Some seem concerned because they feel a resource room is needed at Aspen; others because they feel the resource room is an inappropriate placement for Jenny.

Teacher: "Jenny has been going to the Remedial Lab and that is the same as a resource room. Is a resource room going to help those auditory and visual problems?"

Kathy: "Marty's class is highly structured and that's very different from a regular classroom where directions are given orally. Jenny couldn't handle that."

Mrs. Johnson: "I asked her what she would think about going to a special classroom. She said 'Does that mean I'm not going to pass second grade?'"

Special education teacher: "Are we thinking about next year? I'm not sure that during the last two months of school it is too healthy to take her out the classroom and put her into self-contained. And next year she would be going into Level-II (grades 3 and 4). Now my class has several learning disabled kids in it, but next year it could have almost all SIEBD kids.* I'm worried about that for Jenny."

Karen replies that any decision reached this late in the spring would not be implemented until next fall.

Social worker: "Other schools have resource rooms. . . ."

---

*Significant Identifiable Emotional/Behavioral Disorder, Colorado's term for the emotionally disturbed.

Karen: "I think we have a split decision. I'm on the fence. She is functioning academically below where we would expect but I don't see a significant learning disability here."

Speech-language specialist: "What about the nurse's report (speech retraining after tonsillectomy)? We may be dealing with a very immature auditory system."

The pace quickens. Everyone seems aware that the meeting is coming to an end. The previous comment is ignored and **Karen** presses for a decision. "Since there are so many problems we have to decide on resource room first. We could change at mid-year if necessary. Give her resource room, direct work with a special education teacher *not* a volunteer in the Remedial Lab, and a regular third grade program. It's a problem because there is no resource room here, but there is one at two nearby schools."

There followed a general discussion about the inadvisability of an open-space school for Jenny and the recommendation of a highly structured third grade teacher at one of the nearby schools. Someone recommended summer school. There seemed to be the understanding, although no one said so directly, that Jenny would leave Aspen, either through a change in residence already planned tentatively by the Johnsons, or by transporting Jenny to a neighboring school which does have a resource room. That decision would wait until next fall. For now, Jenny would continue in her regular second grade class and in Remedial Lab.

The group broke into several subgroups, each engaged in a different conversation. Karen passes around the Form C for everyone to sign and explained the due process rights to Mrs. Johnson, who signed the form agreeing to the decision. At this point the meeting became an IEP (Individual Education Planning) conference. Karen recommended a general goal—to improve Jenny's academic performance, and left specific objectives for the resource room teacher to complete. Mrs. Johnson agreed with this goal, and the meeting ended.

The tables and chairs were returned to their places, the participants dispersed--teachers back to classrooms, chairman to another staffing, psychologist to his office where he would test another child, forms A, B C and E filed. But where was Jenny and what would she think when she saw her mother walk away from the school building and her teacher come back to class? And who was Jenny, really? She had just undergone the most intensive investigation education can provide. Yet did anyone know her as anything but a conglomeration of separate psychological traits--high on this one and low on that?   For all that analysis, did anyone imagine that, holding together these traits was a person with ideas and feelings about why she was being examined, seemingly endlessly tested and finally judged by that group of adults? Could she distinguish between their evaluation of her school performance and herself as a human? We can only speculate about her private thoughts, but we must never lose sight of the fact that she has them. One thing we do know. She interpreted her staffing as her own failure, knowing nothing about "neurological impairment." "Does this mean I'm not going to pass second grade?" She didn't blame her reading program that taught her to subvocalize or her teacher who placed her with younger children who needed supervision; she blamed herself. The professionals may argue about whether she is properly compared to her age-mates or her class-mates; but for Jenny, there is only herself.

Comments overheard after the meeting was adjourned indicated mixed reactions to its outcome. Some were disappointed and surprised that it was not decided to provide full-time help for Jenny. One person remarked that Jenny was the first pupil to go through the staffing process at Aspen and be placed in a resource room instead of in a self-contained class.   This person hinted at foregone conclusions, that the staffing conference was only a formality. Another commented that Jenny was marginally qualified as learning disabled even for a resource room placement.

In a interview some weeks later, Mrs. Johnson said she felt relieved that "It went better than I thought it would." She was impressed that so much energy had been devoted to Jenny. She knew everyone sincerely wanted to help, but it worried her to think there were certain people on the committee who were trying very hard to place Jenny full-time in a special education class. Mrs. Johnson has visited that class and didn't like it. Most of the pupils were boys with behavior problems. She felt that Jenny would pick up their bad behavior. During the staffing, however, she felt that there were certain other members who "were on Jenny's side" and she was relieved when the school psychologist had said he didn't see Jenny as a behavior problem. Mrs. Johnson was still satisfied with the school and the staffing decision. She again expressed that Jenny would "come out all right."

In an interview several weeks after the staffing, the school principal expressed his dissatisfaction. Although willing to grant that decision might be reasonable and worth a try, he felt that it should have been otherwise.

"We are not all that comfortable that this child should not have been considered more for self-contained. Remedial Lab help is substantial. Several volunteers are ex-teachers, even one ex-special education teacher. When a kid is really in trouble like Jenny we assign the best one. Jenny has been receiving as much extra help as humanly possible—better than she would be getting in 95 percent of the schools in America. So when we say that a kid needs time out of the regular classroom and in a special environment, we know what we're doing. . . . We don't recommend children for staffing who don't need it. . . . The classroom teacher came to me afterwards kind of discouraged and beaten down. She had thought that Jenny showed greater need. The test scores and the outside consultants carry too much weight in the decisions. We don't want to fill up our program with kids who don't need it. We see the kid 180 days a year in class and have been dealing with the problem and trying to correct it. The people who are responsible for education—the principals—should have involvement in the decision. But the way the law is written the principal has the *least* to say about the decision. . . . We've gone committee-happy."

Jenny's standardized test results became available two months after the staffing. At the time of testing she was, though eight years old, in the seventh month of the second grade. Her total reading score was two months behind her grade placement, her total language score equalled her grade placement and her total math score was three months ahead. In the classroom she continued to be behind in reading. The next fall, as expected, she did not enroll again at Aspen.

Table 1

TEST RESULTS FOR JENNY

Educational Specialist

1. Illinois Test of Psycholinguistic Abilities   February 26, 1979

    Mean Scale 30.5   Psycholinguistic Age = 7.6

	Age Score	Scaled Score	Scale	Age	Scaled
Auditory Reception	7-0	27	Grammatical Closure	6-5	18
Visual Reception	9-3	36	Visual Closure	8-0	32
Auditory Association	7-8	28	Auditory Memory	6-3	30
Visual Association	8-0	33	Visual Memory	9-9	38
Verbal Expression	6-8	28	Auditory Closure	6-1	26
Manual Expression	8-8	35	Sound Blending	8-7	37

2. Pictorial Individual Achievement Test   November 3, 1978

Subtest	Grade Equivalent	Percentile (for eight year olds)
Math	1.9	9
Reading Recognition	1.6	6
Reading Comprehension	2.2	11
Spelling	2.2	11
General Information	3.8	54
Total	2.2	15

Speech-Language Specialist

1. Peabody Picture Vocabulary Test

    Vocabulary Age: 8-11
    Vocabulary Quotient: 99, Percentile: 50th

2. Boehm Test of Basic Concepts

    47 of 50 correct: 50th percentile for second graders

3. Wiig-Semel Test of Language Concepts

Scale	Raw Score	Mean Score (Age Norms)
Comparative Relationships	9	8.1
Passive Relationships	7	7.8
Temporal Relationships	8	6.5
Spatial Relationships	9	7.2
Family Relationships	6	5.2
Total Battery	39	34.9

4. Detroit Tests of Learning Aptitude

Scale	Age Score
Verbal Absurdities	11-6
Visual Attention Span	9-9
Pictorial Opposites	9-3
Memory for Designs	8-3
Pictorial Absurdities	6-9
Auditory Attention Span	5-9

School Psychologist

1. Wechsler Intelligence Scale for Children
   Verbal IQ: 91-99, Performance IQ: 98-106. Total: 95-101

2. Wide Range Achievement Test

Subtest	Grade Equivalent	Standard Score	Percentile (Age 8)
Reading	2.5	88	21
Spelling	2.3	88	21
Math	2.8	92	30

Reading Specialist

    Silvaroli Reading Test

May 19, 1978	Primer Level on Graded Word Lists
October 24, 1978	Primer Level on Graded Word Lists
January 29, 1979	Primer Level on Graded Word Lists

HOW JOHN CAME TO BE CALLED HANDICAPPED

To travel from Jenny's school to John's school is to take a sentimental trip back in time. Old Poplar Elementary School has red bricks, two floors with high ceilings, one of those long spiral fire escapes and an educational climate that matches the building. There are people there who have somehow resisted pressures to bureaucratize and technologize--no management by objectives or criterion-referenced instructional systems.

The teachers are artists and humanists. The principal-- that I unconsciously came to call her Mrs. Smith in my notes reflects my admiration for her--is no less competent a manager for the fact that she most values the lives of children and teachers. Her commitment to teaching and learning and her long working hours have inspired her teachers to an equal effort. The neighborhood served by Poplar is old too , but with economically and socially diverse people. Poplar is one of the few schools in Belleview district with a program for economically disadvantaged children as well as programs for children who speak little English. There are pockets of wealth in the neighborhood as well.

At this school there is a perspective about special education that might be described as accepting but pragmatic. The resource room is regarded as just that, a resource that the school staff can exploit when a child needs its help. It is not regarded as separate or mysterious. This orientation is shared by the special educators and the assessment specialists who work there.

Every Wednesday morning at 7:30, the principal meets with the reading specialist, the resource room teacher, the psychologist, and the social worker to discuss the progress of children who are experiencing academic or personal problems. No representative of the district special education office attends. Teachers bring their difficult cases to this meeting for advice and help. Some of these cases are eventually referred for the formal special education staffing process. But others are short-term situational or instructional problems that can be handled with less radical measures. For example, one little girl who seemed to be immature and troubled in the combined second and third grade class was transferred, as a result of a Wednesday conference, to a class with only second graders. She subsequently attracted no more attention. Another child having greater than usual trouble with oral reading was assigned a volunteer tutor from the local college. Counseling or social welfare programs are sought out and children or parents referred to them. Assignments to Title I programs are made. For some children testing is prescribed and the results presented. Children who have recently transferred from other schools are discussed and placed with the right teacher. Once the teacher of the class for the emotionally distrubed came to say that one of her pupils seemed to be deteriorating and perhaps needed a residential program. Another teacher came to report that an instructional strategy suggested by the psychologist had been tried and was successful.

The specialists play active roles in these meetings even though many of the children discussed are not really the wards of special education. Thus does Poplar's orientation to special education reveal itself--that all the staff are responsible for all the pupils and territorial boundaries are neither honorable nor honored.

It was at one of these Wednesday meetings that John Martin's case first came to light. Yet I want to emphasize that no one at Poplar sounded the alarm. Mrs. Martin agreed to meet with me to discuss the history of John's problem from her perspective.

We met in her home, which placed the Martin family at the upper end of Poplar's social and economic diversity. She was young and friendly, and I played with her baby as she spoke. She said she did not want me to think of her as a pushy or over-anxious mother or that she lacked confidence in Mrs. Smith or John's teacher, but that she was indeed worried about John's continuing inability to read. At the time of the interview John was completing the seventh month of the first grade.

John's older sister, according to Mrs. Martin, had taught herself to read while in kindergarten. John has spent *his* time in kindergarten playing with blocks. During the summer between his kindergarten and first grade the Martins had already sensed a problem and arranged for John to be tested at the University Speech and Hearing Clinic. They had diagnosed an "auditory figure-ground discrimination problem," which meant to Mrs. Martin that he could not hear well in noisy places.

At a get-acquainted party for new first graders and their families, Mrs. Martin expressed her concern that John was not yet showing any signs of starting to read. Both the teacher and Mrs. Smith assured her that, "John *will* learn to read *this* year."

But after a month passed, "I asked him what he was doing in school and he said he was just playing with blocks. So I asked his teacher to push him, because he will never learn anything unless you push him."

At midterm conference time in October, Mrs. Martin was told that John was in the middle reading group. Several children in the class were behind him. Sensing her worry, the teacher and principal again tried to reassure her. They said that girls usually learn to read faster than boys so it isn't right to compare John with his sister.

"But I was worried so I asked if there weren't some games or activities we could work on with him at home. His teacher gave us some concentration games and sight-word lists. I worked with him every night. But it was so frustrating. We made up flash-cards and would drill on the words. One day he would learn a word and the next day, it was just like he had never seen that word before. This went on until Christmas. He learned the whole list before we went on vacation and when we returned he knew only about half the words."

She was getting frantic by this time, she said, because "reading is so *central*. In this society if you can't read, you can't learn anything." The teacher asked her to observe the classroom. Having watched awhile, she left in tears. "He was trying *so hard* and his teacher had the class set up so well but he *just wasn't getting* it."

Again she asked for more teaching aids. But according to Mrs. Martin the teacher was reluctant to do any more or put any more pressure on John. "I think they think I'm an overanxious mother. If it was anything but reading I'd just let it go, but reading is essential."

About that time, Mrs. Martin ran into her daughter's teacher at at Poplar neighborhood party. The teacher told her about the resource room where some children get help with their perceptual and academic problems. That was the first time she knew of such services, and she asked for them in February, John having made no noticeable progress, in her opinion. Mrs. Smith said John might be qualified for the resource room, but that he would first have to be tested. The testing would have to wait because there were several other pupils in greater need of help than John. Frustrated by this anticipated delay, the Martins sought help from the speech and language specialist who operates an evaluation clinic. Dr. James tested John, diagnosed perceptual problems and tutored him weekly. Mrs. Martin said the whole staffing process (she did not use the name, nor that of special education) was frustrating, repetitious and slow.

"The nurse asked me exactly the same questions as I had just answered six months ago on a screening questionnaire. She is only at Poplar one day a week and she has to waste that time asking questions that were right there in the file! And the social worker covers the same ground as the nurse. I asked them about that and they said they were required by law to speak individually with me. So I suppose thay have to do it, but as a taxpayer I resent this much wasted time by trained people."

Mrs. Martin also expressed her concern that despite all this testing, in the end John might not qualify for special help. Still she persisted. Mrs. Smith supplied the school's perspective on John's case.

"John came to us in kindergarten. His teacher felt he did well and saw no indication for concern. There was no significant indication from kindergarten screening (they use a modified version of the Santa Clara Development Inventory) that he would have academic difficulty. Mother came into us at the end of the first quarter (grade one) worried that John wasn't doing as well as she had expected. . . that he didn't know enough words. At that time we tried to reassure her that it was probably maturational, something that he would grow out of. . . .

"In February, we had a second conference. She shared with us the results of an assessment at the University Speech and Hearing Clinic. She also described some problems at John's birth--he didn't start to breathe immediately. (Because of this new information) we decided jointly to go ahead with the staffing process."

Elaine, John's teacher elaborated.

"At first I had no concern, then became worried later when I saw he wasn't retaining words. It was better when he got into his first reader because words weren't in isolation. They were in context. Visual clues from the reader also helped. Now in March, I'm not worried. He is a little behind grade level. There are several children lower than he is in this class. He's okay, not strong, but okay. He should finish the first grade curriculum. With help from summer school he should start second grade at grade level. He tries very hard. Do you look at that hard work as good effort or as struggling? Is the glass half empty or half full? In kindergarten and first grade you don't know what is developmental and what is a learning problem. You just don't know. I have trust in Marilyn (reading specialist) and Julie (resource room teacher). If they say he's going to be okay without a resource room, then I'll rely on that. Their test results confirm his classroom performance. He's mad about all the testing. Each person has pulled him out two or three times. Between the testing, the tutoring he's getting here and the tutoring at home, I think he is going to be overwhelmed. And that is going to hurt his attitude. There's too much pressure."

The difference in perspectives--teacher and principal on one side, the parent on the other--set up tension for the events to follow. The teacher and principal were not out to assign labels, blame the victim, or evade responsibility. I could understand some of the mother's worry and her wish to obtain all the educational help to which she was legally entitled.

Form A for referral had been filed in February. At a regular Wednesday meeting, John's teacher presented his case to Mrs. Smith, the psychologist, reading specialist, and resource room teacher. Together they decided to proceed with the staffing process based on the information presented. Form B, the Request for

Staffing, was submitted and signed by Mrs. Martin early in March. The specialists then began their testing which went on until mid-April. At that time a mini-staffing was held to go over the test results.

According to those present, the mini-staffing was long and complicated. The group heard the reports of the teacher, social worker, psychologist, resource room teacher and reading specialists. They tried to determine whether the test data indicated the presence of a perceptual handicap and whether John would qualify by the official criteria for staffing learning disabilities. The following conclusions were stated in the principal's notes:

1. John does not seem to be frustrated or struggling at school. He gets his work done. He works hard--has good work habits.

2. His Comprehensive Test of Basic Skills (CTBS) reading scores are in line with what would be expected from WISC-R IQ score (CTBS Reading around 50%).

3. He does well in math--Woodcock showed him to be achieving at about 2.0 grade equivalent.

4. Staff feeling is that in general observations and tests indicated John is doing okay. If he has an auditory problem he is compensating adequately at this time.

5. Staff feeling is that John should not be staffed into special education at this time. He should be watched carefully next year. Should try to help parents see there is overall progress and try to relieve some of the concern.

In essence, the decision was reached at this meeting. The data showed John was not qualified. Those at the mini-staffing considered them carefully and weighed them against Mrs. Martin's desire to have John placed in the resource room.

The formal staffing took place one week later, with Gwen serving as chairman and representative of the special education department. Mrs. Smith was there as were the resource room teacher, the reading specialist, John's teacher, the social worker, speech-language specialist, nurse, and physical education teacher. Mrs. Martin brought Dr. James with her, whom she had hired to evaluate and tutor John. Gwen made the introductions and outlined the purpose of the meeting. "We want to go over the information and find out what John's needs are and what services might be available for him." After that introduction, the staffing conference proceeded in its usual sequence: the teacher first, then the nurse, and the others in order. The pace was brisk and the tone business-like. Gwen had already seen the data and seemed to sense the interpretation made of them by the committee.

Teacher: "John is a well-liked little boy, plays well, is occasionally bossy. But the kids don't mind; they see him as a leader. He is short but not rude with kids he doesn't like. He has an *incredible* attitude. He wants to learn, he appears happy, he is warm and open to me now, though he wasn't at first. He doesn't *seem* frustrated. When he is given a task he works on it. He is strong in first grade math, at grade level. At the start of the year there were concerns about sight words. He was very inconsistent. One day he knew them, the next day he didn't. But when he integrated them into reading, he could remember them. He's getting tutoring in my class and from Dr. James. He's doing better. He's succeeding.

Gwen refers to the items on the staffing report. She seems to be trying to find a context for interpreting John's marginal weakness.

Gwen: "Are there kids in your class who are lower than John?"

Teacher: "Oh, yes!"

Gwen: What about his class participation, his verbal skills?"

Teacher: "With a small reading group there is no problem. He doesn't seem nervous about reading in front of me. If it's something he's interested in he will participate when he's called on."

Mrs. Martin breaks in with a question. Although her tone is not at all contentious, she is forcefully asking for clarification. She seems to be trying to interpret John's weakness in a more negative light than the committee does. "In our conference you told me he would get *through* the workbooks but he wouldn't really *learn* it."

Teacher: "He needs reinforcement so he won't backslide. But he has shown improvement."

Gwen: "What about his fine motor skills--his printing?"

Teacher: "He does well. He is proud of it."

Gwen: "Creative writing? Spelling?

Teacher: "He puts in a minimum amount. He will do the assignment but doesn't put much imagination into it. He has a hard time with spelling but I can make out what he is trying to tell me."

Mrs. Martin: "That has been recent."

Teacher: "Of course we are looking at April and not January."

Gwen: "What about his gross motor skills--walking?

The P.E. teacher answers that he walks stiffly and has had problems doing the movement exercises and throwing a frisbee.

Mrs. Martin: "But he has thrown a frisbee many times."

Gwen: "Mrs. Martin, do you see an awkward walk?"

Mrs. Martin: "He has been really awkward with all his physical skills. The previous P.E. teacher said he was slow but within normal range."

The P.E. teacher and Gwen talk about a new consultant in the district who could evaluate John's physical coordination and make recommendations for activities at home and school to help his coordination and movement.

The **school nurse** gives her report. "Mrs. Martin reports that John's gait and physical coordination are the main health problems. The pregnancy was fine. The labor was short. There were difficulties in the delivery. His head turned but his shoulders didn't. Forceps were used to turn the head and then the delivery was manual. He didn't breathe spontaneously, and was suctioned. . . . Because of this he may have soft neurological damage. His developmental milestones were fine. He is healthy. He had croup. He occasionally runs into walls. He can see and hear. The acuity is fine but he has a figure-ground kind of problem. This is okay in Elaine's class but may be a problem in noisy environments."

Teacher: "But the school psychologist observed him during play time and he had no trouble hearing what everybody is saying."

Nurse: "But he is putting a lot of effort into doing it. I would also suggest a test of depth perception. He is up-to-date on his immunizations." General laughter greets this, as the nurses always seem as concerned about the shots as about the staffing.

The **speech-language specialist** begins her report. "I gave him several tests. The Linus test measures part-whole discrimination. Can he hear small words in a long word? This was just not his bag, he didn't do very well. He did all right on a test of temporal discrimination, such as 'Where is the "um" in him.' The Carrow Test of Auditory Discrimination tests what he understands in language. When I asked him to show me 'pair' he was confused on that. Generally his specific auditories are sort of low, although his general auditory is all right."

Social worker: "John's parents are concerned that his current positive attitude will be lost if he continues to spend so much energy and gets no results. (Addressing the mother) You seemed to want him to achieve without all that effort or else he would eventually give up. (Continuing the assessment) He has good expression of feelings. When problem-solving he tries to get his parents to do it for him and when they don't he gives up."

Mrs. Martin asks whether they see that problem at school and everyone says they don't.

Social worker: "That's not inappropriate for kids that age to behave that way toward parents. John is responsible at home. There have been no serious accidents, separations, or illnesses. When playing ball with Dad, John will drop the ball nine out of ten times. But when Dad threatens to quit, John will then only drop the ball one out of ten times. So his motivation and concentration seem to be in John's own control."

Julie, who teaches in the resource room, gives her report. "I gave him a math test. Although math wasn't a concern we thought it would give us a clearer idea. On the Key Math test he did well. His scores ranged from a grade equivalent of 1.7 on money and measurements to a 2.3 on knowledge of fractions. I hand-scored his CTBS tests and they were nearly grade level, but that is a highly visual test."

The **reading specialist** gives her report. "I gave four reading tests plus the Slingerland.* His grade placement at the time of testing was one year, seven months--that will give us a measuring stick. His reading expectancy based on his academic ability is 2.1. The Silvaroli showed he was at the pre-primer or beginning primer level so that puts him about one month behind grade level. Errors were transpositions (switching letters) within words. There were some reversals, but this is developmental and

---

*A test of perceptual processing and integration.

children have to be taught to have this skill. He's not a risk-taker. He says 'I don't know' a lot. He wouldn't use what phonic skills he has and always wanted to be told the answer. When reading in context he used pictorial skills extremely well. . . . Unaided recall of a story was difficult. When my questions aided recall, he did fine and recall on the Slingerland was great. He did fine on vocabularly and direct comprehension but more poorly on inferential comprehension. On the Woodcock he scored 1.5, at the 32nd percentile nationally. There was one significant deficit on word comprehension. . . . He has little word attack skills. On the Slingerland there were 30 errors out of 74 questions, indicating some weak areas, clustering in the auditory. Motor and visual areas are strongest modalities. Performance breaks down in the integration--when things are given orally and he has to retrieve the visual clues and make a response. Processing takes *so* much time. We need to strengthen visual sequential memory because the visual is where the compensation is coming in. We found some perseveration, he got stuck on b's and d's. He got tense."

The **social worker** again tries to supply a perspective to interpret these data. "How discrepant is this, relative to other kids?"

Reading specialist: "It's slightly behind the norm. There is some discrepancy, but his compensation puts him at grade level."

Gwen: "Is it a significant discrepancy?"

Reading specialist: "Not with his current compensation."

Social worker: "What is his prognosis for continuing effort and success in the future?"

Reading specialist: "That depends on how alert we are to his weaknesses and how he is compensating. We can give the teacher many suggestions for strengthening his stronger areas."

Gwen passed around Form C (Report of the Staffing) to
ed. Mrs. Martin seemed frustrated and expressed her reser-
about the second-grade teachers and programs available at
Mrs. Smith promised that John would be watched closely--
veryone at Poplar was now aware of this problem and would
anything bad happen. "We'll always be looking out for John,"
id. I believed that this was true, even if Mrs. Martin didn't.

With Mrs. Martin's concurrence, Gwen and the speech-
age specialist wrote a general goal for the following fall--to
on the auditory problem, reading, and spelling. The IEP was to
ritten in the fall, and Mrs. Martin would have a chance to help
ell as to approve whatever was written. Mrs. Martin seemed
ned to the lack of resource room help for John. She accepted
decision. The meeting broke up amid a general feeling of re-
The business finished, Gwen rushed out; she still had four more
fing conferences to attend that day.

A week after the staffing conference, Mrs. Smith and the
ource room teacher invited Mrs. Martin back to explain again
t the tests measured and what John's results meant. They reas-
ed her that John was everyone's responsibility.

About a month later, I asked Mrs. Martin for her reac-
ns to the staffing.

"I had anticipated the outcome so it was no big surprise
that he didn't qualify. But he didn't qualify because we
got him a tutor and got him caught up to grade level. I
am happy that he's at least getting *some* extra help from
school . . . . It will come--he is doing better. He is always going to have to work harder than the other kids.
People at school are really concerned, they know about
his problems, they are on top of things. They got him a
high school tutor, they got him into the best second grade
class and he will get help from the speech teacher.
That's probably as much extra work as he could stand
anyway."

Concerning the staffing meeting, she said everyone did
their job well but that she felt "stabbed in the back" by the psychologists's report of the sentence completion test and the implication

The principal, **Mrs. Smith** interjects: "As long as we don't
put the extra stress of adult attention to his weakness, as
the psychologist points out in her report."

Dr. James, seemingly vexed at the direction being taken
asks, "How would the school handle a child like this who
looks good on paper but still isn't doing well?"

Mrs. Smith answers quickly and pointedly. "Before we
talk about optional programs we need to finish the reports. Since the psychologist couldn't be here, I will read
her report. The testing was actually done by an intern
under her supervision.

The following are excerpts from the psychologist's report, read by Mrs. Smith at the staffing conference.

"John was referred by his teacher because of slow progress in reading, having specific difficulties with word
retention. Auditory figure-ground discrimination difficulties were also mentioned. A detailed analysis of the
WISC-R profile shows overall difficulties with both short-
term and long-term memory related tasks, suggesting
that more general problems of memory may bear upon his
acquisition of a reliable sight vocabulary in reading. The
suspected auditory figure-ground difficulty was not subjected to direct study; however, informal observation of
John's listenting and comprehending behaviors, with and
without moderate background noise (in the classroom,
hallways, etc.) did not tend to support the hypothesis of
any extensive problem in this area.

"John appears somewhat sensitive about his slow
reading progress. When asked to complete the sentence,
'If I could read better. . . ' he answered 'I'd have a lot
more fun.' 'The worst thing about being myself is . . . '--
'When I get mad at myself'; 'read when I don't want to.'
This apparent overconcern may be self-defeating, if
John's general coping style is to react fretfully when
confronted with demanding tasks, as witnesed by the
examiner. Since John seems to be reacting with considerable discomfort to the perceived emphasis upon his

reading difficulties, especially during recent evaluation procedures, it will be important for members of the school staff to attend to his sensitivities in the area if additional remedial measures are undertaken. In addition, areas of interest and achievement other than reading should also be brought into focus whenever feasible."

Dr. James (private tutor): "I'm hearing many inconsistencies. I'm wondering if I've made a mistake. My evaluation showed higher skills in auditory than visual areas. But my evaluations were therapeutic* so he could relax between questions when he felt stress. I'm worried about the validity of other test results because he tends to give up easily. Generally we can say he has some auditory problems, also some visual problems. Whatever his deficiencies are, they are giving him problems with reading and spelling. He does well one-to-one. He is getting a lot of extra help."

Teacher: "We are worried that he is getting too *much* help."

Mrs. Martin: "He accepts help fine from Dr. James and the school but just won't do homework with me."

Mrs. Smith: This could be some manipulation techniques he used on adults."

Gwen seems to sense that the reporting phase of the conference is over and it is time to summarize and make decisions. It is one of the few cases in which the decision will be negative.

Gwen: "There's been pretty consistent information from several people. Remember the social worker's report of the ball-dropping. . . . In general, we are looking at John having some difficulties with auditory skill, medial

---

*"Therapeutic" or "clinical administrations" of individual tests are frequently given to see how a child can respond to a test stimulus. During these administrations strict time limits are not observed and clues and prompts may be given by the examiner.

sounds, integration, memory prob...
tory. But he seems to be functioni...
try to find the learning disability ar...
from IQ and grade level related to...
He is at grade level, so there is no...
qualify for resource room but coul...
with the speech-language specialist...
watch to see how he progressed and r...
saw he was falling back.

Mrs. Martin addressess the speech-la...
"How often would you see him?" and sh...
a week for a half-hour beginning in the...

Gwen: "All our placements made now...
for the fall."

Dr. James: "Maybe we need to take th...
particularly at home."

Mrs. Martin: "It's with my husband and...
won't do the work. It's hard for me to la...
want him to fall behind. This is not what h...
through when she learned to read."

Teacher" "Please don't compare them, they...
people."

The school nurse speaks with emphasis. "His...
have some difficulties. There's nothing that...
do to correct this. He'll always have this pro...
you can help him compensate. He can't go...
Never! He'll have to detour. He has to be a...
find his own way round.

This comment was received with embarra...
Then everyone began making suggestions about remedi...
for John: "language experience" methods, reading int...
corder. The resource room teacher had prepared a pag...
tions for John's teacher to use such as "write direction...
possible," "stress word families," "Point out word configu...

that too much negative attention from home was being focused on John's reading problem. She expressed dismay over the nurse's comments that John had soft neurological damage (since tests given at his birth had revealed no such problem) and John would never be any better. "No one can possibly know that."

Mrs. Martin understood that John could not go to the resource room because he didn't meet the standard criteria. But the reason he didn't, according to her belief, was that the Martins had solved the problem themselves by hiring Dr. James. But no matter, she remained respectful of the people at Poplar Elementary.

John continued to struggle. By January of his second grade Mr. Martin asked that John be referred again for special education staffing. John's new achievement tests were still not significantly lower than what his ability would lead one to expect. Nor were his perceptual test results definitive. Nethertheless, at a second staffing conference he was placed in the resource room. The decision to place John in the resource room as learning disabled was based on the "professional judgment" of the staffing committee. It was made under the advisement of the district director of special education, to whom Mrs. Martin had taken her case.

POINTS OF COMPARISON BETWEEN THE STAFFINGS OF JENNY AND JOHN

These two staffings share important characteristics. They were both legal and both were expensive. The procedures prescribed by federal, state, and district regulations were followed to the letter. No rights were denied either in substance or procedure. The assessments were by multiple methods and professionals. They were non-discriminatory. The staffing decisions were made jointly by parents and professionals. Parents gave their informed consent for assessment and programs. No expense was spared in studying the characteristics and needs of these children. An analysis of the costs showed that about $1,000 was spent in the assessment and staffing of each one (2 times in the case of John). In these respects these two cases were similar to all other staffings I observed in Belleview.

Jenny and John were alike in that they were both marginal cases; that is, the data that might have identified them as learning disabled were equivocal. In this respect they resembled about half of Belleview's cases of learning disabilities. Others are more like Bobby (described below) or Sean (Chapter Three).

THE CASE OF BOBBY

Bobby's staffing conference occurred within three weeks of his initial referral in March. He was a fourth grader at Tamarac School, in a working class neighborhood. His teacher referred him, citing severe reading problems that she had tried for six months to handle herself. She said she was not surprised that his teachers in previous years had not recognized the problem because his falling behind his classmates had been precipitous. Testing had not been extensive since Bobby's problems were so apparent.

The staffing conference lasted only 20 minutes and was without much discussion because neither of Bobby's parents attended. The staffing chairman ran the meeting. Bobby's teacher was there, the school social worker, the resource room teacher, and the principal. The atmosphere was relaxed, almost free-wheeling.

Teacher: "His mother doesn't want to discuss the problem; the family is not too stable. His strengths are gym and math, provided the math problems are not story problems. Weaknesses are all language. He can't read words longer than one syllable, can't remember spelling lists after 24 hours. Reading at the third grade level is a struggle for him. He's the lowest reader in my class. He is very responsible and warm and nice to have around."

The chairman summarizes the nurse's report in a word: Normal.

The social worker's report was the same: "Within normal limits." Several anecdotes are passed around about his family.

TABLE 2
TEST RESULTS FOR JOHN

Educational Specialist

Key Math Total Grade Equivalent Score 2.0
(Subtests varied from 1.7 to 2.8)

Speech Language Specialist

(Test Scores not filed with Specialist's report.)

Reading Specialist

1. Silvaroli reading Test: 90% correct at pre-primer level,
    35% correct at beginning primer level.
2. Woodcock

Subtest	Instructional Level	Percentile Rank
Letter Identification	1.8	60
Word Identification	1.6	41
Word Attach	1.9	64
Word Comprehension	1.2	4
Passage Comprehension	1.8	59
Total Reading	1.5	32

3. Wide Range Achievement Test

Basal Level	1.3 (grade equivalent)
Instructional Level	1.8
Ceiling	2.7

4. Slingerland
    (Scores not interpretable)

School Psychologist

Wechsler Intelligence Scale for Children
    Verbal IQ: 90 ± 4, Performance IQ: 111 ± 5
    Full Scale: 102 ± 3
California Test for Basic Skills (Grade Placement: 1.7)

Subtest	Grade Equivalent	Percentile
Total Reading	1.8	53
Total Language	2.5	87
Total Math	1.6	44

The chairman reads the evaluation report done by the speech-language specialist. Expressive language is okay. Auditory skills are very weak.

The resource room teacher summarizes Bobby's test scores. "The Woodcock test places him at the 3.0 grade level in reading. Spelling is a year behind the norm. The Slingerland shows definite auditory discrimination and sequencing problems. My recommendation is for placement in the resource room for one hour a day, more intensive work in the classroom, and confidence-building. I have room for him now in my case load."

In the absence of the psychologist, the principal reads the psychological evaluation--average IQ, problems of eye-hand coordination on the Bender-Gestalt indicate severe perceptual problems.

Summarizing, the chairman states "I don't think there is any question of his qualifying. Compared to his IQ he should be performing way above where he is."

There is no argument. The principal has only to get the consent of Bobby's parents and the placement will be settled.

Jenny and John's staffings differed in several ways that illuminate the staffing process. First is who "sounded the alarm," who identified a set of actions and events as problems and then tried to convince others that they signified a problem. It was Jenny's teacher and John's mother. The view of Jenny's teacher spread to the principal and the resource room teacher, but was never accepted by the social worker, the psychologist or the mother. John's mother used data from the University Speech Clinic, the private evaluator plus problems during John's delivery to try to convince the people at school. Although they nibbled at this bait, they did not bite. John's teacher saw him in the context of this class, and he was within her acceptable range of variability. John's mother finally convinced a district administrator of her view. Perhaps the implied threat of litigation aided this change.

The second difference is the school's view of special education. At Aspen here seemed to be the old idea that special education was almost a different school. The children were the responsibility of either regular or special education. Although there was mainstreaming there, once the children were identified as handicapped, they were not really the responsibility of the regular classroom teacher. Poplar was different. Even those children in the full-time class for the emotionally disturbed were watched over by and kept track of by all the teachers. Special education and regular teachers consulted regularly and coordinated the education of their pupils.

The next important difference is the relationship of the assessment specialists to the school. At Aspen, they came and went quietly, participating very little in school life and maintaining their loyalties elsewhere. At Poplar they worked closely and congenially with the principal and teachers, assuming responsibility for all the children. This characteristic affected the two decisions in predictable ways.

How people viewed learning disabilities varied between the two places as well. The staff at Poplar focused on what John could do and what he was likely to do under different conditions. The focus was on his learning and behavior. The Aspen people seemed most interested in some underlying disease, the existence of which they went to great lengths to prove.

The personalities of the parents differed. Although I have no evidence, I may speculate. Jenny's mother never seemed alarmed; indeed she maintained some quiet skepticism about what the school tried to tell her. She preferred to retain her own definition of Jenny's problem. Rather than fight the school, she availed herself of the opportunity to leave it. Why John's mother fought the school is more difficult to understand. She knew John's case for resource room placement was so weak that he would have to wait until other children in greater need could be staffed and placed. With her wealth and her energy, why did she not simply hire a tutor and leave it at that? Perhaps there was some need to shift the responsibility from the family to the schools. One area where assessment is usually deficient is in understanding and confronting the dynamics of the family. Poplar's committee ventured into these murky waters farther than most. In John's case, that was probably not far enough.

The last difference is in the children themselves. Different ages, different sexes, different social classes do not explain all. Both were confronted with the fact that a problem had been discovered and that problem was their own. John denied it. Repeatedly he said, in so many words, "there is no problem, why are you bothering me?" He resisted the testing and he resisted his mother's help. When she brought home more educational games he said, "Not more work!" Later, the speech-language specialist gave up on his therapy. He did not seem to like her; he would leave class reluctantly for their sessions. He said he was doing fine and did not need her help. His mother thought otherwise.

Jenny, as I described before, accepted all, internalized all the blame, the construction of the problem, the sense of failure. What this portends one cannot say, but it is quite distinctly a real and unacknowledged effect of the special education staffing process.

PART II

EXPLAINING THE STAFFING PROCESS

Although the case study does not speak completely for itself, it should have portrayed some of the complexities of the staffing process. What must be explained as well as portrayed is its probable antecedents and consequences. The staffings of Jenny and John did not happen by chance, but were influenced by psychological, intellectual, institutional, and legal forces far beyond the Belleview city limits. In this section I present a series of ideas that explain how the staffing process works, why it works as it does, and what effect it has beyond obtaining special education for the children.

CHAPTER THREE

DEFINITIONS AND DIAGNOSIS OF LEARNING DISABILITIES AFFECT THE STAFFING PROCESS

"I know an LD child when I see one, but defining the term is nearly impossible." (Item from a survey of learning disabilities by Kirk, Berry, and Senf, 1979).

"A stone could be made to look LD." (Anonymous Belleview school administrator).

DEFINITIONS IN PROFESSIONAL LITERATURE

Acknowledging the ambiguities in definitions of learning disabilities is commonplace even among professionals working in the field. The authors of one of the major textbooks admitted that there is "no unanimity for the meaning" of the term learning disabilities but that the best "consensus definition" is as follows:

"A Learning Disability refers to a retardation, disorder, or delayed development in one or more of the processes of speech, language, reading, writing, arithmetic, or other school subjects resulting from a psychological handicap caused by a possible cerebral dysfunction and/or emotional or behavioral disturbances. It is not the result of mental retardation, sensory deprivation, or cultural or instructional factors" (McCarthy and McCarthy, 1969, p. 1).

McCarthy and McCarthy discussed the "variety of seemingly unrelated conditions" that are covered under this umbrella-like term: dyslexia (the inability to read), dysgraphia (the inability to write), perceptual handicap, neurological impairment and autism (the latter is rarely included by other authors who are more likely to include conditions such as hyperkenesis, minimal brain dysfunction, or language disorder). According to this popular text, "Children with learning disabilities come to the attention of schools for a number of reasons ... the ten most frequently cited characteristics of such children, in order of frequency cited (are) ... hyperactivity, perceptual-motor impairments, emotional lability, general orientation defects, disorders of attention (e.g., short attention span, distractibility), impulsivity, disorders of memory and thinking, specific learning disabilities in reading, arithmetic, writing, and spelling, disorders of speech and hearing, equivocal signs and electroencephalographic irregularities" (p. 8). The authors suggested that there are three generalizations about the children who exhibit this variety of characteristics and symptoms. They are all "retarded or disordered in school subjects, speech or language and/or manifest behavior problems" (sic). Mental retardation, deafness or blindness, can be ruled out as explanations for these disorders. All have "some presumed neurologic basis (cerebral dysfunction)" for their observed disability.

Although some other schools of thought on learning disabilities ignore questions of etiology (the factors that caused the disorder) and merely identify and treat the observable symptoms, the McCarthy's belong to the dominant school of thought. To them, as to many medical personnel in the field, it is important to understand the etiology of neurological impairment which in turn causes the behavioral manifestations of poor school performance.

"Typically, cerebral dysfunction in children dates from events preceding or surrounding the birth process. Germ plasm defects, noxious influences and agents affecting the development of the embryo, fetus, or infant, and chemical or mechanical factors may damage, directly or indirectly, the delicate and irreplaceable neural tissue of the newborn. Traumatic, poisonous, or infectious factors may be responsible for postnatal cerebral insult. Verifiable neurological impairment, such as cerebral palsy, is known to be associated with a history of prematurity, anoxia, toxemia of pregnancy, Rh incompatibility, maternal rubella, or unusual delivery. In as many as one-third of the cases of verifiable neurological impairment the cause may be unknown. Minimal brain dysfunction such as is associated with learning disabilities may arise from genetic variations, biochemical irregularities, perinatal brain insults, illnesses or injuries sustained during the years critical for the development and maturation of the central nervous system or from unknown causes." (pp. 11-12).

CHARACTERIZATIONS OF THE PROBLEM

There are several schools of thought about what constitutes the "principal cause" of learning disabilities. Like the McCarthy's, many experts believe that neurological defects underlie learning disabilities. Others think of the source of the problem as attentional, perceptual, or related to language. A very few seek out environmental influences to explain unaccountably poor school achievement.

The Problem is Neurological. The earliest and most persistent explanation is that poor school performance and symptoms of impulsivity and hyperactivity can be traced to a specific, organic injury or abnormality of the brain. This neurological or cerebral dysfunction could have been caused by events such as those listed by the McCarthy's. This theory originated with Strauss (Strauss and Lehtinen, 1947). But the physical evidence of the defect could not be located in those with the familiar behavioral manifestations. According to Satz and Fletcher (1980) who summarized the research, "the vast majority of children who are labeled

60

MBD* have no consistent evidence of soft neurological signs, peri-natal complications or electroencephalographic abnormalities ... there are many severely brain-injured children who show no evidence of academic difficulty nor behavioral impulse problems" (p. 674).

Despite these ambiguities, research on the neurological correlates of learning disabilities continues and has been expanded to topics such as brain hemispheric asymmetry, monoamine metabo-lism, family studies of the genetic basis for learning disabilities, effects of injury and malnutrition on brain and behavior, and so on.

Defining the problem as neurological was common in Belleview's staffings, particularly in the evaluations of school nurses and the few pediatricians that became involved. John's nurse, for example, placed great significance on his failure to breath spontane-ously at birth. She persisted in her judgment that something was wrong with his brain as a result of this neonatal insult (see page 44). Many professionals seemed to believe that learning disabilities are genetically determined and tend to look for symptoms in chil-dren whose siblings have already been staffed. Bobby's teacher had this to say about his perceptual problems, "If you met his mother, you'd see where he gets it."

The Problem is Perceptual. The idea that learning disa-bilities are caused by deficits in the child's perceptual or perceptual-motor apparatus grew out of the work of Orten and Strauss and has been advanced by Kephart, Wepman, Frostig, and others (Kessler, 1980).

"In Kephart's view the body is the zero point, or point of origin, for all movements, and perceptual understanding of outside objects will be disturbed if the body image is disturbed. Laterality, the ability to distinguish the left from the right side of the body and to control these individually or simultaneously, was considered pre-requisite to the differentiation of left and right in space. This would result in the failure to discriminate between a 'b' and a 'd', ...

---

*MBD, or minimal brain dysfunction is a term whose meaning is close to that of learning disabilities. Distinctions in their definitions "have not yet been demonstrated" empirically (Bryan and Bryan 1980, p. 457).

because of the absence of a proper kinesthetic, body reference point" (Kessler, 1980, p. 29).

According to this view, learning to read requires skills of perceptual processing. Academic performance is governed by a complex set of input-output relationships. In a classroom the child is confronted with a huge variety of stimuli--the voice of the teacher explaining the lesson, the writing on the blackboard, the noise of the other children moving around the room. His senses incorporate sensations which are integrated with other sensations coming from other senses, interpreted in the cortex, and must result in some motor or verbal response, such as writing an answer in his notebook or obeying the directions given by the teacher. In this theory, emphasis is placed on the connection between sensory perception (ability to recognize and interpret information coming through the eyes, ears), and the overt, physical or speaking response. Any disturbance in one of the perceptual systems will result in an attenuated ability to respond and thus poor school performance. The neurological connection cannot be observed directly, but only can be inferred by setting up a controlled testing situation to observe the in-going visual or auditory stimuli and the out-coming, elicited responses. Thus, it might be observed in the testing situation that a child's responses were deficient whenever the stimulus was presented auditorily-- through the ears. This is the idea of channel of perception or "modality"; i.e., that there is a deficiency in the visual, auditory, or kinesthetic perceptual system, channel, or modality. By interpreting patterns of test scores, therefore, clinicians may find that a child is relatively stronger in the visual than the auditory modality and therefore is a visual learner and has an auditory weakness.

Implicit in this theory is an assumption about the nature of those intellectual abilities called upon in school tasks. An individual is assumed to have a general intellectual ability plus many separate abilities. There is variability among these separate abilities within that individual so that his rote memory, for example, is very good but his abstract reasoning ability is poor; or his auditory discrimination is low but his visual processing ability is good, independent of his general intellectual functioning. The theories underlying intra-individual variability or trait organization were reviewed by Anastasi (1958) and contrasted with theories that cast intellectual ability as one general trait and theories that cast intellectual ability as many independent traits. There is evidence both for and against these competing theories, and reasonable people disagree about their merits.

The perceptual view of learning disabilities has many proponents (more often psychologists and educators than physicians) and a few critics. One of the latter (Belmont, 1980) demonstrated that the functions of perception cannot be isolated from those of cognition or language. Research and testing based on identifying auditory discrimination, say, as a unitary trait or process are likely to be simplistic and misleading. Furthermore, Newcomer and Hammil (1976) found that perceptual processing abilities do not correlate with academic performance such as reading. This would mean, if the research was sound, that auditory perception, say, was not a skill required for reading. Or it might mean that above a very basic threshold of perception, greater acuity or perceptual power does not enhance reading. Either possibility seriously challenges this dominant perspective on learning disabilities. Looking back to the case histories, one finds that the attention in staffing was paid to finding deficiencies in perceptual modalities or discontinuities between general and specific abilities. John's problem seemed to be localized in his auditory system or in integrating sensations from different modalities. Remember how his speech-language specialist said "his specific auditories are sort of low, although his general auditory is all right" (p. 44).

Attention is the Problem. The trouble experienced by learning disabled children in maintaining attention was first noticed by Strauss and is still identified as the core problem by many experts. Researchers such as Keogh, Messer, Kagan and Meichenbaum have found learning disabled children less able than normal children to scan and focus on relevant stimuli, control impulses, screen out distractions and irrelevant features, and avoid erroneous judgments (according to research reviewed by Bryan and Bryan, 1980). Jenny's problem was thought of as attentional by those who thought she had a problem (see pages 20-24).

Language is the Problem. The overlap of language and learning disabilities has long been known. Clements (1966) included (in his list of the characteristics of MBD) the language dysfunctions of aphasia, impaired discrimination of auditory stimuli, slow language development, and frequent but mild speech disorders. According to Bryan and Bryan (1980), research has shown that

63

children with learning disabilities have problems with language production and comprehension, oral syntax, morphology, and linguistic
competence generally. Language specialists tend to think of the
overlap of language and learning disabilities as derived from the
same source (cerebral or perceptual deficit) and that language itself
is the primary mediator of learning. In fact, Berry (1969) subsumed
learning disabilities as one category of language disorders.

Dating back to Orton (1937), language disorders were
said to be related to perceptual problems. He suggested that
aphasia occurred because of the child's difficulty with sequencing or
ordering stimuli through auditory and visual modes. This theory
spawned much research (reviewed by Weiner, 1980) and probably is
responsible for the current interest among speech-language specialists in perceptual testing of children suspected of learning disabilities (see Table 1). There is also considerable controversy in the field
about the causal link between concepts and language. Therefore,
speech-language specialists venture into the domain of conceptual
development as well.

- The following quotation is an excerpt from an informal
interview with a speech-language specialist, taken from the case
study data.

Question: "You're a speech-therapist aren't you?
What's a speech person doing giving the Tests of Basic
Concepts or the Picture Vocabulary Test?"

Answer: "I'm a speech-*language* specialist. We
understand language disabilities and auditory disturbances."

Question: "But those tests measure concepts."

Answer: "Language *is* concepts. Language is
everything. If you've got a language disability, you have
trouble processing auditory input and you can't perform
in the classroom. So we have to evaluate these functions
too."

Whether there are real differences behind the distinctions between language and thought, language and perception, or

language disabilities and learning disabilities awaits more adequate research and theory. Weiner (1980) reported that an adequate data base does not now exist to answer these questions.

The Problem is Environmental. The classic and still dominant view of learning disabilities places the origin of the problem in the physiological make-up of the individual. This view implies what characteristics the diagnostician should look for, what the clinician should treat, and what the researcher should investigate. A small number of experts have sought the origin of learning disabilities not in the child's head but in his family, social and physical environment. The following research was reviewed and synthesized by Werner (1980).

It has long been established that a child's low birthweight predicts his subsequent identification as learning disabled. Werner, Bierman, and French (1971) in an epidemiological study on the island of Kauai, found that this relationship was mediated by socioeconomic status. "Ten times more children had learning and behavior problems related to the effects of a poor environment than to the effects of perinatal complications. For example, children growing up in (upper) middle class homes who had experienced the most severe perinatal complications had mean scores on the Cattell Infant Intelligence Scale (at this age largely a measure of sensorimotor development) almost comparable to children with no perinatal stress who were living in lower SES homes" (Werner, 1980, p. 215). This relationship was confirmed in two other studies.

Werner also presented research data that linked learning disabilities with a barren physical environment, incapacitating mental or physical illness, disability, or accident on the part of the parents, absence of the father, and mothers' low expectations for behavior and achievement.

"Parenting variables" also relate to learning disabilities, according to the following excerpt:

"Paternite, Loney, and Langhorne (1976) have shown that parenting variables were better predictors of secondary behavior problems in hyperkinetic MBD boys than was SES. For the symptom aggressive interpersonal behavior, the most significant seven predictors were:

father's love-hostility, spouse-reported "mother's short temper," mother's consistency, spouse-reported mother's autonomy-control. For the symptom impulse control deficiency, three predictors resulted: mother's consistency, father's placidity, and mother's short temper. The four significant predictors for the symptom self-esteem deficits were: father's consistency, self-reported 'mother's strictness,' mother's firmness, and spouse-reported 'mother's too easygoing' variables" (Werner, 1980, p. 223).

Premature birth is also related to subsequent learning disability. However, Werner reported that the amount and quality of contact between the premature baby and its mother may moderate the physiological effects of prematurity.

"The diminished contact that mothers have with prematurely born infants may actually diminish the attachment the mother feels toward her new-born baby (Klaus and Kennell, 1970). When mothers of pre-term infants were compared with mothers of full-terms as to their style of contact in the initial meetings, mothers of pre-terms were more tentative in their physical contact and showed less eye-to-eye contact. Increasing the opportunity for early contact with their pre-term neonates in the hospital changed their care-giving styles. Mothers who had been allowed contact during the first 5 days showed many more intervals of cuddling and more en face intervals than mothers separated for 20 days. These differences in maternal behavior persisted and were observed at home one month after discharge.

"Residence in hospital nurseries in isolettes may deprive the pre-term infant of proprioceptive stimulation (Solkoff, et al, 1969) and reciprocal stimulus feedback experiences (Siqueland, 1973) (Werner, 1980, p. 220).

"In the Kauai longitudinal study, at one year a significantly higher proportion of mothers of infants who were later to become learning disabled characterized their offspring as 'not cuddly, not affectionate (and) not good natured; fretful' than control mothers from the same SES and ethnic group. A significantly higher proportion of mothers of infants who later were diagnosed as learning disabled were rated as 'erratic' or 'worrisome' by observers in the home; more control mothers were described as 'energetic,' 'patient,' and 'happy.'

"By two, children who later became learning disabled were characterized significantly more often by both mothers and observing psychologists as 'awkward,' 'distractible,' 'fearful,' 'insecure,' 'restless,' 'slow,' and 'withdrawn.' Controls were more often characterized as 'alert,' 'calm,' 'quiet,' and 'responsive.' Mothers whose offspring were later to become learning disabled were described in their interactions with their toddlers as 'kind, temperate,' 'matter-of-fact,' and 'content.' Apparently a vicious cycle betwen a 'non-rewarding' infant and an increasingly frustrated mother had begun in the first year of life and became aggravated in the second year (Werner and Smith, 1977)" (Werner, 1980, p. 221).

These interactions do not prove that there is no physiological cause of learning disabilities. They do, however, show that the physiological explanations have perhaps been over-stated and may be oversimplified.

Are learning problems really teaching problems? This is a question that is intriguing in itself. Even more intriguing is why virtually no research has been directed toward answering it. Yet it seems obvious that a child's achievement would be significantly lower than his ability if he missed three out of every four days of school. If his parents moved him several times from one school to another, and each school had a different curriculum, he would also fall behind. If he was assigned to three consecutive poor, inept teachers, he would lack adequate opportunity to learn. Any of these events could produce an ability-achievement discrepancy, easily mistaken for a learning disability.

Suppose a teacher knew only one way of teaching two-digit subtraction, and a child didn't get it that way. Wouldn't that lower his achievement to the significant level? And if so, why attribute causality to a deficiency of dyscalculia?

67

Seymour Sarason reviewed his experiences with the Yale Psycho-Educational Clinic and concluded that problem behaviors are never inside the child but a product of the interaction between the child and the teacher, the child and the school, or the child and his parents.

"No teacher (no human being) is equally effective with all kinds of children. It may sound like an extreme statement but we have never seen a child labeled a serious classroom problem who could not be effectively managed by another teacher in that school if one disregarded grade levels. Just as we have emphasized that some parent-child relationships founder because of a mismatch between the child's and parent's characteristics or vulnerabilities, the same principle holds between pupils and teacher" (Sarason and Doris, 1978, p. 31).

Ignoring environmental explanations may simply represent bad mental habits. Or it might be ideological. In either case, environment was given only lip service by staffing committees in Belleview.

Social workers invariably gave detailed descriptions of the pupils' emotional, social, and family status. Good data and clinical judgments on emotional and environmental patterns were therefore available. Yet the social workers seemed to defer to the judgments of the psychologists and others concerning whether a child was learning disabled. Data produced by the psychologists, learning disability and speech-language specialists were not only quantitative and therefore more credible, but focused on the psychological characteristics of the child rather than the characteristics of his environment. Definitively, the problem was located "inside" the child.

Problems in the child's home, such as divorce, were frequently mentioned in the assessment reports, but this was in passing, as it were en route to the cerebral explanation. Emotional problems were usually seen as secondary to, rather than a cause of, poor school achievement. There was little recognition that impulsivity, preserveration, and hyperactivity can be caused by anxiety or depression (in reaction, perhaps, to a family crisis) rather than by a mimimal brain dysfunction.

UNANSWERED QUESTIONS ABOUT DEFINITIONS

The experts have foundered upon three issues: whether learning disabilities represent problems of deficit or development, whether they are single or multiple syndromes, whether learning disabled children are only quantitatively, not qualitatively different from normal children. The research that should have provided the field with a valid set of definitions has not done so. Many studies used the design of comparing samples of children identified as learning disabled with samples of children identified as normal. The dependent variables on which the two groups were compared were myriad, everything from "skill in matching familiar figures" to teachers' ratings of pupil attentiveness. Differences on the dependent variable were then attributed to the group (i.e., "learning disabled children have shorter attention spans than normal children").

These studies suffered from a variety of shortcomings. Regression to the mean is the most technical. Frequently, the studies used samples of learning disabilities with mixed levels of intelligence, socioeconomic status, sex, age, and severity of disability. Thus findings were confounded with these other variables.

Studies suffered for having retrospective or expost facto designs. That is, they used as subjects children already identified as learning disabled and tried to establish a pattern of characteristics and events such as prematurity or breech delivery. Biases from poor memory, absence of a reliable record, or selective reporting are notorious in research of this type. Most importantly, the studies confounded the disorder with the identification of the disorder. Some members of the sample were truly learning disabled, but others might have been falsely labeled.

Psychological theory demands that traits be validated by constructing a "nomological net" that links measurable characteristics logically and empirically. The medical model of diagnosis requires establishment (for any disease) of the cause, lesion, pattern of uniform and invariate symptoms, course of illness and treatment of choice. Whether the clinician is a psychologist or a doctor, he must look to research studies to verify the existence of a disease or trait. Although research studies that examine characteristics of learning disabilities are many, their results clearly define neither nosology nor trait validity.

Routh (1980) who undertook to validate the trait minimum brain dysfunction (a term he used synonymous with learning disability) reported on his failure to find patterns of uniform symptoms:

"Our inital study (Routh & Roberts, 1972) concerned the covariation of these deficits among a sample of 89 school-age children attending the Child Development Clinic. Most were referred for evaluation of poor school performance. All children with either mental retardation or gross neurologic defect were excluded from the sample, as the review done by Clements' (1966) task force suggested. Some of the deficits of these children were defined by teacher ratings (e.g., attentional problems), others by psychological tests (e.g., the Bender Gestalt Test) and others by consensus based on multi-disciplinary examination of each child. After partialling out the covariation among the aspects of MBD due to age and IQ, we found that there was virtually no common variance left among the measures of different types of behavioral deficit. Thus in this sample, one could not predict from the degree of rated hyperactivity how much visual motor difficulty a child might be having, or predict how much of a reading problem a child had from knowing the child's degree of incoordination, and so on. The results of the study were considered 'somewhat damaging' to the idea of an MBD syndrome.

"One negative study does not destroy a concept. In the case of the concept of MBD as a behavioral syndrome, however, there seem to be many negative studies (Dreger, 1964; Paine, Werry & Quay, 1968; Rodin, Locas & Simson, 1963; Werry, 1968b), and no positive ones. Before I will seriously wish to use the concept of MBD again, I will wait to be shown that such a syndome exists (p. 62).

The concept of learning disabilities is illusive. Some writers have even called it illusory. Schrag and Divoky (1975) referred to both hyperactivity and learning disabilities as "myths," "created" by venal professionals and overanxious parents. This judgment must seem incomprehensible to the resource room teacher who struggles daily with yet another technique to penetrate Jimmy's inability to read or change Jackie's tendency to reverse her digits in an arithmetic problem. As one Belleview teacher said to me "The tests are baloney; what the professors tell you about LD is baloney. But you work with these kids everyday and you *know* that *something* is wrong with them, but no one, *no one* really understands what it is."

DEFINITIONS IN LAW

The special education staffing process--deciding who will and will not receive special education--is no longer the sole prerogative of professionals, but is governed by a variety of state and federal mandates. Therefore professional definitions of learning disabilities, like those of the other handicapping conditions, must give way officially to very specific operational criteria. If a child meets these criteria the school must provide services for him, some agency reimburses the cost of both his staffing and treatment, and he falls under the jurisdiction of that agency to insure that his civil rights are not violated and he receives an education appropriate for his needs.

Definitions that appear in laws and the agency rules and regulations that elaborate the laws are more political than professional. They are framed as a result of the testimony before the relevant legislative or executive department of myriad and variegated experts and special interest lobbies and of the political compromises among these groups. The federal definition, from Public Law 94-142, is as follows:

'Specific learning disability' means a disorder in one or more of the basic psychological processes involved in understanding or in using language, spoken or written, which may manifest itself in an imperfect ability to listen, think, speak, read, write, spell, or to do mathematical calculations. The term includes such conditions as perceptual handicaps, brain injury, minimal brain dysfunction, dyslexia, and developmental aphasia. The term

71

does not include children who have learning problems which are primarily the result of visual, hearing or motor handicaps, of mental retardation, of emotional disturbance, or of environmental, cultural, or economic disadvantage."

"Criteria for determining the existence of a specific learning disability. A team may determine that a child has a specific learning disability if:

1. The child does not achieve commensurate with his or her age and ability levels in one or more of the areas listed in paragraph (1) (3) of this section, when provided with learning experiences appropriate for the child's age and ability levels; and

2. The team finds that a child has a severe discrepancy between achievement and intellectual ability in one or more of the following areas: 1. (i) Oral expression, (ii) listening comprehension, (iii) written expression, (iv) basic reading skill, (v) reading comprehension; (vi) mathematics calculation or (vii) mathematics reasoning.

The team may not identify a child as having a specific learning disability if the severe discrepancy between ability and achievement is primarily the result of:

1. A visual, hearing, or motor handicap;

2. Mental retardation;

3. Emotional disturbance; or

4. Environmental, cultural or economic disadvantage."

Definitions vary slightly from state to state. Colorado, of which Belleview schools are a part, has a different name, but not a different meaning for the learning disabilities. The definition of Perceptual-communicative Disorder is as follows:

"A perceptual or communicative disorder is indicated when there is a significant discrepancy between estimated intellectual potential and actual level of performance and is related to basic disorders in the learning processes which are not secondary to limited intellectual capacity, visual or auditory sensory impairment, emotional disorders, and/or experiential information. One or more of the following measurable disorders are observed:

1. Significantly impaired ability in pre-reading and/or reading skills.

2. Significantly impaired ability in reading comprehension.

3. Significantly impaired ability in written language expression, such as problems in handwriting, spelling, sentence structure and written organization.

4. Significantly impaired ability to comprehend, apply and/or retain math concepts."

Both the federal and state definitions demand that the staffing committees look for children with manifest school problems--primarily low achievement--exclude those children whose problems are explained by deafness, blindness, low intelligence, emotional disturbance, or socioeconomic or cultural disadvantage, then infer the presence of a neurological or perceptual disorder. According to the legislated definitions, if a child is a "slow learner" (has a low IQ but not so low as to be classified as mentally retarded) or is achieving poorly because he is Chicano or poor or mentally ill, he cannot be classified as learning disabled. He is excluded from qualifying for the rights of the handicapped to a "free and appropriate education," and the school cannot be reimbursed for the extra costs of his education. This is the law; in practice this exclusionary definition is regularly ignored by staffing committees.

IMPLICIT DEFINITIONS

Professional and legislated definitions are public. An individual's personal constructs are internal, often poorly articulated and may only by discovered through intensive interviews or long-term, first-hand observations of his actions. His public declarations of what he conceives learning disabilities to be are deceptive, and he may assert that he follows professional and legislated definitions. But when it comes time to decide whether a particular child should be staffed as learning disabled, the basis of his decision-making is his personal constructs or implicit definitions.

The most common personal construct among people studied in Belleview was this: The learning disabled is the "child who needs extra help." That is, the child who needs more individual attention and time than the classroom teacher can provide or a different kind of instruction from that which his classmates are receiving. If the majority or influential members of the staffing team hold this implicit definition of learning disabilities, then room is made in treatment programs for children that would be excluded if the legislated or professional definitions were strictly followed. "Slow learners," those who have below average intelligence but not low as to be classified as retarded, "need extra help" and thus are labeled and treated as learning disabled by staffing committees.* Such teams defined as learning disabled the child who was having trouble in school because he was emotionally disturbed, another because his cradle tongue was not English, the one who had suffered from inferior schools in a poor community, maybe even the child who just did not try very hard to learn to spell. All of them "needed extra help."

Another common personal construct or implicit definition about learning disabilities is "the child who is behind his age-mates." Parents and teachers have strong normative expectations. They believe that the group of children they face directly--the population of children within their immediate personal experience--will

---

*According to Shepard, et al., 1981, 12% of the learning disabled population in Colorado are really slow learners, not learning disabled.

differ from each other in their abilities only to a moderate degree. A child who is very discrepant from the average of this personal population violates their mental images about normal variability. In other words, children of the same age should be nearly alike, and if one departs from the expected range of abilities something is wrong. There seems to be a powerful motive on the part of both educators and parents to provide an explanation for the deviation. The professional literature provides a ready explanation--that the child in question is learning disabled.

The testing profession reinforces the obsession with age-mate expectations by publishing age norms and encouraging their use. Age norms are the principal technique for assigning meaning to test scores. Jenny was eight years and three months old when she was administered the Illinois Test of Psycholinguistic Abilities (see page 35). Her score on the Auditory Reception subtest of 27 was not meaningful in itself. But the test publishers say that a score of 27 is equivalent to the average score obtained by persons of exactly seven years old. By using these age-norms the clinicians concluded that Jenny was a year and three months behind where she should be in Auditory Reception. The next step in their chain of inference was that she had a perceptual deficiency in the auditory domain; i.e., she was behind her age-mates and therefore learning disabled.

Age-mates expectations affected John in slighty different ways. When his older sister was John's age she could already read by herself and loved doing so. This established an age-mate expectation in the mind of their mother, who felt that John must have a perceptual problem that explained his lag in learning to read.

Causing a child to repeat a grade is one of the most stressful decisions educators and parents make. It violates the age-segregation of classrooms and confuses age-mate expectations and grade level expectations. Because of what was called immaturity, Jenny had been retained for a second year in kindegarten. She was eight years-old and in the second grade (typically made up of seven year-olds) when staffed. The clinicians used norms for eight year-olds to decide that her achievement was sufficiently discrepant from her ability. They thus penalized her for not knowing words and sentences typically encountered by third graders not second graders. She would not have qualified for special education if they had compared her to children of her same grade level.

Placing a child in special education is often used as a substitute for causing him to repeat a grade. By declaring this child as learning disabled, the school releases itself from obligations related to accountability or grade level performance standards for him.

Age-mate expectations are created by only those children within the teacher, parent, or clinician's personal range of experience. Therefore a child who is normal and unremarkable in an urban or poor rural school district might be discrepant and declared handicapped when compared with children in a richer, suburban district such as Belleview.

"The lowest child in my class" is another variation on this implicit definition of the learning disabilities. One Belleview administrator pointed out that referrals for learning disabilities staffing will continue to pour in as long as regular classroom teachers hold this definition and desire to deal with more homogeneous groups of children.

Another class of implicit definitions exists in Belleview. These are imposed by teachers and parents who have a smattering of knowledge about special education so that they hear a term, have only a loose understanding of it, and then apply it inappropriately to the children they encounter. For example, teachers frequently used the designation "auditory discrimination disorder" to identify children who do not pay attention to them. "Fine motor problems" designated the child with poor handwriting and "hyperkinetic" described the child who runs around the class and upsets the teacher.

The final category of implicit definition I call LD-Speak. LD-Speak is a puzzling phenomenon, for it abides chiefly in the leaflets and conversations of parental and advocacy groups. Occasionally newspaper or magazine articles contain it, or it is presented on television talk shows. It consists of statements about the nature, cause, and treatment of learning disabilities. An activist parent recently stated, in a tone that pre-empted any question or challenge, "Most LD children don't ever get better, so it's ridiculous for the legislators to criticize us for lack of turnover in our programs." Later in the same meeting, another activist parent pleaded for more resources: "Unless these kids get special treatment they will invariably have failed lives."

LD-Speak usually consists of empirical generalizations or scientific-sounding statements about learning disability. Some of them may be true. The truth of LD-Speak, however, is not as important as its function, which I believe to be a kind of ideological sloganeering. It functions as a way of unifying a set of individuals into a faction and convincing the society at large that the personal problem these parents have is really a legitimate social problem for which society's resources must be devoted. (The theory of social problems of Blumer, 1971 applies here.) LD-Speak is political rhetoric. Its relationship to science is tenuous, for the critical, disinterested stance of the scientist is antithetical to the colorful, committed moral fervor of statements designed to motivate action on behalf of the cause (Geertz, 1973). A statement such as, "Twenty-three percent of children have learning disabilities" draws on no body of scientific evidence, but is meant to sound scientific so that members of the advocacy groups will work harder to convince the public and its legislators to take action.

Another purpose must be mentioned. These statements may be a way that troubled parents have of resolving dissonance, of breaking our culture's connection between achievement and love. Attaching these labels may be a culturally acceptable way for parents to prize a child who is not doing well.

Examples of LD-Speak
(taken from advocacy groups, magazines,
television shows and popular books)

1. Learning Disabilities are not something kids grow out of.

2. Albert Einstein, William James, Thomas Edison, Nelson Rockefeller, August Rodin, George Patton, and Woodrow Wilson suffered from learning disabilities.

3. Urging the learning disabled child to try harder will just compound the problem.

4. Blond, blue-eyed kids are more susceptible to learning disabilities.

5. Almost all juvenile delinquents are learning disabled.

6. The learning disabled are superior problem-solvers.

7. LDs have an extra eye-fold.

8. Learning disability is genetically determined because it runs in families.

9. LDs lack binocular vision so vision training can help most of them.

10. Children who can't follow directions are apt to have a dysfunction in auditory memory.

11. There are disproportionately more adopted children among the learning disabled.

12. There are six million dyslexic children in the United States.

13. Even the best parenting cannot offset the damage resulting from a physical insult to the central nervous system.

14. Learning disabled children have above-average or superior intelligence.

15. A child who says emeny instead of enemy and aminal instead of animal has a dysfunction of auditory sequentialization.

16. Vestibular dysfunction causes LD and vestibular stimulation can cure it.

17. An LD child may have a white chalk spot on one cheek.

18. A 9 year-old who has trouble walking the balance beam is likely to be learning disabled.

19. LDs have clinical signs resembling those of sleep-deprived adults.

20. LDs seem to need to read or watch television while lying supine.

21. A child with poor perceptual motor development was a floppy baby.

22. Breech delivery leads to central nervous system dysfunction.

23. Ambidexterity is a reflection of poor neurological organization.

24. All hyperactivity is a result of allergic reaction to foods and food additives.

25. There are 7 million children with learning disabilities.

26. A learning disabled child will explode at minor irritations and slip into temper tantrums at the slightest provocation. It is best for parents to ignore them.

27. The vast increase in learning disabilities is related to the increased use of sugar, additives, and chemicals.

28. When an infant of low birth weight survives only because of intervention of new medical techniques, there will inevitably be some degree of neurological deficit.

29. Emotional and behavioral problems in the learning disabled are the inevitable and understandable *result* of the physiological problem.

30. More than three out of four youngsters with learning disabilities appear to be clumsy and awkward.

31. Every child who has normal intelligence and is seriously behind in reading has a specific language disability that is the result of Minimal Brain Dysfunction.

32. No learning disabled child is exactly like another.

33. Initial diagnosis will confirm--or refute--the presence of learning disabilities in your child.

34. I have proved that dyslexia is caused by problems of the inner ear.

35. Your child might not like the special class at first. Don't panic if he regresses.

Effects of Ambiguities

The condition called learning disabilities is ambiguous. The scientific research that ought to have reduced the equivocacy has not done so. Implicit definitions of those on staffing teams carry more weight than professional and official definitions in determining whether a child is learning disabled. These personal constructs depart from the clinical patterns established in the professional literature to unknown degree and to unknown effects. One thing is clear about these personal constructs. Learning disabilities have usually been considered a characteristic of the child who had one; they have seldom been considered to be characteristics or effects of the environment, the relationship between parent or child and virtually never considered to be the result of ineffective curriculum or teaching.

Yet to be discussed, in subsequent chapters, are various legal, economic, and social pressures to identify individuals as handicapped. These pressures, when coupled with the ambiguous definitions of learning disabilities, result in a high probability that any child who is referred will be staffed and placed. This in turn produces overidentification.

Diagnosis

With the definitions so ambiguous, valid recognition and assessment of learning disabilities is troublesome. Tests proliferate. Clinicians test with abondon. The pressure to conduct more assessments comes from all directions. Psychometricians (experts in the theory and mathematics of testing) have objected to the kinds of test used in special education. Yet special educators either do not know about these objections or fail to recognize their validity. The unsurprising result is controversy. Three models of recognizing learning disabilities can be distinguished--the mechanical, the medical, and the psychometric.

Mechanical

Without regard to etiology or clinical signs, a child can be diagnosed simply by application of a statistical formula. With this procedure one can estimate the size of the discrepancy between a measure of the child's intellectual ability and another measure of his achievement in reading or arithmetic. If the discrepancy is large enough to exceed chance expectation (i.e., said to be "statistically significant") then the child is declared to be learning disabled. This method fits the operational, legislated definitions of "school performance lagging behind potential." It eliminates the need for elaborate clinical assessments and the judgment by the staffing teams that the discrepancy is due to some underlying neurological or perceptual processing disorder.

Although it is undoubtedly the least expensive and probably the most impartial of the procedures, the mechanical has few adherents among special educators in Belleview or elsewhere. Although it is the district's officially recognized method of identifying learning disabilities, it is virtually never used. It also fails to meet the requirements laid down in Public Law 94-142 that every potentially handicapped person be evaluated on individual rather than standard criteria.

Using the discrepancy between ability and achievement as a sign of learning disabilities fails to consider alternative causes. Discrepancies can result from frequent absences or changes from school, from poor teaching or lack of effort. Discrepancies can be produced simply because the tests are unreliable or because of differences in the samples on which the two tests were normed. Although the procedure seems objective, it can be manipulated by the choice of tests. By picking Test A, an administrator can be sure that a fifty percent discrepancy will qualify many more children than would be qualified by the use of Achievement Test B. True learning disabilities can be missed by this process, as when a child's perceptual problem depresses both his achievement and ability scores so that no discrepancy is observed.

Medical

Also called the clinical model (Meehl, 1954), the medical model operates on the recognition of one or more observable symptoms or indicators and the inference by a skilled clinician that those indicators are connected to an underlying condition or disorder. For example, Gofman (1969) listed ten indicators of learning disabilities and recommended that the clinician examine the child to see if he displays any of them. If he displays several of them (Gofman did not specify the minimum number), the clinician may infer that the underlying learning disability exists. Her list of "Physician's Index of Learning Disorders" follows: sex (males are more vulverable), "family history of reading, spelling, or speech disorders," illness of mother during pregnancy, birth history including prematurity, prolonged or precipitous labor or unusual delivery, perinatal anoxia," neonatal course" including sucking ability and general activity compared to that of siblings: a history of poor sucking, excessive sleeping, apathy or increased irritability may indicate deviation in central nervous sytem function," developmental milestones in comparison with siblings (including awareness) and hyperkinetic syndrome. She recommended attending to the total profile of such indicators rather than to any one or two of them, but was vague on the question of what profile dissimilarities might imply.

Mercer (1979) explained the medical model and how it works in the diagnosis of the handicapped (pp. 94-96).

"The medical model is designed to answer questions about the state of the organism. . . . An abnormality in the organism is defined as a process that tends to destroy the biological integrity of the organism as a living system and to interfere with its functioning. Such pathological processes are identified by their biological symptoms. In the medical model, normal tends to be a residual category which consists of those persons who do not manifest the symptoms of pathology. In some situations . . . behavioral patterns are interpreted as symptoms of organic malfunctioning. In such cases, there is the assumption that the behavior is the result of pathological conditions in the organism and not the result of learning . . . . The medical model assumes that the symptoms are caused by some biological condition in the organism--a disease process, lesion, chromosomal anomaly, or other pathological condition. When the only observable symptoms are behaviors and the organic basis for the condition cannot be specifically identified, the burden of proof rests with the evaluator who uses the medical model to present evidence that organic inferences are justified.

"A second assumption of the medical model is that the sociocultural characteristics of the individual are irrelevant to making a diagnosis or prescribing a treatment. The medical model is based on a universal set of values derived from the fact that the human organism is similar in all human societies. There is a single, cross-cultural status of any human being, regardless of cultural setting. These norms are based on the nature of the human organism and do not vary with language or culture. . . In the medical model the organism is the focus of assessment and pathology is perceived as a condition existing in the person, an attribute of the organism. Thus, we say a person is tubercular or has scarlet fever. It also holds that a pathological condition can exist, unrecognized. Hence, within this model, it is logical to 'screen' populations for undiagnosed or undetected pathologies . . .

"The validity of the medical model measure is determined by the extent to which it predicts pathology . . . Operationally, validity of medical model measures is determined by intercorrelating scores from a variety of medical model measures, i.e., health history, physical dexterity, sensory-motor coordination, medical history, etc. Correlations should be statistically reliable but we would not expect them to be large. Conversely, correlations with sociocultural characteristics should be low unless there is a clearly established genetic or other biological link between such characteristics and pathological symptoms."

For learning disabilities the correlation between observable or measureable symptoms and the underlying disorder is neither large nor significant. Coles (1978) showed the poor validity of neurological examinations and assessments made by electroencephalogram. As for "suspicious" behavioral signs such as impulsivity, non-disabled children are also quite likely to display them.

People on staffing teams at Belleview tended to focus on one or two signs (rarely attending to the whole profile as Gofman recommended) or become fascinated by isolated indicators such as anoxia at birth. They seemed not to recognize the base rates of such phenomena; that is, the distribution of such characteristics across affected and unaffected groups of children. For example, the staffing team at Poplar was reluctant to staff John until the nurse heard that he had anoxia at birth. She considered that as a positive sign of learning disabilities. She ignored, however, the completely normal results of the neurological examination given to John shortly after his birth.

Mercer (1979) described the medical model as more concerned with "false negatives" than false positives.

"The pervasive code in medical decision making holds that it is worse for a physician to overlook a pathology than it is for him to suspect pathology, continue to make diagnostic tests, and later to find that there is no pathology . . . . The belief that a 'false negative' is more serious error than a 'false positive' is based on the presumption that an untreated pathology may worsen and eventually lead to death, while additional diagnostic tests will not be harmful to the patient" (p. 96).

However, when the disease is learning disabilities the consequences of this frame of mind may be severe. There are myriad positive signs, but not one negative sign, i.e., not one litmus test that tells that a particular child is *not* learning disabled. Classes for the learning disabled are a club that your child or mine could easily get into, but would have a difficult time avoiding.

Clinical methods of diagnosis have had a checkered career in both medicine and psychology. Meehl (1954) reviewed evidence on clinical judgment and found it consistently less reliable than statistical (mechanical) methods. Goldberg (1968) found evidence that accuracy of clinical judgments was unrelated to the amount of professional training and experience of the clinicians. Furthermore, he found that the amount of information available to the clinicians was unrelated to the accuracy of their predictions.

Sadler (1981) reviewed studies of person perception and warned that clinical judgment could be adversely affected by the following perceptual tendencies.

1. There are "severe limitations on the amount of information able to be perceived, processed, and remembered" (Miller, 1956; Summers, Taliaferro, and Fletcher, 1970.) This is a particularly evident problem in the diagnosis of learning disabilities where the number of discrete pieces of information runs into the hundreds. Table 1 (p. 35) contains only a portion of the total number of test scores and evaluations gathered from Jenny. There was little sign that any person could or did deal effectively with all of it.

2. The clinician's first impressions carry undue weight (Poulton, 1968; Tversky and Kahneman, 1974). In the staffing process, the first piece of evidence is the judgment of the teacher or parent who refers the child and whose implicit definitions have construed that a problem exists. That initial judgment colors all subsequent evaluations. Jenny's teacher, for example, regarded Jenny's inattentiveness, impulsivity, and bossiness as indicative of learning disability. One can track that teacher's construction of the problem, even her words, throughout the reports of the other clinicians, even though the latter had no opportunity, or failed to observe the same symptomatic behaviors.

3. A clinician's judgment is heavily influenced by information that is in the more readily available and interpretable form (Tversky and Kahneman, 1974). In the staffing process, the numerical, test score data produced by the psychologist, learning disabilities and speech-language specialists were more readily interpretable and carried more authority than the verbal, but no less valid data of the social worker. It was easier to deal with information that seemed to state "exactly" that John was two months below grade level in reading achievement than that he might be actively resisting his parents' pressure to achieve.

4. Information that is in conflict with a previously held hypothesis is ignored. Confirming evidence is given more consideration than negative information (Wason, 1968). Witness the complete disregard by the staffing committee of the possibility that Jenny's problem might have been caused by the reading program. Their prevailing hypothesis was that Jenny's problem was endogenous and they attended to data that supported this idea.

5. Judges treat poor, unreliable data as equal in importance to good quality, reliable data (Kahneman and Tversky, 1973). Clinicians never questioned the reliability or validity of tests given by themselves or each other. Jenny's staffing committee credited the data from the Detroit Test of Learning Aptitude (a test with poor technical adequacy) with as much respect as data from the Wechsler Intelligence Scale for Children (WISC-R), a much better test. In this respect the committee was like clinicians throughout Colorado (see Chapter 10) the majority of whom could not tell the difference between technically adequate and inadequate tests.

6. Judges are insensitive to base rates or normal variability of characteristics in a population and thus are likely to view an individual as pathological when in fact he is within the expected range of persons (Peterson and Beach, 1967). Clinicians misunderstand randomness, over-interpret correlations, and mistake correlation for causation (Smedslund, 1963; Tversky and Kahneman,

1971). Much is made by staffing committees of a significant difference between the verbal and performance subtests of the WISC-R. This is regarded by psychologists as indicative of a perceptual processing disorder. Careful study of the standardization research on this test reveals that a significant verbal-performance subtest was obtained by a large proportion of the sample and must therefore be regarded as *normal*, not pathological.

Psychometric

The preeminent idea among special educators concerning the recognition of learning disabilities holds that such recognition depends upon an inference made by a clinician based on his interpretation of the patterns of a child's scores on batteries of tests. (The word battery might evoke an association with artillery. Indeed, children in the assessment phase of the staffing process are bombarded with tests and afterwards their parents are bombarded with test scores.) That is, particular configurations of high and low scores on tests are supposed to indicate the existence of an underlying neurological or perceptual impairment. The clinical diagnosis thus derived by the test scores is designed to lead to a "prescription" of educational or psychological treatments to remedy or compensate for the impairment discovered in the child. An intelligence test such as the Weschler Intelligence Scale for Children (WISC-R) is commonly given to a child suspected of having a learning disability. This test is given to establish that the child's intellectual abilities are "within normal range" for his age, or nearly average (approximately 100 points on the standard IQ scale). Then an achievement test is given to establish that his school performance is below average for his age, grade, or intellectual abilities. The combination of these two test scores meets the operational definition of learning disabilities and thus establishes his eligibility for the status of handicapped. Yet many additional tests are nearly always given to determine his "educational needs". The additional tests serve three functions. First, they anticipate a positive decision by the staffing committee by providing diagnostic information and prescriptions that the special education teacher can fill. Second, the tests appear to be a response to the state and federal rules and regulations specifying that each child suspected of being handicapped must undergo a "wholistic assessment". A wholistic assessment means that the staffing committee must gather data on all aspects of the child: intellectual ability, academic performance, physical health, vision, hearing, social development, emotional status, motor abilities, language functioning, and in the case of Colorado law, his perceptual processing abilities. Data must be gathered by professionals in various specialties (e.g., health must be assessed by doctors or nurses, intellectual ability by psychologists, and language functioning by speech-language specialists). The rules state that all these data do not necessarily need to come from tests, but specialists may rely on observations and professional judgments. In practice, tests represent the dominant mode of data collection.

In Belleview schools all these data are routinely collected. But the bulk of the assessment time and energy is taken up in the testing of perceptual processing. This is not unique to Belleview (see the cases described by Weatherly, 1979), but illustrates the third reason for these additional tests: the blind devotion of special educators to perceptual testing. The reason for this devotion appears to be that the tests seem to provide explanations for a problem that otherwise defies explanation. When a distraught parent asks, "But, why is my child not learning to read if he is smart enough?" the special educator can point to the child's pattern of test scores and say, "It is because he has a visual perception problem; he can't see letters and mentally process them."

The psychometric model follows the intra-individual or trait variability theory of intellectual functioning. Academic performance is said to be the product of a general ability plus a number of discrete abilities such as memory, language, reasoning, and perceptual processing. In this model it is assumed that in normal children all these discrete abilities will develop at the same rate. But a child whose discrete abilities are not approximately equal is suspected of having a learning disability. This condition is manifested in test score profiles from ability tests batteries, which are made up of more than one subtest. Each subtest represents a separate ability. A normal child will have a "flat profile" because all his separate abilities will be about the same. Patterns of highly variable scores indicate, to adherents of this model, that the child has a learning disability. Looking for these patterns is called an "intra-individual diagnosis" or "profile analysis." The child is not compared with others his own age, but instead his separate abilities are compared with each other. On a series of tests or subtests of separate abilities the scores of even a normal child will differ from each other by a small degree due to presence of error of measurement in each test or subtest. Therefore one task of the profile analyst is to determine whether the difference between two scores is small enough simply to be error (i.e., random or due to chance) or large enough to exceed chance. Chance differences between two scores will not support an inference of underlying learning disabilities. Nor is a difference greater than chance inevitably due to a learning disability. Salvia and Ysseldyke (1981) stated the conditions under which profile analysis could be validly used. These conditions were not recognized by Belleview clinicians, who frequently misinterpreted or over-interpreted random profile differences.

Table 3 presents hypothetical subtest profiles for two children on the ITPA. Using the criteria of the test developers, Child A is normal; all his subtests are the same or differ so slightly that the differences are due simply to chance. Child B has evidence of auditory problems. Child B scored relatively low on the subtest Grammatic Closure (wherein the tester reads incomplete sentences to the child who is asked to complete them with the missing words, "Here is a dog; here are two _____.") A low score was also obtained on the subtest, Auditory Reception (wherein the child is asked to answer yes or no when the tester asks a question such as "Do birds fly?"). Scores on Auditory Closure, Auditory Association, and Verbal Expression were also low, whereas those measuring visual processing abilities were relatively high. The clinical inference about a specific learning disability in the auditory domain rests on the pattern of auditory subtest scores that were low relative to subtests measuring other abilities and to the over-all average of all subtests.

When mental tests are used, the theory and mathematics of testing (psychometrics) come into play, though the mathematical constraints are seldom welcomed by special educators. Psychometricians demand that the error of tests be small; that is, the scores on Auditory Reception earned by Child B on Monday should be numerically close to scores he would earn on Friday if he took the same test. Numerical consistency is called *reliability*. To meet the standard of *validity* there must be a measureable relationship between a score on an auditory test and the auditory ability itself.

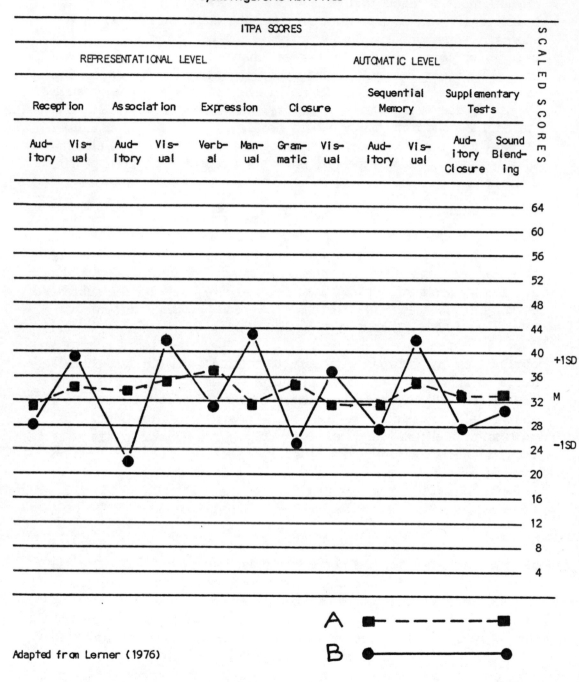

Table 3
A Child's Profile of Scaled Scores on the Illinois Test of
Psycholinguistic Abilities

Adapted from Lerner (1976)

Two different measures of the same ability ought to produce roughly equivalent results. Furthermore, children whose scores on these batteries indicate learning disabilities also ought to be those who have difficulty reading, writing or calculating in the classroom, since the perceptual theorists say these abilities are related. Federal rules and regulations specify that the tests used in the staffing process be reliable, valid, and match the standards of the major professional organizations concerned with psychometrics. These organizations--the American Psychological Association, National Council on Measurement in Education and the American Educational Research Association--have published joint standards for determining the quality of tests, and psychometric specialists use the joint standards in reviewing available tests.

In recent reviews, psychometricians have condemned tests used to recognize learning disabilities. Some tests were condemned because of low reliability. The Detroit Tests of Learning Aptitude have subtest reliabilities so low that the flip of a coin might be as good a way to determine if a child has auditory problems. Some were condemned on the basis of poor validity, e.g., that patterns of subtests on the Frostig Developmental Test of Visual Perception failed to correlate with reading performance. Some were condemned summarily, "The Illinois Test of Psycholinguistic Abilities should never have been published, at least in its present form . . . . . It is as if the APA standards had never been written" (Lumsden, 1978). In general, these condemnations have gone unheeded.

Criticisms by Coles (1978), Lumsden (1978), Shepard (1979), and Ysseldyke (1979) of commonly used tests contrast with the claims made by test developers, who have an obvious stake in the special education staffing process and the use of such tests. The users of these tests are called upon daily to diagnose and make prescriptions for the learning disabled and tend to disregard the criticisms of the tests in their arsenals. Learning disabilities specialists in Belleview were asked to read and respond to a critical review by Shepard (1979). They refused to acknowledge the substance of her arguments and vowed to continue the practice of testing for perceptual processing deficits. The Director of Special Education stated that he had no confidence in reviews of the *Mental Measurements Yearbook* such as that of Lumsden. "Like the Bible," he said, these reviews "are written by people with prejudices."

DIAGNOSIS IN BELLEVIEW

No policy on the use of tests existed in Belleview. The director of special education left the choice of what test and how many tests to use to each professional on the assessment team. Thus the Illiois Test of Psycholinguistic Abilities was given by the special education teacher in one school, the speech-language specialist in a second school, and even the reading specialist in a third school. No one questioned this practice so long as the specific test was not given more than once to a child by two different specialists. Occasionally a specialist used observation or professional judgment rather than a psychometric instrument, but this was rare. Tests were the preferred mode of gathering data for the staffing decision.

Autonomy in this selection and use of tests was extreme. No member questioned another's choice of test even if he had private doubts about its validity. Furthermore, no one questioned if the conclusion from one specialist's test failed to corroborate, or even contradicted that of another specialist's tests. In the case of Jenny, for example, Kathy identified auditory problems from subtest scores on the Illinois Test of Psycholinguistic Abilities but the speech-language specialist found no evidence of auditory problems from her administration of the Wiig-Semmel Test. Connie interpreted evidence of conceptual development problems, but the school psychologist found no such evidence from the tests he gave. These contradictions were available for everyone to see, yet they were not acknowledged. If a discrepancy in test results was pointed out it was rationalized in terms of the differences in content or process of the tests--that Test A is presented auditorily whereas Test B is a visual test. Never was such a discrepancy viewed as indicative of the invalidity of the test itself. The only occasion on which I ever heard the issue of validity raised was when an independent evaluator, hired by the parents, produced test conclusions contradictory to the results produced by the school's assessment team.

Technical standards about the reliability and validity of tests were not part of the consciousness of the people on the assessment teams. They looked at the content of test items and checked face validity, perhaps the table of age and grade norms.

They studied vigorously the interpretations that result from various patterns of test results. Occasionally a person specialized in a particular instrument such as the Slingerland, even attended schools and training workshops on how to administer and interpret the test. Even these people were unlikely to be aware of the research on reliability or validity of their favorite instruments.

The amount of testing was uncontrolled. It was not unusual for five different professionals to come into a child's classroom, remove him to a quiet office, and give him tests or interview him. Sometimes an evaluation specialist pulled out a child more than once--at worst four or five times. The effect of this singling out of the child can only be guessed, as can the effect of the loss of learning time while he was out taking tests.

The costs of this open-minded commitment to testing were considerable, certainly amounting to $500 for each child. The cost of the entire staffing process was estimated at $1000. But the Colorado reimbursement formulas permit the school districts to bill the state for all the costs of assessment with no official maximum amount. Therefore assessment is an expandable resource, a characteristic which makes Belleview very different from the Massachusetts school districts studied by Weatherly (1979).

Although nothing limited the amount of testing in Belleview, there was much to encourage its proliferation. The pressure to produce an explanation for a child's poor performance in school was overwhelming. The more tests given, the greater was the likelihood that one low score would be produced and provide the staffing team something to point to for an explanation. The sigh of relief was almost audible when the poor performance was given a reason, even when that reason was without valid justification. The need of the school to avoid outside scrutiny and lawsuits or appeals hearings also motivated the staffing team to conduct more and more assessments. Tests became a totem that would keep one's house safe from the evils of litigation and administrative review.

Tests, by virtue of the mathematical form of their scores and the opacity of their language, convey status and the appearance of scientific expertise to the clinicians using them. For the same reason they may reduce skepticism and induce parents to comply with what the school people think is the best decision. They rationalize the clinical judgments of those on staffing teams. Therefore tests serve functions besides diagnosis.

EFFECTS OF AMBIGUITIES

The technical problems of measurement and controversies in the diagnosis of learning disabilities are acute. When it confronts the test scores and symptoms of a referred child and tries to match these with the definitions of learning disabilities, the school staffing committee is faced with the equivalent of a Rorschach ink blot. All of the social, legal, and economic needs of the committee are projected onto this ambiguous stimulus. The resulting decisions are sometimes irrelevant to the needs of the child.

Each model of recognizing learning disabilities is plagued with error and controversy. Yet clinicians devote more and more time and energy to diagnosis, looking for explanations that prove to be illusive, and hiding scientism behind a mask of medicine and science.

CHAPTER FOUR

DECISION-MAKING IN THE STAFFING CONFERENCE

Those things that make the definition and recognition of learning disabilities so troublesome also complicate the decisions the staffing committee must make. The official function of this committee is to decide whether or not a child is handicapped. If the decision is affirmative, the child is not merely automatically eligible for special education, but he is also endowed with the rights and privileges that the federal government has guaranteed to the handicapped. Once an affirmative decision is reached, the committee must then determine what specific educational needs the child has, what program of services the school is to provide, by whom and for how long, what objectives should be written, and how and when performance will be evaluated. These latter decisions are, however, only subsidiary to the primary question, "Is this child handicapped?"

For handicaps such as blindness, deafness and severe mental retardation, this primary decision is generally unambiguous. A child is either blind or not, and reasonable people have little argument about whether he should be classified as handicapped. For cases of suspected learning disabilities, like those of emotional disturbance and speech pathology, the decision is not so simple. Problems of definition and identification arise. On what bases, therefore, do staffing committees decide and how does decision-making proceed?

THE PROCESS OF DECISION-MAKING

WHO ATTENDS THE STAFFING MEETINGS?

In Belleview school district, large numbers attended the staffing conferences where the decision is reached. Of the conferences I observed and those whose minutes I read, the number of people attending averaged ten, and ranged from six to eighteen. Almost everyone was a professional. Parents of the child under study were there about seventy-five percent of the time. The child attended only about one time in twenty.

The presence or absence of the parent was critical to the atmosphere, speed, and tone of the conference. Professionals were always solicitous of parents, asking for their description of the problem, their point of view, explaining the tests and the options available to them.* There were times, however, when technical terms were not explained nor the confusing welter of test scores integrated into a coherent picture. When the parent was present, sensitive information, even though pertinent to the decision, was frequently left unspoken so that feelings could be spared. The word "handicap" was never used and the phrase "extra help" became a euphemism for special education. Symptoms of emotional disturbance or family conflict were underplayed.

When a parent failed to attend the staffing meeting, the members worked very rapidly, responded more informally, and discussed sensitive information more readily. The case of Bobbie is

*This was in marked contrast to the treatment of parents in the Massachusetts schools studied by Weatherley (1979).

96

illustrative (see pages 52-54). The teacher's comments about Bobbie's mother would never have been spoken in her presence. The final decision would not have been different, however.

WHAT TOPICS ARE COVERED?

In Belleview the conferences typically lasted ninety minutes, the time governed rather strictly by the schedule of the chairmen, who frequently had as many as six staffing conferences a day in two or more school buildings. Of the allowable time, typically eighty-five percent was spent in reviewing the results of the assessments done by the professionals. This left little time to resolve differences, reach a decision and write objectives for those children declared handicapped. Few staffings were carried over to a second session due to the complications of getting parents and all the professionals there at the same time.

The content and the sequence of topics were remarkably consistent from conference to conference. The sequence was the idea of the chairmen, who had carefully worked out a plan that was efficient and thorough.

WHO INFLUENCES THE DECISION?

According to the prevailing philosophy and the legislated rules and regulations, the staffing decision is to be made by consensus, with each person present at the conference (parent and professional) having equal influence over the decision. In practice, however, some voices are louder than others, some roles in schools carry more authority, and as a result the distribution of influence is unequal.

The principals are sometimes more influential than other members. The classroom teachers, the special education teachers and such clinicians as spend most of their time in that building are under the principal's authority and thus may defer to him or her in the placement of the children. Clinicians who work only part-time in a school building are less responsive to the formal authority of the principals. Psychologists and others who claim expertise in the technology of testing may have more influence. In any school building there is an informal power structure. A member of the staffing team with informal power or a strong personality may exercise more than one share of influence in the staffing decision.

In Belleview school district no category of person or position uniformly dominated staffing. A principal in one school, a psychologist in another, a special education teacher in a third school may be more influential than other individuals on the committee. In others, everyone had equal voice. Classroom teachers were more active and influential in some schools than others. In Poplar, for example, the teacher of the child being staffed was considered by the other members of the team to be the special expert on what the child was like or could do. In some schools the teachers seemed tongue-tied, awed by the technical language used and deferred to the clinicians. In still other schools the teachers were assertive, had adopted the technical language of learning disabilities and seemed quite confident in their newly assumed role as diagnostician. The absence of a general pattern of influence suggested that even in a highly centralized system, schools had idiosyncratic histories and patterns of face-to-face relationships that governed their patterns of decision making.

The staffing chairman played an important role in the staffing decisions. Since she was not in the chain of command from the school principal and spent no time in the school other than for the conferences themselves, she was outside both the formal and informal authority structures of the schools. By virtue of her training and experience (all the chairmen in Belleview had been special education teachers), she was sympathetic to the children and wanted to do what was best for them. By virtue of her role (making sure all the schools use the same standard criteria) she had to represent the special education department and place external restraints on a schools' decision making. By virtue of her status as outsider, she sometimes opposed what the staff wanted to do. The pressure from these conflicting demands could become enormous. She routinely had to buck the group pressure that built up when a school staff and parents wanted a child to be declared handicapped yet that child did not meet the district's eligibility criteria. She did not always resist this pressure, but that she was able to do it at all was remarkable.

WHEN IS THE DECISION MADE?

Occasionally a staffing team avoided the official policies and made its decision *in camera* or during a mini-staffing. Mini-staffings are not as regimented as formal staffings in that parents may not necessarily be asked to attend. Nor does the staffing chairman attend. The latter fact decreases outside influence on the school by the district. When the decision is made in a mini-staffing, the staffing becomes a formality. The case of John illustrates this phenomenon (p. 41).

OUTCOMES OF DECISION-MAKING

When a child was suspected of having a learning disability, the staffing committee evaluated the clinical evidence and came to one of four possible decisions: (1) the child was declared not to be handicapped and consequently was not placed in special education of any kind; (2) the child was declared to be handicapped (by virtue of having a learning disability) and was placed in a self-contained or full-time program; (3) the child was declared to be handicapped (learning disabled) and placed part-time in a resource room; or (4) the child was placed part-time in a speech-language remediation program. The latter option seemed to be used as a safety valve for children with few indicators of learning disabilities but insistent parents.

There were four main influences on the decision. These were (1) the wishes of the staff; (2) the wishes of the parents; (3) availability of a program; and (4) the definitiveness of the data that showed that the child matched the official definition of learning disabilities. A secondary and infrequently observed source of influence was the veto from the district special education administrators, going against the wishes of the staff and parents.

A surprising observation from the analysis of the decision-making process is that, unless the clinical evidence is unequivocal and indicative of a severe disability, it bears less weight than do the staff and parent wishes. When a child's achievement is statistically significantly lower than his ability (the legislated definition of learning disabilities) and his clinical pattern of symptoms is severe, the decision that he is handicapped is automatic. Then the only remaining question is whether a program is available. Parental objections will be overcome. Staff wishes will conform to the data. In cases where the data were less definitive or clear-cut (by far the majority in Belleview), data were secondary to staff and parents' wishes. If data were clearly negative, but both parents and staff favored placement, only the administrative veto prevented placement.

The presence in a school building of a self-contained class for the learning disabled increased the likelihood that a child would be placed there, rather than part-time in a resource room. Thus two identical children would receive quite different programs depending on what was available in their two different schools. There are legal limits for the number of children that can be served by a special education teacher. Availability of space in either a self-contained class or a resource room affected the decision. But when a program was full, space could generally be created by dismissing a currently enrolled pupil, adding a teacher's aide, or convincing the special education teacher to take an over-load temporarily. It was rare that a special education program had less than the maximum number of pupils so that definitions of learning disabilities seemed to be loosened or tightened to maintain this steady state.

The wishes of the parents were powerful and only resisted when the data and wishes of the staff were extreme in the opposite direction. Administrators seemed to be acutely sensitive to pressure from assertive parents. They wished to avoid lawsuits and appeals hearings, sometimes seeming to feel that placing a marginal pupil was less costly than resisting the wishes of the parents to obtain extra help for their child.

The wishes and judgments of the staff -- those people who spent most of their time in the school of the child being staffed -- carried great weight in the decision. Data influenced these judgments, but in many instances a staff "policy" developed, a group-conceived implicit definition about the nature of learning disabilities and about what characteristics of a child indicated that he needed extra help. The pressure to act on this judgment became hard to resist, either by parents, clinicians outside the face-to-face group of staff members, or the district administrators. Attempts were made to rationalize this judgment by gathering more and more test data. (It is a principle of psychometrics that a discrepancy will eventually be found if enough unreliable measures are given.) As in the case of Jenny, clinicians manipulated the norms of tests given so that the child appeared to have a significant discrepancy between her ability and achievement (see page 35). If these attempts failed, the staffing committee could resort to the legal loop-hole of "professional judgment" as the basis for declaring a marginal child to be learning disabled.

The decision-making system was under particular stress when the parents and the staff disagreed. Parents increased their power by bringing in outside evaluators with their own sets of tests and client loyalties, or by threatening legal action against the school. The conflict could be resolved by moving the child to a new school, putting him in speech-language therapy or temporarily delaying the decision for a few months. The district administrators of special education could resolve the conflict, but usually the outcome was reached as a balance of the forces within the school itself. It is clear that the most powerful sources of influence resulted in placements, and few forces exluded children from placement in programs for the learning disabled.

CHAPTER FIVE

HOW PREVALENCE ESTIMATES AFFECT THE STAFFING PROCESS

"Everybody knows what the scream limits are"*

How schools decide whether a particular child is learning disabled depends in a complex way on authoritative estimates of the prevalence of learning disabilities in the nation. Why should this be so? The first reason is the ambiguity built into the definition of learning disabilities coupled with the vagaries of diagnosis. Second is the political and economic implications of adding a child to the roster. Third is the nature of the methods by which prevalence is estimated.

---

*Quotation from an administrator in Belleview school district.

By knowing the number of Americans afflicted with a disease, say diabetes, the Department of Public Health can determine the extent of the problem this disease causes to society. It can report on the number of afflicted individuals who are treated and untreated and can estimate the costs of programs to diagnose, treat, and prevent the spread of the disease. Prevalence can be estimated in two general ways. The department can document the number of new cases of diabetes reported each year by physicians or medical facilities. Or it can conduct epidemiological studies: selecting a representative sample of persons, performing medical examinations to determine the rate of the disease in the sample, then generalizing that rate to the population as a whole.

Short of these expensive and difficult means, the department might accept the judgment of experts on diabetes about the extent of the disease. It might solicit testimony from members of the "American Diabetes Foundation." Although these experts would be knowledgeable about and close to the problem, they would not necessarily have reliable data on which to base their estimates. They might be tempted to exaggerate their estimates to intensify the department's sense of what social problems would be created by having large numbers of unrecognized and untreated cases of diabetes. Perhaps increased money and attention would result from this heightened awareness on the part of a government agency.

Estimates of the prevalence of learning disabilities as well as other handicaps are more likely the result of expert testimony than rigorous research. Based primarily on the testimony of experts and special interest groups, Congress determined that there were eight million handicapped persons under the age of 21, and less than half were receiving services from schools. This finding was one of the bases for passage of P.L. 94-142; the Education for All Handicapped Children Act.

But one must distinguish research findings from findings of legislative bodies and courts, the latter having standards for evidence quite different from those of the social sciences. In the critical P.A.R.C. case (P.A.R.C., 1971), for example, the court found that there were 50,000 unserved mentally retarded persons in Pennsylvania. However, a census conducted subsequently by the state department of education turned up only 7,000, a fraction of which had not previously been identified (Kirp, Buss, and Kuriloff, 1974; Craig and McEachron, 1975).

The choice of Congress from among available prevalence estimates had enormous economic significance. The Institute for Research on Educational Finance and Governance at Stanford described estimates as "not based on educational theory or research; they are defined differently from state to state and are subject to political, social, and historical influences . . . . It is interesting to note . . . a one-percent increase in incidence rates, holding all other variables stable in the most likely estimate, raised the projected costs (of legislation for the handicapped) by $708 million, the number of pupils by 470,000 and the required number of teachers by 22,000" (p. 6).

Hammil expressed the problem more colloquially: "See, you can't divorce specific learning disabilities from the institutional aspects. It's big money. There's big money in materials. There's money in the schools. There's big money in this delinquency side. If LD becomes three percent instead of thirty percent, there are people who will be out of business (Lynn, 1979, p. 21).

Prevalence estimates were used as an instrument to provoke the Congressional action desired by the advocates of the learning disabled. The estimates had to be large enough to document the existence of a significant problem worthy of federal intervention. Yet confronted with too big and expensive a problem, Congress might have balked and excluded learning disabilities from P.L. 94-142. Thus, the claim by one advocacy group that the prevalence of learning disabilities was twenty-five percent was downplayed by the government. The figure presented to Congress as official was two percent, a figure with more political than scientific meaning, neither too big nor too small.

Upon recommendation of the Office of Special Education, Congress arbitrarily determined the prevalence rates for handicaps by setting limits on the number of handicapped children for which it would reimburse schools. According to Kakalik (1979) this limit of twelve percent of the children ages 5 to 17 "represents a somewhat liberal estimate of the number of handicapped children" (p. 202). In the original regulations on P. 94-142, a limit was also set on the percent of the population that could be identified and served as learning disabled. This limit of two percent was placed because of legislators' concern about the open endedness of the category. After approval of the regulations specifying the selection criteria, the legislature lifted the ceiling.

After the act was passed, Congress assigned to the Bureau of Education for the Handicapped (later the Office of Special Education) of the United States Department of Health, Education and Welfare (later the Department of Education) the task of determining more scientifically the prevalence rates for all the handicapping conditions. The contract for studying this question was given to SRI, a prestigeous research organization. The SRI researchers (Stearns et al., 1977) evaluated several procedures for estimating prevalence rates and several existing estimates. They found that existing estimates of the rate of learning disabilities varied, depending on the expert who made the estimate and the method used to arrive at it, from 1 percent to 26 percent, and the median estimate was 1.12 percent. (The rates for all handicapping conditions varied from 8.69 percent to 35.05 percent, with a median of 10.47 percent.)

The methods by which these estimates were made varied from the rigorous to the ridiculous. One was based on a survey of school principals who were asked to supply the number of pupils in their schools with perceptual handicaps, minimum brain dysfunction or brain injury (excluding those with mental retardation or environmental disadvantage). The rate from this source (Silverman and Metz, 1973) was determined to be 3.1 percent.

Craig (1976) reported an anecdote about the origin of prevalence estimates of another ambiguous handicap--emotional disturbance: every expert had estimated the rate at 2 percent.

"Since emotional disturbance is one of the more subjective and controversial classifications, it is surprising that there is no variation whatsoever in reported prevalence for this handicap. Searching for a clue as to why this might be true, a prominent scholar (who wishes to remain nameless) related that he was once asked to estimate the prevalence rate for emotionally disturbed children. He replied that he suspected it was around two percent. The next thing he knew he saw his 'guess' in print; much to his dismay, it soon became the 'official' number" (p. 328).

Researchers who have attempted to base prevalence estimates on the actual characteristics of children (rather than on guesses and hunches) have encountered a variety of problems. For example, Meier (1971) and Schumaker* et al., (1980) produced imperfect prevalence estimates because they selected their samples from children who had already been identified as learning disabled by their schools. Using this method confuses the disorder with the identification of the disorder, which, as I have argued, is not always valid. Identification of learning disabilities comes about because a teacher or parent recognizes troublesome symptoms which may or may not be caused by something neurological.

Only epidemiological studies or studies in which the researcher is blind to the prior classification of his subjects are trustworthy sources of prevalence estimates. For example, the epidemiological studies of children on the Isle of Wight (Rutter, Tizard, and Whitmore, 1979) and of four Illinois school systems (Myklebust, Killen, and Bannochie, 1971) revealed rates of significant ability-achievement discrepancies of about four percent. Such discrepancies may have other causes besides an underlying neurological or perceptual impairment (see page 81) so these percents would be liberal. Even with these studies, however, we cannot say if their findings are true of American children as a whole.

A nationally representative epidemiological study of learning disabilities has not been conducted. The National Health Examination Survey which produced data on the prevalence of mental retardation, emotional disturbance, and other handicaps, provides some clues to the prevalence of learning disabilities (Craig, Kaskowitz, and Malgoire, 1978). Data were collected on the characteristics of a representative sample of school children. They were independently evaluated by multiple means--medical examination, achievement and psychological tests, teacher and parent assessment. This evaluation produced reliable estimates of the prevalence of mental retardation, speech, emotional, orthopedic, hearing, and vision handicaps. Considered together, the prevalence for these categories totaled nine percent, a figure close to the estimates

---

*The series of studies by Schumaker and colleagues produced valuable information on the characteristics of pupils identified as learning disabled, e.g., that they differ little from control groups of low-achieving pupils who have not been identified as learning disabled.

officially accepted by the Office of Special Education. Considered category by category, however, the National Health Examination estimates differed from the officially accepted ones. The differences were significant at the elementary school level for those categories, like learning disabilities, for which identification is highly subjective (Craig and McEachron, 1978).

Furthermore, the National Health Examination Survey data revealed how much error there is in identifying the handicapped. Even though the overall prevalence rates for the *group* were reasonably consistent, reliability in identifying *individuals* as handicapped was abysmal. Teachers identified one set of pupils as mentally retarded. Parents identified another set of children as mentally retarded. Pediatricians identified another, and those children falling below a cut-off score on psychological tests formed another set, with very little overlap in the sets of individuals identified. These sources of data were collected independently, and each source of data identified *different* individuals as handicapped and in need of services. This variation was documented for identifying emotionally disturbed children as well as mentally retarded children. The situation can hardly be better for learning disabilities, an even more ambiguous category than those studied directly by the National Health survey.

Estimating the prevalence of learning disabilities is not science; it is bureaucracy. Although the estimates are not credible, they have been assigned an important status in the governance of education for the handicapped. As revealed in the First and Second Annual Reports to Congress on implementation of P.L. 94-142, they are key data in determining the extent to which the goals of the law have been met.

The first of five evaluative questions in the First Annual Report *(Progress Toward a Free Appropriate Education,* 1979) is this, "Are the intended beneficiaries being served?" To answer, the Office of Special Education compared the percentage of children currently served with the percentage in the prevalence estimates. It is clear that OSE's assessment of success on this evaluative question hangs on a convergence of the two numbers. The difference between the two numbers (7 and 12 percent) was seen by OSE as the failure of schools to satisfy the provisions of the law (to identify and serve all handicapped children). The difference is the number of handicapped children who have so far escaped detection and service.

"The total number of 3 - 21 year-old children served as handicapped during the 1977-78 school year approaches four million. However, previous estimates of the prevalence of children with handicapping conditions suggest that four million may be significantly short of the actual number of handicapped children in the 5-17 year-old population. If current estimates of 11-12 percent of the school-aged population are accurate, there should be more than five million school-aged handicapped children, and from seven to eight million handicapped children in the 3-21 year-old age range" (Progress Toward a Free Appropriate Education, 1979, pp. 15-16.)

OSE was dismayed by the variation among states in percentages served as handicapped (Puerto Rico served 1.8 percent and Utah served 11.5 percent) as well as the small over-all rate compared with prevalence estimates. Four possible reasons were given to explain why the percent served was so much smaller than the prevalence percent: backlogs of assessments, overlap of programs for the handicapped with programs for the disadvantaged, variation among the states in the ages eligible for school services, even that the U.S. Census figures on which the percentages were based were too high. But the obvious explanation was not posed—that the prevalence estimates might be invalid standards by which to compare the rates of children served. The implications of such a question were apparently too severe to be considered. If there were only four million truly handicapped and all of them were currently served, there would be no room for the enterprise to expand. Bureaucracies grow in part by documenting unmet needs.

OSE proposed four methods for correcting the discrepancy between the accepted prevalence rate and the rate served. The problem of assessment backlogs should be corrected by the passage of time, it was said. The program called Child Find should be stepped up. Early screening programs should be intensified. Lastly, the Commissioner of Education "will advise those states serving less than ten percent of their schoolage population of the need to assure that all handicapped children are identified and served" (p. 23).

In September, 1978, the Office of Special Education undertook a campaign, according to a subsequent report of the General Accounting Office

"to reduce the discrepancy between the number of handicapped children counted and its 12 percent national
prevalence estimate ... (O)fficials have contacted at
least 50 states and territories that counted less than 10
percent of their total student population as handicapped
to 'Strongly urge' them to accept OSE technical assistance on increasing the childcount. OSE plans also call
for asking states to 'set specific (numerical) targets of
their own for finding and serving handicapped children'
and following this up with monitoring and assessment
activities, including 'careful review' of states' annual
program plans before awarding grants and 'special site
visits' to key states ... OSE officials also contacted
advocate groups, urging them to become more involved in
finding and serving handicapped children" ("Unanswered
Questions on Educating Handicapped Children in Local
Public Schools," 1981).

By the time of the Second Annual Report to Congress,
these programs and pressures had been effective and progress was
made to close the gap between the rate served and the prevalence
estimates (*To Assure the Free Appropriate Education of All Handicapped Children*, 1980). Between 1979 and 1980, 117,146 persons
had been added to the roster of handicapped individuals. Inspection
of the tables reveals that additional cases of learning disabilities
accounted for all of the increase and more, the number of LD added
being 145,820. Among the population of the handicapped, the share
taken up by the learning disabled rose from 29 to 32 percent. The
emotionally disturbed was the only other category of handicap to
expand. The unambiguous categories of visual, hearing, orthopedi-
cally, and health-related handicaps all decreased, probably in the
same ratio as the total school age population decreased. By 1980,
seventy percent of those labeled handicapped (plus an unknown number of marginally mentally retarded) fell into the ambiguous categories of learning disabled, speech impaired, and emotionally
disturbed.

By 1980, those labeled learning disabled accounted for
three percent of all children between the ages of 3 and 21 years.
(By changing the base rates on which the percents were calculated--
from the school aged population to the population of 3-21 year-

olds--OSE rendered difficult the analysis of trends from the First to the Second Annual Reports.) The figure of three percent, it should be noted, is one percent higher than the original cap placed on the federally reimbursible cases of learning disabilities and two percent higher than the median estimates of their prevalence.*

That OSE made so little of this epidemic of learning disabilities is itself remarkable. The increase was noted almost in passing in the Second Annual Report and explained by saying (erroneously) that schools only recently have had programs for the learning disabled. New programs had apparently resulted in the identification or creation of new cases. Several alternative explanation, overlooked by OSE are intriguing to contemplate. That learning disabilities are so subjectively defined and diagnosed, that learning disabilities is a label more benign than mental retardation (so that children previously labeled mentally retarded were changed into cases of learning disabilities), that schools with low rates were encouraged to identify 12 percent of their children as handicapped (and enough "learning disabilities" can always be found to make up the difference)--these explanations did not enter OSE's analysis.

OSE seemed more interested in how much of the gap had been closed between the overall rates of handicapped served and the overall prevalence estimates, disregarding the disproportionate share of learning disabilities and the change in the base rate. By 1980, the percent of handicapped in the general population was 9 percent, gradually converging--at least on paper--on the magic 12 percent estimated prevalence. This was regarded as a positive

---

*By 1981 the fervor of OSE to identify the maximum had diminished. An official attributed this to the Reagan administration and the end to expansion of appropriations for the handicapped. He acknowledged that the original estimates had been inflated to ensure that the legislation would pass. The great discrepancy between the 1978 childcounts and prevalence estimates had been embarrassing. Still, as recently as July of 1980 the head of OSE testified to the validity of the 12 percent estimates and refused to honor the GAO recommendation that the estimate be revised downward and no longer used as a lever against low-prevalence states ("Unanswered Questions . . ., 1981). Using the same circular and self-fulfilling reasoning, he cited the fact several states were approaching the 12 percent rate as evidence of the validity of the original estimates.

response to the evaluative question, "Are the intended beneficiaries being served?" However, using the base rate of school age population, the percent was 7.78, only one-half of one percent higher than the previous year, a fact not detailed in the narrative of the report.

But, are simple numbers of children served and percentages in the population the appropriate statistics for answering this question? Are the individuals served the ones actually handicapped or some other individuals? In the 1979 report, OSE asked, rhetorically and as an afterthought, "Are we serving the right children?" No data were supplied in answer.

The authors of the OSE report acknowledged the possibility of erroneous classification, that some non-handicapped children may be among those identified, served, and counted. Yet the philosophy was clear:

"Weighing the possible harmful effects of a label versus the benefits of an appropriate education suggests that there is a risk of being so diverted by the potential ill effects of labeling as to lose sight of the value of special education. Less often has it been recognized that the *failure* to identify a child who is handicapped is also a serious type of erroneous classification, which results in the denial of the Act's benefits to the very children it was designed to serve. Yet the degree of confidence one can place in correctly identifying a child as handicapped may be inversely related to the degree of confidence one may have that the child is *not* handicapped. Stated in another fashion, if primary concern is directed toward preventing the incorrect classification of children as handicapped, many eligible handicapped children may not be identified and served" (Progress, 1979, p. 24).

Using frequencies and percentages and comparing percentages with prevalence figures assumes that prevalence does not vary among races and socio-economic groups. This assumption of uniformity is probably false. Might not children in Puerto Rico be more subject to prematurity, bad nutrition, less intellectual stimulation than children in Minnesota? If so, should not one expect that learning disabilities occur more frequently in the former? Yet Puerto Rico served .36 percent of their children (ages 3-12) and

111

Minnesota 4.52 percent. OSE would say that Puerto Rico has failed to identify and serve enough of their learning disabled. But they do not seem concerned that Minnesota serves too many. The variation in the rates from state to state (1.05 percent in New York, 6.27 percent in Delaware) defies explanation. It is arbitrary and artifactual, reflecting differential eagerness and propensity to identify the learning disabled as well as relative laxness in diagnostic criteria.

During 1978-79, the year of the case study presented in Chapter Two, 3 percent of Belleview's children were considered learning disabled. By 1979-80 that rate had increased to 5 percent. These figures were slightly higher than the rate for Colorado, which in turn was higher than the national rate of identified learning disabilities. But because the rate for all handicaps was less than the legislated ceiling (there being relatively fewer children with more severe handicaps), no special note of the learning disabilities figure was taken by the special education administrators at the district or state level.

The general education administration did take note, however. They openly complained about the rapid growth of special education, highlighted as it was by the coincident decline in the population and budget of regular education. An enormous amount of the time and energy of teachers and principals was being absorbed in activities related to staffing. Money was being re-directed as well, for neither state nor federal governments had provided as much money for special education as they had promised. District funds had taken up the slack. The "scream limit" had been reached.

Estimates of the prevalence of learning disabilities affect the staffing process by generating expectations about personnel needs. The state uses these estimates and provides reimbursement to the district based on standards for pupil-teacher ratios. Thus, indirectly at least, there is a financial incentive to identify pupils as learning disabled up to the ceiling for all handicaps. In Belleview, there are few under-enrolled special education programs. The state specifies that there should be no more than fifteen pupils assigned to a resource room teacher. If more than that number are identified by a school as learning disabled, some pupils currently enrolled must be released or a teacher's aide hired. Both actions can be disruptive, and the district special education administrators tend to resist the latter. Hiring an additional resource room teacher would be almost unthinkable. New space in the school would have to be found, the state department would have to be petitioned. The principal's energy would be consumed. Therefore the figure of fifteen becomes a maximum.

On the other hand, a resource room teacher with only five children assigned to her excites the envy of the regular teaching staff--"What does she do with all that free time?" The teachers are apt to fill that free time with newly found cases of learning disabilities. "As long as there is a bottom kid in the class, we will never run out of new referrals," said one special education administrator. Thus the state standards become a minimum. There exists only a small range of acceptable variation for identified learning disabilities cases within a school, notwithstanding the true extent of need there.

A normative standard has thus been established wherein the numbers of learning disabled identified by a school closely parallels the national prevalence estimates, regardless of the validity of the latter and the actual incidence of the disorder locally. Reimbursement formulas and programs of case-finding maintain the standard. State officials keep the districts in line and the federal officials keep the states in line, but only with respect to the percent of over-all handicapped.

This normative standard affects the staffing of the individual pupils by generating probabilities in the minds of those on staffing committees as illustrated in the following fallacious analysis of the prevalence of hyperactivity.

"The prevalence rate of four percent can often help decide doubtful situations. For example, if a school already has fifteen percent of its students diagnosed and/or medicated, the probability plummets to near zero. The pool of undiagnosed hyperkinetics in that school should be exhausted already. (Of course, it is possible that the wrong ones have been diagnosed and the real hyperkinetic children missed thus far, but this would be betting against the odds.) On the other hand, if few students (much less than four percent) in a school have been diagnosed, we may assume the presence of a residual pool of

113

undiagnosed hyperkinetics. In such circumstances, the appropriateness of diagnosing a given suspected child soars" (Arnold, 1973, p. 511).

Staffing committees tend to be relatively more strict when the local percentages being served exceed prevalence estimates. When school and district rates are low, the gatekeepers will tolerate, albeit unconsciously, the placement of children whose ability-achievement discrepancies are less than statistically significant and whose processing deficits are unverified.

CHAPTER SIX

HOW PROFESSIONALIZATION AFFECTS THE STAFFING PROCESS

"Every profession is a conspiracy against the layman"
(Attributed to George Bernard Shaw)

The staffing process is both affected by and contributes to the professionalization of schools. In the staffing process tests serve several purposes. Diagnosis is the only official one. Enhancing status by associating a clinician with the quasi scientific languauge of tests scores and trait measures is another. Avoiding resistance and parents' legal challenges is a third. One other must be considered. Tests are the means by which one profession stakes out and protects its territory from other professions and the non-specialist teaching staff. The net effect of expanding professional territory is to increase the number of children identified as learning disabled.

Because of the political motive to avoid the misidentification of minorities as handicapped, the courts and legislatures required that each potentially handicapped child be evaluated by more than one professional group and by more than one assessment technique. This official policy was justified by experts such as Mercer and Ysseldyke (1977) who testified that multi-professional and multi-modal assessment are reasonable guarantees of valid evaluation and non-discriminatory identification. Federal law requires parent and teacher participation in the evaluation, "that no single procedure is used as the sole criterion . . . the evaluation is made by a multi-disciplinary team or group of persons . . . the child is assessed in all areas related to the suspected disability including where appropriate, health, vision, hearing, social and emotional status, general intelligence, academic performance, communicative status, and motor abilities." (20 U.S.C. 1415(b) (2)(B) (121a. 532a-F).

Colorado statute requires that every child suspected of a handicap undergo a "wholistic assessment," that is, be evaluated in these areas of functioning: educational, psychological, vision, hearing, development, adaptive behavior, and health. The assessments are made by trained psychologists, social workers, special educators, teachers, speech-language specialists, nurses and others (as indicated by the child's characteristics) employed by the school districts. Like most Colorado school districts, Belleview district policy insures that each of these professional groups examines each child whether majority or minority, destined for a half hour per day in the resource room or a full-time residential placement. Other professionals are brought into the staffing process as requested by parents, suggested by some special characteristics of a child, or the availability of such personnel in a district's employ. These are occupational therapists, adaptive physical educators, and bilingual specialists.

Furthermore, federal law requires that schools pay for supplemental evaluations by independent professionals when the parents desire them. Thus, if there is some conflict between the school's professionals and the parent concerning the child's characteristics, the parents can hire a professional outside the district to re-evaluate the child. The district must bear this expense, and the report given by the independent evaluator must be considered at the staffing conference. The intent of this policy is to remove the politics from the staffing. For example, a district-employed psychologist who knew that there was no room for a child, might be

116

pressured to underestimate the severity of the child's problem. The rationale of the policy holds that a psychologist in private practice might not be subject to this pressure and provide a more valid report. The assumption that the outsider may produce a more valid report is probably mistaken. Evaluations commissioned by parents are no less political than school based evaluations. The independent evaluators consider the parents as clients and actively work to obtain the services desired by the parents, skewing the data accordingly. Dr. James, hired by John's parents (p. 39) is a good example of the role of the independent evaluator. The validity of John's staffing was enhanced not a bit by her assessment, which was aimed at a placement for him in the resource room.

Besides school psychologists, language and special education specialists, and occupational therapists, independent evaluations are sought from such professionals as pediatricians, pediatric neurologists, psychiatrists, clinical psychologists, physical therapists, rehabilitation therapists, and optometrists. There is probably no more obvious effect of the special education laws than in the increase in number and variety of professionals that schools have had to hire or buy services from. Besides this change in their number, the professionals have had their roles changed. Whereas they formerly spent much of their time providing therapeutic services, now almost all of their time is spent in testing.

Each of these proliferating professions has its own special language, its own collection of tests and diagnostic devices, its own training program and standards for professional behavior. Each has a professional association with a lobbyist to appear at legislative hearings and testify to its importance. Each calls its members "child advocates." Each profession claims unique expertise in the assessment or treatment of learning disabilities. These claims ought to be critically appraised, yet they rarely are. Most laymen feel helpless and ignorant when they hear a pediatrician or occupational therapist toss off statements like "In the neurological examination quality of binocular fusion should be examined, and the presence or absence of strabismus and nystagmus should be recorded." They are in no position to question the scientific basis of the assertion. A claim without sound basis must be regarded as an expression of the interests of the group to enhance its authority and privilege over schools, parents, and competing groups.

When Jenny's speech-language specialist (see page 64) said "language is everything," she was not only expressing her implicit beliefs about the nature of learning disabilities, she was staking a territorial claim for her profession. She claimed not only the traditionally held ground of the assessment and correction of stuttering, poor articulation and fluency, but that of deficient "receptive and expressive language" (read, "vocabulary") as well as "auditory perception" and poor school performance in reading, spelling, writing, and oral storytelling. Her statement implied that to detect and remedy problems in any of these areas, it is necessary for the school to employ people trained as she had been. Clearly there is overlap in what the speech-language specialist "specializes" in, and what is done by learning disability specialists. The commonality of their expertise is covered over because the tests used have different names, and the argot varies. On closer examination, the underlying constructs measured are the same. At Aspen school, the learning disability specialist routinely administers the Illinois Test of Psycholinguistic Abilities, which is instead given by the speech-language specialist at nearby Tamarac School. The Wiig-Semmel Test of Language Concepts usually given by speech-language specialists has been found in validity studies to measure verbal intelligence, which is also measured by the Peabody Picture Vocabulary Test, ostensibly given to gauge "receptive language."

Some speech-language therapists feel that learning disability specialists are the claim-jumpers. Learning disabilities specialists feel the opposite is true, and one told me privately, "First they were speech correctionists, then they called themselves speech therapists. Now they're language specialists. I think they are just looking for a home, drumming up business."

Pediatricians play a substantial role in identifying learning disabilities and are frequently brought into the staffing process by parents seeking services for their children. This is particularly true for those with implicit beliefs about the neurological, organic basis of learning disabilities. If it is organic, it must require the attention of a physician. The leading textbook* on the role of the pediatrician in learning disabilities lists a dozen functions including

---

*Levine, Brooks, and Shonkoff, 1980, recommended by staff at the University of Colorado Health Sciences Center.

community education, advocacy of public policy, continuity of care and counseling and "demystification." Only the evaluation of neurological functioning is a role unique to the medical profession, however. Of the entire contents of this leading textbook, only about fifteen percent is devoted to providing information that is unique to technical pediatrics (neurological examinations and medical treatments). The remainder of the book resembles nothing more than the standard learning disabilities textbook, explaining tests such as the Wechsler Intelligence Scale for Children ("owned" by psychologists) or the Illinois Test of Psycholinguistic Abiltities ("owned" by learning disabilities and speech-language specialists) or describing treatments encountered in most resource rooms.

Even the uniquely medical expertise of pediatricians in learning disabilities has been challenged by Coles (1978) and Grossman (1966) who questioned the reliability of neurological examinations and the scientific validity of the connection between "soft signs" (equivocal signs of an organic lesion) and academic problems.

Nevertheless, the physician's claims are more likely than those of any other profession to go unchallenged. School nurses share a bit of the medical authority. A school psychologist expressed the underlying resentment of this status: "The baby boom is over. Pediatricians have fewer patients and spend less time treating sicknesses that have been prevented. Medical schools are pouring out more doctors, and they are looking to the schools for a practice."

Few professions have undergone transformations as radical as that of occupational therapy. As recently as 1969 a professional handbook (Meldman and Wellhausen, 1969) listed the activities of an occupational therapist as providing for hospitalized patients or the aged a milieu of therapy, recreation and activities such as crocheting, knitting, weaving, painting, and woodworking. Now occupational therapists are experts in the assessment and treatment of sensory integration (read "perceptual-motor") dysfunctions and as such claim a role in assessment and treatment of learning disabilities. This transformation is due to popularity among occupational therapists of work of Jane Ayers (cf. Ayers, 1969, 1972). An excerpt will give the reader a flavor of this work (Ayers, 1972, p. 342).

"Basic brain research demonstrates the importance of the brain stem in organizing auditory and visual processes and the dependence of the neocortex upon adequate organization at the brain-stem level, for the two levels of the brain interact together. Disorders consistently observed in learning disabled children that are suggestive of inadequate sensory integration in the brain stem are immature postural reactions, poor extraocular muscle control, poorly developed visual orientation to environmental space, difficulty in the processing of sound into percepts, and the tendency toward distractibility. The statistically significant increased ability of the experimental group compared to the control group to blend sounds and auditorily to remember and reproduce a sequence of numbers suggests that increased reading skill may have been related to those abilities.

"The intervention program provided considerable vestibular stimulation, received either passively or in connection with some goal-directed activity such as riding a "scooter board" down a ramp. Postural mechanisms were normalized by inhibiting the primitive postural librium reactions, especially in the prone and quadruped position. The tactile system was stimulated as a means of normalizing brain function in general and specifically to provide a somatosensory basis for motor planning and to lower the level of excitation of the reticular arousal system. Proprioceptive input through muscle and joint receptors was also carefully planned. Manipulatory puzzles were employed about 5 to 10 percent of the time.

"It is proposed that the carefully controlled sensory input through vestibular and somato-sensory systems enhanced the capacity of the brain for intersensory integration between these sensory modalities and the visual and auditory inputs that were a natural component of the gross motor experience employed to elicit much of the stimuli. Mechanisms for these integrative processes believed that considerable processing of visual stimuli occurs in the brain stem and that at that level it is intimately associated with postural and ocular mechanisms."

It is easy for the layman to be carried away with such language, but the ideas have not gone unquestioned. A psychologist (Reed, 1978) doubted the psychometric validity of the tests commonly used to assess sensory-integrative functions. A pediatrician (Sieben, 1977) doubted the scientific validity of Ayer's theory,

"It remains to be shown . . . that children with learning disabilities have anything demonstrably wrong with their brain stems. The lack of any postmortum studies or accepted sign of brain-stem malfunction must lead one to seriously question Ayers' theory. Ayers further proposes that carefully controlled stimulation through vestibular (balancing) and somatosensory (positional awareness) systems somehow improves the brain stem's integration between these systems and the eyes and ears. Just how stimulating these systems in certain ways is supposed to make them form the right nerve connections is not made clear.

"There is no convincing evidence that mastering such postural skills carries over into academic skills such as reading . . ." (Sieben, 1977, pp. 142-43).

Despite such counterclaims, occupational therapy of the new variety is part of the services mandated by P.L. 94-142. School districts are increasingly called upon to hire or contract with this professional group. Resistance by schools to this dubious service is futile as an interview with a child advocate makes clear ("Paralegal an angel to State's handicapped," 1981).

"To parents of handicapped children across the state, Lynn Finer of the Legal Center for Handicapped Citizens is a guardian angel . . . In Penrose, she helped Mr. and Mrs. Steve Rhoten get occupational therapy for their handicapped son, Mark. Although outside evaluators had said Mark needed therapy, the school district, which didn't have a therapist on staff, said he didn't. Ms. Finer helped the Rhotens through the appeals process and, finally, the school district was ordered to provide the therapy", (p. 8).

By resorting to a clever trick, a pediatrician (Lerer, 1981) showed how an occupational therapist diagnoses sensory-integrative dysfunction and prescribes sensory-integrative therapy

121

to almost every child (even two normal ones sent by the peditrician) referred to her. Nevertheless, the mere recommendation of therapy by a professional activates the legal mechanisms. It is sufficient evidence to require that schools provide or pay for that therapy. The open-endedness of the statuatory commitments has proved to be a bonanza for the professions.

Having watched for several months the various specialists dealing with each other, I believe that with few exceptions they had the childrens' interests foremost in their minds. They had something to contribute, yet their political maneuvers were unmistakable. Each used its battery of tests, its specialized language, its "scientific" theories to advance its position, enhance its status, ensure the expansion of its clientele.

Because of the open-endedness of the federal, state, and district commitments to special education staffing, the various professions did not have to compete with each other for scarce resources. Disputes about the validity of relative claims (illustrated above) were never voiced in staffings, and professional courtesy was the usual mode of behavior.

One simply made room for the others, never questioning the validity of their tests and theories. Nor did they question the redundancy (e.g., when members of three professional groups each administered tests of verbal intelligence), or resolve the discrepancies in information provided by one another (such as the reading diagnostician placing the child's reading at the 3rd grade level but the special educator indicating he reads like the average fourth grader). There was really no need to notice or resolve the contradictions so long as there were no restrictions on the number or quality of tests given. The assessment pie is expandable, and each new professional group can ask for a piece without the others being denied.

The proliferation of professionals in the staffing process and the uncritical attitude of one group toward another probably leads to over-identification. Each profession has a perspective on learning disabilities that differs slightly from that of the others. If a child matches any of these he will be placed. The increased numbers of unreliable tests administered by the various professionals will yield test or subtest scores that are discrepant. This will be simply due to chance, but is very likely to be interpreted as an abnormality, and the child will be placed.

There can be little doubt that each of these professions has something to contribute to the study or treatment of learning disabilities. Yet because of legal requirements and reimbursement policies, diagnosis is consuming a greater share of the financial resources available for special education. If the scientific basis of this diagnosis were more sound, then the current policies would be correct. So much professional attention would lead to better prescriptions and more effective treatments. Such is not the case, and the therapeutic, remedial, and educational functions* are becoming secondary to and diminished--in money and status--by the over-commitment to diagnosis. That over-commitment is in part the result of the increasing professionalization of special education and the openhandedness of government agencies to promote it.

---

*Wolcott's (1977) analysis of the inherent discontinuities between teachers and technocrats (read here, the professional diagnosticians) is germane to this problem, as is Lortie's (1975) finding that teachers feel little kinship with specialists such as psychologists.

CHAPTER SEVEN

THE EFFECT OF LAWS, JUDICIAL DECISIONS, AND BUREAU-CRACIES ON THE STAFFING PROCESS

"Lawyers are our heroes" (Blatt, 1972)

"Woe unto you lawyers also! for ye load men with burdens grievous to be borne, and ye yourselves touch not the burdens with one of your fingers." (Luke II:46)

"If one or more special educator tells me, 'It's the law,' I'll scream." (A Belleview Administrator)

LAWS AND CASES

The staffing process was born in the courts and nourished in the legislatures. It carries the marks of this heritage. The rights of the seriously handicapped to a suitable education at public expense were dearly won in the courts. Legislation extended these rights to all the handicapped and rendered the mandates so open-ended that an army of attorneys will be needed to settle claims on the schools.

In a difference context, Moynihan (1980, p. 40) wrote, "organizations in conflict become like one another." To survive the legal onslaught, schools have had to adopt legal forms. To avoid the courts, schools have had to function more like the courts. Nowhere is this more obvious than in the staffing process. The decision to place a child in special education, once considered a matter of educators' professional judgment, now resembles a legal hearing in which the child's parents are the plaintiffs or petitioners and the school is the defendant. Thus the staffing process assumed the familiar form of the landmark judicial decisions—with parents of the handicapped (or public interest lawyers acting for them) suing schools to provide services or standardize decision-making processes. The judge asks: "Does this party have a right?" Does that party have a duty?"

The cases that changed staffing from an educational to a legal form were *P.A.R.C.*, *Mills*, *Diana*, and *Larry P.* (see, for example, reviews by Nystrom and Staub, 1978; Kirp, Kuriloff and Buss, 1975, and Burt, 1975). In 1971, the Pennsylvania Association for Retarded Citizens brought suit against the state school system for excluding retarded children from public education. According to Abeson, Burgdorf, Casey, Kunz and McNeil (1975), retarded children had been excluded from public education through a variety of mechanisms. State constitutions like that of New Mexico prescribed compulsory education for children "of school age and of sufficient physical and mental ability," thus exempting the retarded. A Nebraska law exempted the retarded from compulsory education because their "physical or mental condition or attitude is such as to prevent or render inadvisable their attendance at school or . . . application to study." A few states that provided education for the handicapped managed to exclude a few because they had a combination of disabilities or were not mentioned on a list of disabilities the state agreed to treat. Other states refused to provide tuition to private schools for the handicapped. Sometimes handicapped children were denied services because the responsibility for treatment was divided among schools, public welfare agencies and so on.

The P.A.R.C. case was meant to end this exclusion by appealing to two legal principles embodied in the Fourteenth Amendment to the U.S. Constitution: equal protection and due process. These principles were to apply to the retarded as a class, based on the fact that exclusion constitutes unfair discrimination or unequal treatment and that arbitrary and unfair procedures were used by schools to classify children as retarded.

The Fourteenth Amendment implies that all states (and schools, by extension) must treat all citizens equally and fairly and cannot discriminate against any class or citizen. It prohibited states from violating the rights guaranteed in the first ten amendments: ". . . no state shall make or enforce any law which shall abridge the privileges and immunities of citizens of the U.S., nor shall any state deprive any person of life, liberty, or property, without due process of law; nor deny to any person within its jurisdiction the equal protection of the laws."

The principle of equal protection had already been applied to school children in the *Brown v. Topeka* decision and related to the retarded children who had been excluded from public schools. According to the Supreme Court in the *Brown* decision, "the opportunity of an education, where the state has undertaken to provide it, is a right which must be made available to all on equal terms." The P.A.R.C. case was settled by a consent decree agreed to by the plaintiffs and defendent, and ratified by the presiding federal judge. Pennsylvania could no longer exclude the retarded from public education. The state was required to find and evaluate the excluded ones and provide at public expense education suitable to the abilities of the individuals. The principle of "least restrictive environment" was introduced, specifying that the retarded children should be educated in as normal conditions and as close to non-handicapped children as possible. Not to do so was a violation of equal opportunity. Furthermore, a 23-step procedure was prescribed for evaluating and deciding the appropriate education of the retarded. This was to guarantee their rights to due process.

The *Mills v. Board of Education* case was brought by a public interest law firm on behalf of all those in Washington, D.C., who were excluded from public education because of their handicaps. These included, beside the retarded, those with brain damage, hyperactivity, epilepsy, and orthopedic handicaps (Zettel and

Abeson, 1978). The plaintiffs also claimed that the procedures for excluding the handicapped from public schools violated rights to due process since no formal hearings were held, no reasons for exclusion provided, and periodic reviews of the decisions did not take place. Procedures had been arbitrary and did not conform to the due process requirements specified in the Fifth Amendment. Plaintiffs were "excluded and suspended without: (a) notification as to a hearing, the nature of offense or status, any alternative or interim publicly supported education; (b) opportunity for representation, a hearing by an impartial arbiter, the presentation of witnesses, and (c) opportunity for periodic review of the necessity for continued exclusion or suspension."

The Mills decree included, according to Zettel and Abeson (1978, p. 196),

"(a) a declaration of the constitutional right of all children, regardless of any exceptional condition or handicap, to a publicly supported education and (b) a declaration that the defendant's rules, policies, and practices which excluded children without a provision for adequate and immediate alternative procedures denied the plaintiffs and the class rights of due process and equal protection of the law.

Due process rights were also appealed to in the *Diana v. Board of Education* case, which resulted in the principle that a child being considered for a special education placement must be tested in his own language. In the *Larry P. v. Riles* case the court ruled that disproportionality of minorities in special education constituted violation of equal opportunity and resulted from the use of culturally biased tests in special education placement. Thereafter the staffing process was required to include multiple assessment devices, multiple assessors, culturally unbiased tests, and periodic reviews of placement already made.

All these ideas were embodied in the federal legislation P.L. 94-142, the Education for all Handicapped Children Act of 1975. In that act Congress acknowledged the rights of the handicapped to an education at public expense, appropriate to individual needs, and required the public schools to provide it. It extended the rights, won in the courts for retarded and excluded children, to all handicapped children, including the learning disabled and speech impaired. One might question the legal logic of this extension, since the learning disabled and speech impaired were rarely excluded from public education, except in the most severe instances.

The education was to be provided in the least restrictive environment. The law provided procedural safeguards in the decision-making process such as

1. Opportunity for parents to examine all relevant records with respect to the identification, evaluation, and educational placement of the child . . . and to obtain an independent educational evaluation of the child;

2. Procedures to protect the rights of the child whenever the parents or guardian of the child are not known or are unavailable, or of an individual (who shall not be an employee of the state educational agency, local educational agency, or intermediate educational unit involved in the education or care of the child) to act as a surrogate for the parents or gaurdian;

3. Written prior notice to the parents or guardian of the child whenever such agency or unit proposes to initiate or change, or refuses to initiate or change the identification, evaluation, or educational placement of the child;

4. Procedures designed to assure that (this) notice . . . fully informs the parents or guardian, in the parents' or guardians' native language;

5. An opportunity to present complaints with respect to any matter relating to the identification, evaluation, or educational placement of the child, or the provision of a free appropriate public education to such child.

Parents not satisfied with the decision had the right to appeal "to an impartial due process hearing," as Zettel and Abeson (1978) recorded:

". . . at which all persons concerned shall be guaranteed (a) the right to be accompanied and advised by counsel and by individuals with special knowledge or training with respect to the problems of handicapped children; (b) the right to present evidence and confront, cross-examine, and compel the attendance of witnesses; (c) the right to a written or electronic verbatim record of the hearing; and (d) the right to written findings of fact and decisions."

The language of lawyers is evident in these passages. The action of lawyers could be expected by a school district that violated these laws or deviated from the prescribed procedures. The Office of Civil Rights is the agent of enforcement. Compliance by schools is further assured by application of the Civil Rights Act of 1964 which was extended to the handicapped under Section 504 of the Vocational Rehabilitation Act of 1973:

". . . no otherwise qualified handicapped individual . . . shall, solely by reason of his handicap, be excluded from the participation in, be denied the benefits of, or be subjected to discrimination under any program or activity receiving federal financial assistance."

Failure of a district to comply risks the loss of federal funds.

What emerges from these rulings and laws is the notion that the handicapped have been established as a class with special legal status and protections not provided to the non-handicapped. For example, a non-handicapped school child has no legal right to an education "appropriate to his needs" nor must he have an Individualized Educational Plan. Nor are decisions about his education governed by due process procedural guidelines. Whether he is to be placed in an open-space or self-contained classroom, for example, is a matter of educators' judgment, perhaps done in consultation with the child's parents.

This analysis will leave aside further consideration of the right of the handicapped to free, public school education and the principle of least restrictiveness. The first seems a logical extension of Constitutional protections. The latter, though it lacks an empirical basis, reflects a sound ethical value and one whose effects will eventually be understood. Neither concerns the staffing process directly. What must be considered are the due process rights and the rights of the handicapped to an "appropriate" education.

Except for a few items specifically excluded from P.L. 94-142 (e.g., medical treatment), what constitutes an "appropriate" education is nearly without boundary. There is no legal test of appropriateness, and schools have been forced by law to provide an astonishing array of direct and related services. Psychotherapy is a service many school districts have resisted providing. Such resistance has produced several law suits, as noted in a recent publication of the National Association of State Directors of Special Education (Liaison Bulletin, 1981). In these cases the schools argued that psychotherapy was a medical service and therefore excluded from the school's responsibility. Parents argued that it was a psychological service and therefore the schools must provide or pay for it. The Office of Civil Rights sided with the parents on the more liberal interpretation. It found that if psychotherapy was listed on a child's Individualized Educational Program as necessary to enable him to benefit from special education, the school was obliged to provide it.

One might speculate about the possible collusion between parents who want a special service for their child, a few professionals who may declare without much fear of contradiction that the child needs such service, and the legal structure that forces compliance by the school district. Psychotherapy is not the only example of this. Residential, private-school treatments are claimed by parents and professionals as "appropriate" and therefore must be paid for by reluctant school districts (Weatherley, 1979). A Denver "paralegal" reported with pride about how she successfully fought the school district that resisted paying for occupational therapy, which had been recommended by two occupational therapist-evaluators as treatment necessary for the special education of two pupils ("Paralegal . . .", 1981). The schools have little protection against an expanding notion of "appropriate education." They cannot specify that "appropriate" must mean the treatment most efficacious or most cost-effective. Neither the science nor technology necessary to establish whether, say, Montessori is more beneficial than Doman-Delacato for pupils of type A, is yet available (see page 159 below). The only tests of the appropriateness principle are professional recommendation, parental satisfaction and whether the decision was reached under due process guidelines. This is a very shaky principle indeed. Its application is guaranteed, however, to expand the rolls of the learning disabled.

The legal right to due process has been critical in shaping the staffing process. Yet whether it insures justice and fairness is debatable. What cannot be debated is its excessive cost. The staffing process absorbs about $1000 per pupil in Belleview, provided that the decision of the staffing conference is not challenged. Appeal to fair hearing may double that amount. Rebell and Block (1979) reported the cost of the appeals process may vary from $1,000 to $10,000. Against these costs the benefits of due process procedures must be weighed. Buss, Kirp, and Kuriloff (1975) described other contexts in which due process is applied.

"Procedural due process in its most classical form is represented by the procedures designed to prevent a criminal defendant from being wrongfully convicted. But procedural due process has also been applied in a variety of contexts outside the criminal law-to juvenile justice, discharge from government employment, student discipline, revocation of motor-vehicle licensing, and distribution of welfare benefits. In all of these contexts, due process is invoked because of two fundamental elements: (1) governmental action threatens to cause deprivation of a vital interest such as personal freedom, college enrollment, or welfare payments; and (2) the facts that might lead to the deprivation (whether the defendant 'broke and entered' at night, whether the student participated in an unlawful demonstration, or whether the welfare recipient had received income in excess of permitted amounts) are disputed. Due process, then, requires some proceeding that will protect the individual's asserted interest by ensuring careful determination of controlling facts. Due-process proceedings are also designed to achieve other goals: to ensure that facts will be measured against appropriate criteria; to guarantee that decisions will be made carefully and impartially; to afford opportunity for participation to affected persons; and to preserve public confidence in the integrity of governmental decision making (Buss, Kirp, and Kuriloff, 1975, pp. 388-89).

These authors questioned whether the special education classification decisions threatened the vital interests of children. If not, there may not be a "protectable interest" that due process is

131

designed to guarantee. They asked whether the information gathered and reported in staffings was similar to the hard and fast "facts" that are usually the object of due process hearings (facts are scarce in staffings). They questioned whether there were any definitive standards for determining what was a correct decision. They cited court cases which concluded that due process is not an absolute right when the cost of its guarantee exceeds the risks of failing to guarantee it. Such may be the case with the staffing process.

Buss, Kirp, and Kuriloff (1975, pp. 393-94) offset these arguments by listing the proposed benefits of due process:

"First, when facts are explored in a formal due-process proceeding, they are fully exposed for analysis and contradiction. It is arguable that due process would contribute to improving the content of special education because the reasons for each classification would be out in the open; if the reasons were invalid, they would be exposed, and the resulting public disapproval would force adjustments in a salutary direction . . . Second, decisions made with due-process procedures are ordinarily accompanied by a statement of reasons. Such statements articulating the grounds for the classification decisions might result in greater consistency. Third, it is claimed that due-process procedures increase the competence and impartiality of decision making. A fourth claimed benefit is that due process facilitates participation in determining one's own fate.

"Finally, due process is said to increase public confidence in the integrity of decision making."

The regulations of P.L. 94-142 make these arguments irrelevant. Whatever the relative costs and benefits of due process, due process there is. The rules have been laid down and the schools that I know have scrupulously followed them. The rules are not difficult to adopt, only costly. Whether one believes they assure correct classification and fair treatment depends on one's belief that human behavior changes in accordance with legislated rules (Wise, 1979, p. 125). I have seen too many counter-instances to believe it. Tests can be given that are non-discriminatory, but the interpretation of their scores can determine that the outcome will be discriminatory. Every rule can be followed and still incorrect results can eventuate. What little discrimination and incompetence exist are simply driven underground. The staffing process has become so complicated, legalistic, and technical, that only the most sophisticated and persistent parents can cope with it.

Legal remedies were sought for racially segregated schools. Social scientists testified in *Brown v. Topeka* that segregated schools harmed black children. The court ordered the schools desegregated. Rules and attendance boundaries were changed accordingly. Many whites left the newly desegregated schools for suburban or private schools, leaving the schools more segregated than ever. The court had the authority to change schools, which are the agents of the state, but no authority over where people chose to live. There exists a realm of human behavior that fails to conform to the legal view of man. That realm may likewise go untouched by the reforms for the handicapped.

DEALING WITH RACE, LANGUAGE, AND GENDER

Many provisions of the law reflect the controversies of the 1960's and early 1970's about the disproportionate numbers of minority children who were in special education, particularly classified as mentally retarded. Judgments in class action suits were generally based on the assumption that such placement was unfair, permanent, racist, and ineffectual. Children placed in special education were destined to be there forever and take on the characteristics of children who were truly retarded. Mercer (1973) reported that such disproportionate misplacements occurred as a function of the use of racially and culturally biased tests.

The federal government included in Public Law 94-142 several provisions to ameliorate this situation. Staffing committees were required to use unbiased assessments. The Office of Civil Rights was empowered to make sure that minorities do not make up a disproportionate share of the special education population. There are implicit quotas operating within each district. If the district enrollment is ten percent black but black children make up twenty-five percent of its special education rolls, that district invites investigation and sanctions by the Office of Civil Rights. The costs to the district of subsequent legal defense and reevaluation of minority children in special education are considerable.

Disproportionate numbers of minorities were no problem for Belleview schools, there being relatively few minorities enrolled in the district. The single complaint lodged against it was judged to be unfounded. The Office of Civil Rights has taken action against several other Colorado school districts, however. The chief result in those districts seems to be, as an attorney involved in these cases reported, that a wholesale reduction of minorities in special education is imposed, without regard to whether the children dismissed were handicapped and needed the help.

Staffing a potentially handicapped child is complicated if he is black or Chicano. The team must determine the racial bias inherent in the test, judge what program would be most efficacious for the child and still keep one eye on the "quotas" being monitored by the Office of Civil Rights. Minorities whose symptoms are marginal are most likely to be rejected for classification as learning disabled, as compared to majority children with equivalent test scores and behaviors. The costs of overinclusion of most children are low, except when a school has exceeded the maximum numbers allowed by official policy. For majority children it is cheaper to provide a resource room placement than it would be to fight legal battles with insistent parents. For minority children this cost equation is reversed. Staffing committees think twice before placing them in special education.

There exists a contradiction in the conception of special education held by special educators (that it is an efficacious and not unpleasant place to be) and the conception of special education held by civil rights activists. Embedded in the judgments and consent agreements in cases such as *Diana* and *Larry P.* is the notion that special education classes are places where minority children languish and deteriorate.

Staffing children with native languages other than English is even more complex. The interference of a second language can produce test profiles that look almost exactly like the test profiles typical of processing disorders. Measured non-verbally, a Spanish-surnamed child's intelligence may be significantly higher than his verbal intelligence score. His reading, writing, and spelling may be significantly below what his over-all ability scores predict them to be (even with the low verbal IQ averaged with his higher quantitative score). His math achievement may be up to his proper grade level. All three of these characteristics are said to be indicative of perceptual processing disorders and very likely would result in placement in a program for the learning disabled. One set of symptoms, therefore, can be explained by two very different underlying traits. The Spanish-surnamed child with the misleading test profile would be misplaced, particularly in a program that emphasized perceptual-motor training. Although I saw no instances such as this in Belleview, there are many in Colorado. Stories of two of them are told in Chapter Ten.

There remains the problem of gender. There is almost universal acceptance of the notion that boys are more likely than girls to be learning disabled. Boys outnumber girls by three to one in programs for learning disabilities in Colorado. Boys are in general more variable than girls, so true differences may be plausible. On the other hand boys also cause more trouble for teachers, who may refer them disproportionately for that reason.

Are learning disabilities distributed equally across social and economic classes? In a careful analysis of this question, Kavale (1980) found conflict between reality and official policies. He pointed out that provisions of Public Law 94-142 specifically rule out learning difficulties that result from cultural or economic disadvantage. However, many characteristics that may be responsible for brain injury occur most often to poor children. He reviewed studies that showed the possible connection of brain injury with malnutrition, prematurity, low birthweight, lack of proper medical care during pregnancy, accidental head injury, lead poisoning, sensory deprivation, and the like. He reviewed other studies that indicated a greater probability of malnutrition and the rest of these characteristics among poor children. He concluded that poor children were at greater risk for learning disabilities and ought not be excluded from official definitions of that handicap. One may readily extend his reasoning to minority children, for they are disproportionately represented in lower social and economic classes. Franks (1971) surveyed Missouri school districts and found that children in programs for the learning disabled were disproportionately white and middle- or upperclass. Programs for the educable mentally retarded were disproportionately black. Despite this greater risk for learning disabilities among minorities, they are excluded from programs that might help them. As reflected in present policy, learning disability seems to be a middle class disease.

SCHOOLS AS BUREAUCRACIES

The staffing process is a product of an increasingly popular but erroneous conception of the nature of schools. School systems are coming to be regarded as bureaucratic organizations. In this respect the staffing process, as dictated by the federal and state laws, is similar to reforms wrought by accountability laws, minimum competency testing programs, court-mandated school finance plans and due process procedures in employment of teachers and discipline of pupils. Policies resulting from these laws, decisions, and programs were intended to right wrongs, equalize opportunity, and insure justice; in short, to reform schools by fiat, from the top down.

In *Legislated Learning*, Arthur Wise (1979) argued that the effect of these reforms has not been to change practice but to bureaucratize schools. What he meant by bureaucratic schools is an organization with a small, agreed upon set of goals, that is hierarchically arranged with a high decree of central control, in which decisions are made by a formal set of rules and procedures, that employs scientific management techniques to increase efficiency, with a functional division of labor. In a bureaucratic organization, it is assumed that means and ends are logically related, that people behave rationally and are virtually interchangeable. Reformers and policy-makers believe that schools operate this way. According to Wise:

"The theory of education which underlies much policy development includes at least the following additional rationalistic assumptions about human behavior and learning:

1. The child is pliable, at least within the range of normal aptitude and normal expectations. As noted, an ambivalent attitude is held toward children who arrive at school displaying less than normal aptitude.

2. The teacher is pliable and will modify his or her behavior to comply with legislation, court orders, regulations, or scientific knowledge about education.

136

3.   A science of education exists which yields treatments that can be applied by teacher to student.

4.   If shown the way, people will prefer cost-effective behavior over behavior which is not cost-effective.

Since not all of these assumptions can be validated, one wonders whether a policy based on them could be expected to have its antici- pated effects" (Wise, 1979, p. 57).

Wise disputed each of these assumptions about the nature of schools. There is no science of education such that means and ends can be linked. The behavior of teachers and pupils is rarely rational or predictable and they flaunt the rules rather than comply with them. Schools have multiple goals and values, some of them implicit and in mutual conflict. What actually occurs in classrooms is not closely coordinated from higher levels of authority and emanates less from centrally-determined objectives than from indi- vidual teachers' values and experiences. Furthermore, according to Wise, informal structures may be more potent than formal ones. Decisions are highly personalized and frequently result from bar- gains and compromises rather than from the application of formal rules and procedures. Schools are places where the effects on chil- dren of policy changes are not predictable because the elements within the system are so loosely coupled.

Because of these characteristics, Wise states that these centrally-determined policies are ineffective. Despite accountabili- ty and minimum competency laws, achievement still declines. Schools are still segregated. Some schools are vastly richer than others, and so on. What does occur as a result of these policy re- forms is that a greater share of educational resources, both time and money, is absorbed in creating and maintaining the systems of rules and procedures and the technological apparatus of "scientific man- agement" e.g., objectives, tests, accounting and recordkeeping sys- tems. Authority over these rules and procedures is centralized, particularly at the level of state government. As this process con- tinues, the conception of schools as bureaucracies is strengthened.

If the local educators accept this conception, the schools will in fact become more bureaucratic. If, as Wise hypothesized, local educators reject this conception, schools will go on as they are but the new policies will fail.

The federal and state laws for the handicapped and the agencies enforcing them seem to rest on the assumption that schools are bureaucracies. The reforms were instigated centrally, from the seats of government. Congress became, in intent if not in effect, a "super schoolboard," according to Terrell Bell, Commissioner of Education when the law was passed. The law granted authority to the federal Office of Special Education to initiate the reforms and monitor the state offices of special education. The states were empowered to monitor the compliance of local districts. (Only one state elected not to participate, and compliance suits were launched against it.) In turn the local authority for special education was supposed to control the actions of individual teachers and administrators in the staffing process.

The assumption of a single centrally controlled, hierarchically arranged organization is obvious, but easily disputed. In Belleview school district, which is as compliant as most districts, the teachers (including the special education teachers) reported to their school principals, and the line of authority from the special education office was fuzzy. Neither did the assessment specialists fall under the jurisdiction of special education. The director of special education was under the authority of the district superintendent, not the state department of special education. The state department of special education had to answer first to the state's education authority (commissioner and state board) and after that to the U.S. Office of Special Education. Within the schools (e.g. Aspen School) informal status and communication carried greater weight than the formal organization in determining the outcomes of staffing. Decisions were made that reflected local criteria and personal motives and beliefs and idiosyncratic pressures from parents. Explicitly they followed the official rules, but implicitly the school people followed their best instincts and local necessity.

A bureaucratic organization has a small set of goals, but American schools are pluralistic in goals and values. The policy reforms for the handicapped have as their aim to make one educational value, equity, preeminent over the other values honored in schools. Because federal and state appropriations have not increased as special education budgets have grown to pay for the mandated reforms, local districts have had to make up the difference. Local district monies now make up just over fifty percent of special education budgets. The question of providing occupational therapy instead of a music teacher illustrates not only budget priorities but a competition of values. New educators aver (sometimes self-righteously) that the choice is obvious; the Belleview Association of Band Parents may not be so sure.

CHAPTER EIGHT

HOW SOCIAL THEORIES HAVE EXPLAINED THE STAFFING PROCESS

The staffing process culminates in the attaching of a label and the assignment of the child to a category. The committee says, in effect but rarely in words, "Jenny is learning disabled," or "John does not qualify for the resource room because he is not learning disabled." Mention labeling in the company of academics and civil rights activists and you are almost always guaranteed a lively conversation. The conventional wisdom of the 1960's and 1970's held that when a child was given a label, expectations were induced in his teachers and parents, the expectations were self-fulfilling, and the result was poor achievement, low self-esteem, insane behavior and whatever else the label suggested. The opinion was widespread-- labels were bad. The source of much of these beliefs was the "deviance" theories of sociology (cf. Becker, 1963), that society created deviance by attaching labels.

If these theories are true (evidence is mixed and MacMillan and Meyers, 1979, questioned whether the detrimental effects of labels had ever been demonstrated empirically), the advocates for the handicapped are in a paradoxical position. Classifications are necessary so that a special service can be provided to those in need of it (Hobbs, 1975). With the classification comes the label.

Two radical criticisms of the identification of learning disabilities will be reviewed here. *The Myth of the Hyperactive Child* (Schrag and Divoky, 1975) attempted to debunk even the existence of hyperactivity and learning disabilities. The authors reviewed the theory and research on this topic and found it both deficient and fanciful. Although the syndrome of learning disabilities had been defined in the 1920's, the real growth of the movement coincided with the Nixon administration. It resulted, according to these authors, from the conjunction of two social themes. One was the sentiment that society must control individuals who transgress or threaten against it. The other was the belief that medical and behavioral sciences were able to diagnose, prevent, and treat psychological and social problems. Later, because learning disabilities were linked to juvenile delinquency, they were considered one form of social and academic deviance that must be diagnosed and prevented if possible or treated if necessary. The programs to identify and treat children with learning disabilities were always said to be for the benefit of the child. In reality these programs benefited society and social institutions by labeling troublesome behavior as deviant. Controlling deviance was a way of increasing the power of the institutions over individuals. Programs were always couched in medical and scientific language even when these concepts lacked scientific validity. Thus the attempts to control deviance were rationalized by making school problems appear to have medical origins. Diagnostic systems were created to find children who were having problems in school. Syndromes such as minimal brain dysfunctions were created to explain these learning problems (most were the result of poor teaching but could subsequently be blamed on the child's neurological system).

"A whole new demonology has sprung into existence: the predelinquent, the learning disabled, the minimally brain damaged. Since a small percentage of children could be shown, through medical tests, to be

141

organically brain damaged, a substantial number of other children who had trouble learning to read and who showed some, though not all, of the same 'behavior syndromes' were labeled 'minimally brain damaged' (or MBD) even though no one could find any sign or organic damage and all tests showed that there was none. Subsequently MBD was further broadened to mean, among other things, 'minimal brain dysfunction' and invoked to explain everything from learning difficulties to divorce and homicide" (Schrag and Divoky, 1975, p. 27).

The authors described tests and diagnostic systems as ideological instruments of control.

"(They) enhance the mystical powers ascribed to the tester, the therapist and the institution. They tend, among other things, to confirm institutional legitimacy by reinforcing the corresponding illusion that there are legitimate, universally accepted norms underlying the practice. The teacher may be capricious, brutal and stupid, but if you test the child with the most difficulties for MBD, or if you test all children, you reinforce the assumption that the teacher, the school and the system are functioning properly. The frequent argument that test data will enable the system to make proper adjustments (to individualize instruction, for example) is simply a self-serving argument about its own flexibility and universality and therefore another point for legitimacy. As long as the ideology focuses on diagnosis and treatment it tends to confirm the belief that the system can know and do things which the individual cannot know or do for himself: the individual who fails or cannot adjust requires further treatment" (Schrag and Divoky, 1975, p. 38).

If the institutions initiated this movement as a means of controlling deviant children, parents were willing confederates, for different motives.

"In the symbiosis between parents and professionals, everyone has something to gain: for the parent, the payoff comes in the alleviation of guilt and in the protection of social status and self-esteem; for the practitioner, it lies in the generation of new jobs, specialties and funds, and in the creation of a new mystique enhancing professional status. For both, it is a way to maintain belief in the dynamics of class, the belief that white, affluent, well-manner parents simply cannot produce offspring who can't behave or can't learn and are therefore no better than ghetto blacks" (Schrag and Divoky, 1975, p. 65.).

For the children whose test profiles predict learning disabilities (deviance from the norm, according to this view) a variety of programs were in store--special classes, behavior modification, drugs, aversive conditioning and the like. In these programs, children would be reshaped, homogenized, and made to adjust in the name of individual benefit but in reality to enhance social order.

Less flamboyant but more scholarly was Coles's (1978) paper on the learning disabilities test battery. To evaluate the "special knowledge" the field claims to possess, Coles reviewed research on the reliability and validity of tests typically-used to diagnose learning disabilities. Not finding the evidence credible, he used social conflict theory to explain why this test battery has been used in spite of its poor psychometric characteristics.

"The reason, I believe, lies to a great extent in our social system--a system now requiring vast structural changes to remedy its present state of instability. Unable to make these changes, and in an effort to make unassailable its deteriorating institutions, the system, in its own defense, has generated and nurtured the growth of such fields as learning disabilities--providing, in other words, biological explanations for problems that require social solutions ... (such as) poverty, agression, and violence, as well as for educational underachievement" (Coles, 1978, p. 332).

"By positing biological bases for learning problems, the responsibility for failure is taken from the schools, communities, and other institutions and is put squarely on the back, or rather within the head, of the child. Thus, the classification plays its political role, moving the focus away from the general educational process, away from the need to change institutions, away from the need to rectify social conditions affecting the child, and away from the need to appropriate more resources for social use toward the remedy of a purely medical problem. It is a classic instance of what Ryan (1972) has called 'blaming the victim.' That is, it is an explanation of a social problem that attributes its cause to the individual failings, shortcomings, or deficiencies of the victims of the problem" (Coles, 1978, p. 333).

Coles also gave another reason for the popularity of the learning disabilities test battery. Diagnosis creates patients, patients require treatment, and the clinicians and pharmaceutical industry profit thereby. A further reason for biologizing of learning problems is the enhancement of prestige and economic advantage for specialists of learning disabilities. He quoted Friedson (1970) as follows:

". . . (T)he characteristics that mark a 'profession' are its claims of 'knowledge of an especially esoteric, scientific, or abstract character' and of work that is 'extraordinarily complex and nonroutine, requiring for its adequate performance extensive training, great intelligence and skill, and highly complex judgment" (pp. 106, 153-54). Of all professional groups, it is the medical profession which has the clearest claim to this kind of prestige and authority, particularly in its prerogative to diagnose, treat, and direct treatment. Thus, in a professional relationship where there is the opportunity to share assumptions about the biological nature of a 'disorder,' the closer a profession comes to acquiring the terminology and characteristics of the medical profession, the more that profession can increase its prestige and 'its position in the class structure and in the market place' (Friedson, 1970, p. 153).

These criticisms by Coles and Schrag and Divorky have much to recommend. The theories they invoke explain some things about the staffing process but not (I believe, except in my darker moments) all of it. They do not square with facts and ideas such as the following:

(1) Both are based on the argument that because re-search has failed to validate the trait of learning disabilities and the tests that measure the trait, one must look for alternative, social explanations to account for the popularity of the trait and its measures. But proving the existence of a negative is impossible. That research failed to confirm the existence of a trait can mean either (a) that the trait does not exist or (b) that present research techniques are not adequate for finding it. Either explanation is possible; that these authors did not raise the second one identified their approach to inquiry as more polemical than even-handed. The open-minded person must consider both hypotheses.

(2) Social theories generally fail to account for individual differences in that they regard personal motives, characteristics, and consciousness as subordinate to social forces. When I consider the professionals, parents, and children in Belleview, I can identify the social forces described by Coles, Schrag and Divoky as plausible explanations for the actions of some, but not all these people. Certain teachers obviously wanted to rid themselves of troublesome children and perhaps rationalize their own teaching failures. Some parents seemed desparate that their children be declared learning disabled so that their poor handwriting or clumsiness would have a medical explanation. Some doctors, psychologists, speech-language specialists, occupational therapists, nurses and others used medical and psychological concepts I knew to lack foundation. They did so seemingly to establish their expertise and authority and to rationalize what were little more than common-sense personal judgments. There were many of all roles who blindly accepted the jargon and used it to mystify parents, each other, and themselves.

But there were many on the other side; for example teachers who referred children with learning problems only after months of effort to remediate the problem in class. There were many teachers who still considered naughty boys to be just that and not as children with hyperkinetic syndromes. There were many psychologists and special education teachers who refused to use the hocus-pocus of neurological and cerebral dysfunctions. Instead they considered learning problems to be something to work on by providing remedial tutoring techniques or emotional support. There were many skeptics among both parents and professionals.

Individual differences were not considered by these criticisms in another way as well. In labeling theory, individual differences are assumed to be products, not causes of the labels attached to people by society. Yet studying the children labeled learning disabled--not in the abstract, but in person--leads even the most radical environmentalist to wonder whether *some* of them might not be impaired by nature or early experience.

(3) Theories presented in this section do not account for the fact that, among labels, learning disability is a benign one. In fact, even that label is rarely used in the staffing process by parents, clinicians, or teachers. For the most part, treatments given to the learning disabled are part-time, short term, and mild, hardly the instruments of social control posited by Schrag and Divoky. Children are placed. Half are dismissed as cured after a year. The vast majority are treated only one hour each day. They get better. They graduate. Some only graduate because they are so labeled. The dire and deleterious consequences predicted by these theories are not evident.

CHAPTER NINE

TREATMENT OF LEARNING DISABILITIES: WHAT HAPPENS AFTER STAFFING

Almost everything--and more--that can be known about the child is discovered during the staffing process. But what will happen to him after placement remains unknown.

Belleview's psychologists assume that once a clinical assessment and differential diagnosis are completed, the special education teacher can design a program to remediate the difficulties discovered. They further assume that the program, whatever it is, will be effective. Once the child is staffed, he is the responsibility of the special education teacher and department. The teacher works from the child's Individual Educational Program (IEP) but decides how to achieve the goals of the IEP, what materials to choose, how rapidly to move through the curriculum, how to monitor progress and revise the instruction, even whether to change objectives or dismiss the child having achieved them, all matters of professional judgment. The teacher has latitude that is astonishing when compared to the strict limits placed on teachers in the staffing process prior to placement.

State and federal special education officials would no doubt deny this, for they generally believe that the IEP guides the treatment of children staffed as handicapped. Morra (1979, p. 7) described the Individual Educational Program, or IEP, as follows:

> "A major purpose of Public Law 94-142, the Education for All Handicapped Children Act of 1975, is to assure that all handicapped children have available to them a free appropriate public education which emphasizes special education and related services designed to meet their unique needs. According to the law, an Individualized Education Program (IEP) is to be developed and reviewed jointly for each handicapped child by a qualified school official, by the child's teacher or teachers, the parents or guardian, and when appropriate, the child. The developed IEP document is to specify the child's present level of educational performance, annual goals, short-term instructional objectives, the types of educational and/or related services the child is to receive, a time line for the delivery of those services, the extent to which the child will be able to participate in regular education programs, and objective criteria and evaluation procedures and schedules. The IEP document serves as a guide for the delivery of special education and related services to the child."

A properly developed IEP insures "FAPE," a "Free and Appropriate Education" which is the right of the handicapped. This is the federal view. For the IEP to be properly developed, parents must have played an active role in supplying information about the child's characteristics and proposing goals and programs. Although the federal law specified the procedures for developing the IEP and obtaining parental consent for it, laws do not regulate the provision of treatment nor the progress of children in meeting IEP goals. On this they are mute. (But regulations do require a triennial evaluation, and parents may request a repeat of the staffing process.) One can guess from this omission either a lack of concern about effective treatment or an assumption amounting to blind faith that the IEP and effective treatment are magically linked.

In use, the IEP is merely a set of objectives (a national average of 3.3 objectives per child according to a survey by Pyecha, 1979). Objectives are statements of the projected or desired status of a child as a result of treatment. According to the technology of objectives, the status is stated in behavioral or test-specific terms. But the means for achieving these ends are usually left unstated and in the hands of those who deliver the treatment--in this case, the teachers. One can only remark that it was the teachers and schools that were considered culpable and untrustworthy before the passage of the laws for the handicapped. Now, treatment is not only in their hands but there is no redress if objectives are not met in a reasonable time. Table 4 contains examples of IEP objectives taken from representative files of learning disabled children.

Given that treatment cannot be predicted from the IEP, then what happens to children staffed as learning disabled? Over eighty percent are treated in resource rooms. Fifteen percent are placed in self-contained classes. The rest are served indirectly by the special education teacher's monitoring their progress and providing consultation to their classroom teachers.

The resource room is a part-time treatment, a manifestation of the concept of mainstreaming. The child remains in the regular classroom for most of the day, but leaves it for the resource room for anywhere from 30 minutes to two hours. The program may occur every day or every other day, but the typical pattern is one hour per day. In the resource room a special education teacher, usually a learning disabilities specialist, teaches him individually or in a group of two or three. The specialist maintains a file of test results and academic work performed by the child, and makes decisions about how the child is progressing through the program planned for him at the staffing conference. The specialist may or may not consult with the regular classroom teacher to coordinate the child's activities in the two places. Such coordination was quite variable in Belleview as it is elsewhere (Stearns, Green, and David, 1980). For example, a child who was working in the resource room on reading skills might leave his regular class while it was doing social studies

Table 4

Examples of IEP Objectives for Learning Disabled Students

"The learner will gain six months progress in reading as measured by the PIAT."

"The learner will master two-digit subtraction problems by May."

"The learner will learn to sit quietly during class time."

"The learner's auditory discrimination will improve significantly as measured by the Wepman."

"When walking the learner will hold body in proper verticle alignment using a smooth heal-toe gait and relaxed alternative arm swing, observed 70% of the time."

"The learner's self-concept will improve."

"The learner will complete the *Auditory Discrimination in Depth* program to the satisfaction of the teacher."

"The learner will improve ability to sequence sounds presented auditorily from K-level to end of second grade level as measured by the LAC test."

"The learner will improve visual memory for sequenced objects and letters from 40% for 4 items to 90% for 4 items as measured by teacher test."

"The learner will read and write the 100 most common words from 13/100 to 80/100 in spelling and from 60/100 to 95/100 in reading by May, 1981."

Table 4

Examples of IEP Objectives for
Learning Disabled Students
(continued)

"The learner will complete language arts writing task, using a student dictionary and independent spelling skills from a zero-word story to a 8-word story as measured by teacher test."

"The learner will cross midline with both arms in order to catch a ball thrown to the right or left from 0/5 times to 4/5 times as measured by crossing the midline activities."

"The learner will continue responsibilities in completing regular class assignments as measured by teacher observation."

"The learner will reproduce a multi-colored, overlapping design from 0/5 times to 3/5 times as measured by DLM pegboard designs, by May."

(thus getting a double dose of reading) or else leave while the regular class was receiving instruction in reading.

The content of the treatment children receive can be roughly categorized into four groups: medication, behavior modification, the pure forms of perceptual-motor or attentional training programs, and the eclectic treatments.

Medication

Whether a child is diagnosed as hyperactive or learning disabled is sometimes a function of who sounded the alarm. The two "syndromes" have several symptoms in common. Parents troubled by symptomatic behavior may seek explanations and relief from pediatricians; teachers may likewise be troubled and seek comfort from psycho-educational clinicians. Stimulant treatments such as amphetamines, methyphenidate, and pemoline can only be prescribed by physicians and are called by Cantwell (1980) the "treatment of choice" for the ADDH syndrome. (Attentional Deficit Disorder with Hyperactivity, also a covering term for Minimal Brain Dysfunction.) Educators have no role in this kind of treatment (although school nurses and secretaries sometimes administer the medication) and tend to dissociate learning disabilities from hyperactivity. In the Colorado rules, for example, hyperactive children are not categorized with the learning disabled but with "medical handicaps."

Behavior Modification

Although many special educators employ some concepts and techniques derived from behavioristic psychology, few adhere exclusively to this approach. Behaviorists ignore underlying neurological or perceptual dynamics or states. They concentrate instead on the concrete, observable behaviors of the learning disabled child. According to Kanfer and Phillips (1970), the behavioral approach involves selecting specific interventions to alter the symptoms, monitoring progress continuously and changing the intervention as necessary to achieve the desired end-state. In the arsenal of behaviorist tactics can be found reinforcement techniques, shaping, charting and counting a child's behaviors, task analysis, role playing and model reinforcement, systematic desensitization of specific anxieties, training in the skills of self-monitoring, contingency management, and "the engineered classroom." One unique feature of behavioral treatments is that the child's environment is "diagnosed" and treated as well as the child himself. The behavioral psychologist attempts to discover what elements in the child's "social ecology" are controlling his behavior. These elements may then be the object of intervention, or the therapists may work directly on changing the child's behavior.

Perceptual-Motor Training Programs

Like behavior modification, many resource room teachers employ some ideas and techniques adapted from perceptual-motor training programs, but few use them exclusively. Those who do so tend to be disciples of developers of such programs: Barsch, Cratty, Delacato, Frostig, Ayers, Kephart. These programs share the assumption that academic failure is due to some underlying dysfunction or developmental lag in the motor or perceptual systems. Thus, the treatment must be aimed at identifying and remediating the underlying disorder or strengthening an unaffected ability to compensate for the disability. Diagnosis, therefore, is the *sine qua non* of effective treatment.

Kephart's theory and related treatment as described by Myers and Hammill (1976) are based on the notion that all learning depends on sensory-motor abilities, particularly in the child's ability to orient the physical body to the external world. Administration of the Perceptual Motor Training Scale yields information about the developmental stage of learning and what training activities should be chosen. Traits measured and training to match these traits fall into four categories: visual-motor, sensory-motor, ocular control, and form perception. If the weakness or arrested development is diagnosed as being in the visual-motor abilities, treatment would be chalkboard training,

"beginning with random scribbling and progressing through directionality exercises, including those that require the child to cross the midline, to orientation exercises in which the child copies forms, reproduces them from memory, and varies his reproductions with respect to size, speed, direction, etc. Throughout these activities the child is taught to attach the verbal symbol to his productions. In general, however, the child is experimenting with movement patterns and observing closely the pattern left on the chalkboard which results from his activity; both activities comprise the essentials of visual-motor perception" (Myers and Hammill, 1976, p. 322).

"Sensory-motor training emphasizes the development of balance but progresses through the development of body image and bilaterality and unilaterality. The child is taught balance through a number of activities requiring a walking board: walking forward, backward, sidewise, and turning and bouncing on the board are typical exercises. In addition to the walking board, and usually after proficiency on it has been attained, the child is introduced to the balance board and taught many of the same skills he has learned on the walking board. The trampoline is used in this phase of training as well as the walking and balance boards. Other activities included in the sensory-motor training program include:

1. Angels-in-the-snow--used in teaching bilateral, unilateral, and cross-lateral movements and in teaching the child to change the time and position of his movements.

2. Stunts and games--for example, the duck walk, rabbit hop, crab walk, measuring worm, and elephant walk; all aimed at teaching variations in movements patterns and providing the child with opportunities to elaborate movement patterns which he has learned.

3. Rhythmical activities--both bilateral and unilateral" (pp. 322-23).

Ocular Control Training is required so that the child can match what he perceives visually with the motor and kinesthetic patterns he has learned in earlier stages. It proceeds from stage one to stage five.

154

"Stage one. The child is taught to follow with his eyes an object, such as a pencil, while it is moved first laterally and vertically and then moved diagonally and in rotary fashion. The latter movements are the more difficult and are not employed until the child is able to follow lateral and vertical movements of the target . . ."

"Stage five. The fifth stage of ocular training requires the use of a ball, first large, such as a beach ball, then smaller, such as a baseball. In this stage, the teacher places both hands, palms flat, on one side of the ball, and the child places his hands on the opposite side. The teacher moves the ball in lateral, vertical, diagonal, and rotary patterns carrying the child's hands along with him and encouraging the child to keep the ball in sight as it is moved" (Myers and Hammill, 1976, pp. 323-24).

The training of Form Perception involves matchsticks, pegboards, and puzzles for the child to use in matching and copying patterns presented to him by the teacher.

According to Myers and Hammill teachers of the learning disabled "have reported positive results from the use of the materials and activities recommended by Kephart" (p. 325).

The Doman-Delacato method for treating learning disabilities "is based on the theory that neurological development follows 'ontology recapitulates phylogeny' . . . that human development repeats the pattern of man's evolutionary development" (Myers and Hammill, 1976, p. 335).

"With the completion of (normal) developmental processes, usually by the age of eight years, a child is said to have achieved a state of Neurological Organization. If injury to the brain occurs at any level or if environmental factors restrict the child's development in his natural progression, the child will show evidence of neurological dysfunction or disorganization in either language or mobility. Children who have problems in language, particularly in reading, almost always demonstrate incomplete attainment of cortical hemispheric dominance. Children who do not establish this dominance usually also evidence incomplete development at one or more preceding stages of brain development."

Extensive diagnostic procedures are used to determine at what stage of neurological development the child is fixated, then the therapists train him to master each successive level.

"The method of treating the brain itself instead of the results of the brain injury was developed at the Institutes and is called 'patterning.' A group of patterning movements was devised to manipulate the limbs of brain-injured children to produce movements which are the responsibility of the damaged level. The levels considered are medulla, pons, midbrain, and cortex. Patterning (the manipulation of arms, legs, and head) is based on the theory that all cells in an area of the brain are not usually affected by injury and that activation of live cells is possible. Intensity, duration, and frequency of the exercises will enable the brain to receive the sensory messages" (Myers and Hammill, 1976, p. 342).

"Training for children determined to be disorganized at spinal cord and medulla level, opportunity is provided to use the basic reflex movements available to him by placing him on the floor for most of the day. In addition, undulating, fishlike movements are imposed on the child's body for prescribed periods during the day" (p. 344).

"For children at the cortical dominance (highest pre-remedial) level, patterns of sleep consistent with sidedness are emphasized. Activities such as kicking, stepping off, and hurdling are used to help develop a dominant foot. Skills such as throwing, cutting, using tools, and picking up objects are used to develop handedness. Eye dominance is taught through the use of games involving telescopes for far-point vision and microscopes for near-point vision. Delacato also favors the use of a device called a Stereo-Reader manufactured by the Keystone View Company. It has the effect of occlusion while giving the illusion that both eyes are seeing the training material. This material consists of exercise cards of visual-motor activities, word families, visual discrimination, phrase reading, reading for interest, and speed reading. Two twenty-minute periods per day are usually prescribed" (p. 346).

Although the Doman-Delacato method has many loyal supporters, it has aroused considerable controversy. Critical statements have been issued against it by such organizations as the American Academy of Pediatrics and the Canadian Association for Children with Learning Disabilities.

Eclecticism

Most special education teachers practice eclecticism in the treatments they provide the learning disabled. They feel free to select from many methods what they think best fits the children in their charge. In Belleview, this freedom resulted in great variety, owing to the differences in training and philosophy of individual teachers. Three patterns were observed.

The first pattern, characteristic of only a few teachers, resembled psychotherapy. These teachers viewed their primary role as that of providing emotional support to psychologically needy children. Remedial academic work was pursued, but primarily as a vehicle for maintaining a healing interpersonal relationship between the teacher and child.

The second pattern differed little from remedial tutoring. Teachers determined what academic skills were lacking in each child and then conducted activities to master the skills. For example, if the staffing committee determined that a child was learning disabled because his achievement tests scores in arithmetic were far below what is expected, the special education teacher might determine that he doesn't know his teen-numbers (between 10 and 20), and that problem has kept him from being able to add two-digit numbers. Then the teacher invents ways to teach him the teen numbers, so afterwards he could progress normally. The emphasis is placed on modifying instruction to overcome a temporary learning block or area of poor learning or teaching. Many materials are available for the teacher's use, including phonics kits, language development exercises, spelling games, math flashcards, and the like. Teachers who follow this model are more likely than others to define learning disabilities by whether a child needs extra help and less likely to take seriously the neurological and perceptual definitions.

The third pattern is characterized by perceptual-motor training, based more or less on some of those programs listed above. The main focus is on identifying the specific perceptual-motor disability a child has, and remediating the disability directly. According to the philosophy behind these programs, the learning difficulties that were the original reason for referral and staffing will be remedied as a result of the improvement of the perceptual-motor ability. This is sometimes called the diagnostic-prescriptive model of treating the learning disabled.

Teachers also attempt to identify the "dominant channel" by which the child learns best and the channel (auditory, visual, or haptic) that is deficient. Then the teacher either attempts to train and correct the deficiency or work around it by emphasizing instruction through the dominant channel. A huge variety of materials are available to assist the teacher in this enterprise. For example, a child such as John, who had a problem with auditory discrimination, might be assigned (if the resource room teacher so decided) to complete the "Auditory Perception Training Figure Ground Program" published by Developmental Learning Materials, a corporation in Illinois (see Appendix C). A child judged to have visual difficulties might be seen stringing beads in a prescribed sequence, cutting, pasting and tracing shapes in colored paper, working with mazes, pegboards, parquetry, or pegboards. A child with perceptual motor difficulties might be found walking the balance beam.

Eclectic teachers seem to vary their techniques among children and on a single child from time to time. Besides the techniques specific to special education, there are some general instructional and organizational practices also characteristic of treatments in special education settings. Reduced class size is one of these. Another is control of student motivation, attention, and time on an academic task. Extraneous stimuli are reduced in a resource room or self-contained class. There are the beneficial effects of attention by the teacher who can provide close appraisal and monitoring of the child's progress. Special education teachers stress the need to be flexible—to present and explain ideas a hundred ways if necessary. Special education treatments also have the effect of removing children from an atmosphere of competition and classroom failure.

Notice, though, that all these conditions are not unique to special education, but are general educational practice.

Benefits of Treatment

Judicial and Congressional fiat can make special education a right, but no agency can make it a benefit. Considering how much official concern is directed toward providing the handicapped with services, there is remarkably little official attention paid to whether the treatments are efficacious. Once the assessments are judged to be fair, multi-modal and nondiscriminatory, the child judged to be handicapped, an IEP written and a "free, appropriate education" provided, federal and state policies are mute. There is no provision in state or federal law for a free, appropriate, and *effective* education for the handicapped. Unless one counts the required triennial re-evaluation of pupils already placed, there are no official demands for accountability for results of treatment.

A few scholars have nevertheless maintained interest in treatment efficacy, and they have painted a bleak landscape. Ysseldyke (1977) reviewed the research and concluded there is little empirical evidence to show that specific treatments for the handicapped lead to desirable academic outcomes. Arter and Jenkins (1979) surveyed teachers of the learning disabled in Illinois and found that 85 percent used the diagnostic prescriptive teaching model. In their review of research, Arter and Jenkins found little empirical support for this model. The reliabilities of the perceptual-motor tests were too low to support diagnoses or even to plan instruction. Test validity was also suspect. Furthermore, they found that measures of perceptual abilities do not correlate with academic measures and interventions in a perceptual disability do not lead to improvements in reading or arithmetic achievement. Identifying modalities or dominant channels does not produce gains in academic skills.

More bad news for the perceptual-motor programs was provided by Kavale and Mattson (1980) who statistically integrated all the controlled studies of the effects of perceptual-motor training programs. They found that children treated with these programs (e.g., by Kephart, Delacato, Cratty, Frostig) were no better off after treatment than comparable children who received no treatment. Hammill and Larson (1974) reached similarly negative

159

conclusions based on their review of research on the effects of psycholinguistic (e.g., traits measured by Illinois Test of Psycholinguistic Abilities) treatments.

There is little evidence to support the specific benefits of special education. Yet the general effects may be beneficial. Educational research has shown that increments of achievement are associated with smaller class size, that tutoring is beneficial, that achievement is related to student engaged time on academic tasks, that counseling and psychotherapy are effective, and that there is a "placebo effect" merely from paying attention to a child. All these work on the average and may work for the learning disabled as well.

From the practitioner's view one can see many children improving. In Belleview, half of each year's group of learning disabilities is dismissed as improved or graduated. When I observed the annual review conferences I repeatedly heard the positive side. Parents expressed their gratitude to the resource room teachers who had done so much for their children, had saved them from academic failure. These expressions were sincere, and I saw no reason to doubt them.

No matter how strenuously bureaucrats or researchers attempt to define special education as an engineering or medical intervention, it remains teaching. As such, it retains its artistic elements, made up of unarticulated knowledge and intuition in the minds of experienced, sensitive, and flexible teachers. When I encountered a Belleview child working with a teacher I usually felt as if something good was happening. If that had been my child, I would have felt secure. But this was a human perception about a human interaction. How different it was from watching the highly bureaucratized, technologized and quasi-legal staffing process.

Two anecdotes remain to be presented. Everyone has war stories about learning disabilities and these are mine. The first is the testimony given to the Colorado Senate by a learning disabled girl. The next is a letter written by a mother who had wrestled with the staffing process. Both pieces came in response to the Colorado study, described in Part III. Unfortunately, they fail to resolve the ambiguities of the staffing process and subsequent treatment.

I'm _____. I'm an 8th grader at
_____ Middle School in _____. I
like drama sports and I play the piano.

After only 2 months in 1st grade my teacher
referred me for testing. These tests determined that I
had a perceptual, sequential LEARNING DISABILITY. I
would need imediate special help to bring me up to the
level of my classmates and then regular monitoring in the
classrom along with the special help in the L.D. lad.

I had and still have trouble especially in the
reading area; this carries over into writing skills. Most
of our curriculum has a lot of reading in almost every
subject so the help I get in special-Ed has also taught me
some other skills such as a special form of note taking
because of poor writing skills.

I didn't qualify for special-Ed one year and I
had a redular classroom teacher who didn't know how to
work with me. She yelled at me a lot and couldnt' understand why I couldn't get things done right like spelling
words. I know how to spell them orally, but I kept
reversing letters and turning the letters wrong when I
wrote them. She wouldn't let me spell them out loud
because nobody else did. I couldent read as fast as the
other kids so I was always behind and sometimes it was
easier to just give up.

The next year I took that grade over again but
I WAS put back into special-Ed. I had to work really hard
to try to catch up with my classmates.

I've had a lot of fun in Jr.-Hi., but I've worked
hard to, harder than most of my friends to keep up. The
special-Ed Lab teacher has been a big help but he expects
me to do as much as I can on my own.

I'll be going into High-school next year and I know I can do well if I have someone who can help me with the English and Algerbra. Without special ed help for students like myself, we would be so far behind by Jr.-Hi, I don't think most of us would make it into High-School.

I hope you will give those of us who need to learn a little differently a chance at the same educational oportunities as the other students.

Thank you.

(Letter From a Mother)

August 3, 1980

To Whom It May Concern:

This is not a vindicative attempt to discredit anyone. I do feel in most cases everyone I have encountered has been sincere. This also is not an attempt to deny that my child does not learn as readily as others, however I've found her capable of learning any subject she is shown and allowed to understand. This is written only after much thought, research and agonizing after which my definite conclusion is that the program did not benefit my child in many ways or the many other children who could benefit in some area of attention. This is a sincere, and objective as possible, attempt to represent my feelings as a parent.

We opted for the special ed placement only as an alternative to holding back a grade since she was an older kindergartener.

I can cope with almost any situation I can imagine. But my experiences with regards to this situation is one area where I admit I feel overwhelmed. I've found most special ed parents a quiet, serious group. I have no doubts that their feelings and reservations mirror mine. These are our children you're talking about--not laboratory specimens or mechanical rejects.

Sincerely,

_____'s development from baby-
dom followed and exceeded in many areas the "normal"
expectations.

Upon entering kindergarten I was surprised to find the
teachers were concerned because she didn't socialize well
and was easily distractable, didn't pay attention, follow
directions, etc. With the advice of our pediatrician we
agreed to have some testing done by the school--this was
in October.

The testing was begun in February. However, before the
results were complete we were pressured to agree to a
special ed placement. This would require _____ to
board a bus every day and be transported by herself to
_____ for a full day's instruction. We refused. Upon calling the State Office of Special Education I was informed that any recommendations made
prior to completion of all testing were in direct violation
of State and Federal laws.

The results of the tests revealed some areas of immaturity. However, no one--the psychologist or teachers could
explain to me what the problem was. When they complained that she could't properly write her letters I sat
with _____ over a three day holiday weekend
in February and she learned how to write her name
properly and successfully from all of the capital and
small letters in the alphabet. All I needed to do was
guide her hand in the initial formation of each letter.
This was accomplished in three days and still, mastery of
this skill and others would not result in promotion to the
first grade.

Could it have been the 48 children in her class that precluded her from receiving individual help from the two
teachers? We felt that that was the problem and expressed our opinion. A fifth grade neighbor who assisted
in the Kindergarten class on occasion related to us that

an oriental child who couldn't speak English was given a lot of individual attention by the teachers.

In not being able to see where _____ had problems learning at home, we couldn't understand any reason for her not to learn at school except due to the children to teacher ratio. At that point we inquired about "resource room" assistance at school and was told it could not be accomplished without a staffing meeting with the teachers, psychologist, school nurse, principal, social worker, resource teachers and us even though resource facilities were available. This meeting was scheduled in late May after _____ was "tolerated" for a full year.

The results of the staffing meeting: All in attendance recommended full time special ed placement next year and _(Principal)_ proclaimed that "obviously this child is incapable of learning." Our choice: Agree or repeat kindergarten. We decided to have additional testing done before replying.

We had extensive testing done at JFK* which did reveal some maturation lags in some areas. (Some areas, however, were evaluated as up to two years above age level.) Their recommendation: A Special Education placement in which she would participate with regular first graders in art, music, gym, etc. and extra-curricular activities but yet receive special ed assistance in areas where warranted. Their results were furnished to our pediatrician and the District Special Education Office.

The result: A placement with five other children her age or younger in a Pre-academic class. This was staffed with a Special Ed teacher and assistant, and classes with a Special Ed music teacher, a Special Ed speech teacher, a Special Ed art teacher, and occupational therapists with no daily exposure to the regular classroom. I was

---

*A university-run facility for evaluation and treatment of developmental disabilities and delays.

upset to find this class joining the kindergarten class for parties and this wasn't all. Many "special" things this class got to do was with the severly retarded children from _____ which I, as well as other parents, felt was very inappropriate and offensive.

_____'s classroom work consisted of extensive work in following lines for remedying "perceptual-fine motor" problems. She seemed to progress in some areas and the first half of the year apparently went well--per a mid-year conference with her teacher. However, this is when I discovered that the teacher did not have copies of any of _____'s testing results nor had even seen her file to know what areas needed remediation! These were furnished to the teacher by JFK upon her request.

After Christmas a couple new students were placed, some of whom were labelled "behavior problems." Shortly thereafter _____ began bringing home notes of displaying "inappropriate" behavior. She would slide down the stairs on her bottom, stare at the ceiling, hug a boy she didn't know, etc. She also increased her finger sucking habit and began making a variety of obnoxious sounds at home and laugh about how funny they are when she and several of the boys do it at school and on the bus. Several other parents commented to me about behavior changes in their children at home--blaming the behavioral placements at school.

It was about this time of the year when began being upset by the sad faces on some of her papers. She brought home a folder of words to copy and return. I watched her and felt she did a real nice job making the letters and writing the words. When she brought the folder home again I was shocked--and upset--to find red marks throughout most the words where the letters weren't perfectly shaped or exactly aligned.

We also objected to the artificial environment where everything was "super," "hooray" and other such terms.

The moderated tones and over-positive emphasis was totally unrealistic and not preparatory to the real world in which we live.

In spring notes were sent home advising parents of the opportunity to listen to __(Psychologist)__ discussing parenting. The first meeting parents were required to list problems with their children. One mother dropped out immediately since she felt compelled to "make up weird stories." I felt I could learn more about some of the other kids and the class so I attended a few more sessions. Interest died dramatically and I was with one other mother and then alone till it dissolved. These discussions amounted to my being "railroaded" in that _____ was targeted by the psychologist. His observations were that _____ had severe emotional problems evidenced by her unconscious desire to receive negative attention through her inappropriate behavior. His recommendation: The whole family receive counselling. This conclusion was arrived at without any familiarity with our family. I later found out how conveniently Mr. _____ is affiliated with the _____ County Mental Health Center. (This recommendation was made at the Staffing Meeting for next year's placement.) Also during this time the teacher began a daily log of _____'s bad behavior." We did, however, not seek family counselling.

We felt any inattentiveness at school was due to _____'s being bored and ready for higher level learning, as she copied lines and did repetitive work all year. At home she could read Dr. Seuss books, remembered stories I read her (at school she remembered only what she wanted), she knows her sounds, letters, numbers, and this summer has begun doing color-by-number pictures with plus and minus problems. (She'd had minimal exposure to addition problems at the end of the year.)

The result of the staffing meeting: Presentations by Special Ed teacher, assistant, Special ed speech teacher, Occupational Therapist, special ed office representative, psychologist, and one other special ed office person, and principal was nearly unanimous for full time special ed placement next year. The criteria-_____'s speech is immature. We were never aware of a "speech" problem to this point. The first grade teacher who had _____ for short periods a few times a week at the end of the year saw no specific problem. Mr. _(Principal)_ also agreed that if we weren't comfortable with special ed we should take her out.

The result: We were allowed to place her in a regular first grade against the Special ed persons recommendations.

One specialist even recommended a kindergarten placement to our dismay.

The attitude in the recent staffing meeting was one of "you're on your own" after we rejected their recommendation for another full-time placement next year. Not one member even suggested resource room or any other attention was necessary. _____, the special ed teacher, expressed that _____ was ready for regular first grade next year during the mid-year conference. This we reluctantly began to accept as we hoped not to hold her back a grade. However her recommendation changed by year end.

My husband and I both agree that she definitely regressed during this year's placement. During and after kindergarten she took and loved ballet and had many girlfriends with whom she shared interests. The only other girl in _____'s pre-academic class suffered from cerebral palsy and although they were friends, the age and physical differences precluded many shared interests. At the end of _____'s pre-academic year she had no girlfriends from school and exhibited behavior more immature than a year ago in many play areas, i.e., playing with younger children in the neighborhood, talking baby talk on occasion, expecting pre-determined rewards for any accomplishment-- then becoming upset when she doesn't ger her way, etc.

She also now is identified as possessing a speech problem. Her year's isolation in so juvenile an atmosphere is apparent. However, over summer, much of her obnoxious and tempermental behavior has disappeared.

(The records will show that _____'s speech did not improve at all in one year. Why? She did mature and learn in many other areas.

Until spring _____ boarded the bus down the street at 7:50 a.m. and made stops at all other schools before arriving for her class at 8:45. She was dismissed at 3:00, yet didn't get home till 3:50. In the spring her class had it's own bus which worked out very well.

I also can't understand the strict adherence and attention to such perfectly written letters, when it seems this skill should improve naturally with use.)

Findings:

In questioning our decision and trying to understand this program despite the nightmares experience I've discovered by researching library books, newspapers and magazines:

1.   There is no way to define learning disabilities, nor no known cause or effective remediation.

2.   The State of North Dakota conducted a statewide study and declared "that most learning problems in elementary school are neither emotional or physiological in origin: They are simply children's defensive reactions or curricula that appear irrelevant and to teachers who are overly punitive or judgmental."

3.   Over the past decade the Federal Government has increased spending for special ed programs more than thirty-fold, to $1.1 billion. This funding will increase yearly through Fiscal Year 1982.

4. Special Ed funding is allocated to counties based on placements and needs to be matched by county funds--70% to 30% I believe. This has caused parents and educators to argue that the regular classroom is being shortchanged.

5. *Teaching the Learning Disabled Child* lists seven pages of titles of tests used to discern "learning disabilities."

6. "An estimated 20% of children are affected by some specific, perceptual, motor, cognitive, or behavioral deficit that restricts learning--therefore schools should eliminate the illusion that all children should be fashioned in the mold of 'The North American Child of the Year.'"

7. "Children labelled 'learning disabled' are normal children who learn differently or require more assistance. Provisions of services within the regular classroom is the only way we can hope to offer help to all children with problem learning areas."

8. "It is obvious that many teachers tend to disregard if not actually show contempt for those who do not learn quickly."

9. "Special ed gives regular ed a scapegoat to hide its failures and to provide the quality individualized instruction necessary to remediate even minor academic behavior deficits and perceptual handicaps." This author called it a "Teaching Disability."

10. "'Programming' is a common teaching method used with behavioral modification and psychological conditioning applied to groups as a unit. Lacking is inspiration, individual creativity and acknowledgment in exciting an adventure in learning."

Recap

Only a parent could know the feelings of despair in this type of situation.

First, you're confronted with the "problem." The evaluations are begun and your private life undergoes a most blatant invasion of privacy. Next, in the Staffing Meeting you're met by a variety of "specialists" with sympathetic yet smiling faces. The intimidation is tremendous, not to mention the guilt you must feel for what's "wrong" with your child. The opinions presented make you feel that your child's problem is hopeless in that such a placement is the only way your child can cope.

I can't help but liken it to someone going to a job interview and being confronted by a security representative, someone from the IRS, a medical person, someone with business and personal references, someone representing your moral lifestyle and sexual preferences, a behavior professional to evaluate your personality and presentation for the proper company "image," etc., etc. It is totally ludicrous to think this could happen, but it must excite a similar feeling.

The following to me is comparative to the program: When you purchase a bushel of tomatoes and notice some of the tomatoes have rotten spots what do you do? You could cut off the bad spots and simmer them all and eventually get spaghetti sauce; or you could put all the bad tomatoes in a paper bag - and you know what will eventually happen to the tomatoes and the bag!

In talking to a teacher who highly supports this special ed program and behavior modification, etc., I was shocked to hear her relate that she feels more like 35% (to 20%) of children have specific learning problems, and only the WORST get any help.

Why not concentrate on our children's good points - not their failings?

Educators must be labelling me: neurotic, ignorant, meddling. I could come back with: indoctrinated, arbitrary, cold.

Some may feel this is overly dramatic; others - hilarious. But seriously, the day will never come when I'll look back and see any humor in any of this.

I hope to present my feelings the best I can, and hope someone will share my concern and hope to find out how other parents and educators feel on this matter.

It's no secret that our country's graduates are illiterate. I want to know why and in knowing hope to cultivate our nation's most precious natural resource - our children. They may be the only hope we have left!!

UPDATE - March 5, 1981

Over the summer I'd requested and received records from JFK and the school district regarding my child. It was interesting to note the following:

1. JFK definitely did not feel occupational therapy was necessary. The school's tests rated her lower and that was another area where special education was recommended for the second year.

2. The kindergarten records reflected the child to be very "cooperative and willing to please" as strong points. After one year of special education she became a "behavior problem".

3. The kindergarten records reflected her speech being "satisfactory" on all ratings. A year later she was "two years delayed."

A big change in _____'s behavior became very apparent over the summer. All four of our children were assigned daily chores and _____ was expected to conform the same as everyone else to our family rules. She did this very responsibly and was even very cooperative about being grounded once or twice. The temper tantrums and immature behavior associated with the "rewards system" used at school disappeared.

With extreme apprehension _____ was registered for first grade at the school where the problem originated.

The second day of school I met with the Resource Room teacher and requested testing to determine if resource assistance would be necessary. A staffing meeting was set up for September 17 (in case she would need resource help).

On September 8 the first grade teacher reported the only apparent problem seemed to be following directions at times. She promised we'd work closely together and she'd keep me informed.

The resource teacher also contacted me that day. _____ had some trouble blending sounds and with vowels and was not adding or subtracting. She had good consonant sounds and beginning and ending sounds. She was such a big change from the last time the resource teacher had seen her (in kindergarten). She said by no means was _____ in the low group - we'll wait and see. She said she'd call again on Friday.

Friday - September 12 - The resource teacher called to say the Sept. 17 meeting had been postponed till October 8. _____ worked with the reading readiness teacher and had no problem—she did real well. She's been answering questions in class and raising her hand. The music teacher reported she follows directions well in music. No problems observed as yet - she will watch her longer. Overall _____ has done "real well."

September 10 - Resource teacher called to report _____'s doing great. "She's learning all the new

173

things that are introduced." The October 8 meeting was cancelled. Should she begin to fall behind, the resource teacher and I will be informed.

October 20 - I called for an early conference with the first grade teachers. They reported _____ to be very capable but not following directions well at times. (Her younger brother in the same grade has the same problem - typical of first graders.) I was invited to visit and observe the classroom any time I could.

November 12 - Regular conference with teacher who reported _____ is doing very well. When I asked if she seemed to have a delayed speech problem the teacher told me that "no delay had been noticed. Her sentences and memory do not reflect any delay. She's doing very satisfactorily - not a behavioral problem at all either. She's cooperative, gets along well with the other kids. Her reading comprehension is satisfactory. Also doing well in math."

Her report cards to date reflect her to be where she should be in all areas. She even out-shined her brother in some categories. The second report did reflect a weakness and need to practice her math - "speed addition facts 1-10."

I have no doubt that another year's special ed placement would have made _____ a special ed student for the duration of her education - just by assessing the damage done in one year.

We are even considering a tutorial program to promote her up to where she should be when and if we feel she may be ready.

Taking all things into consideration - "special education" was a traumatic experience affecting our entire family. We're so glad we fought the system to restore our daughter to a "normal" child again.

PART III

EXTENDING THE STUDY OF STAFFING BEYOND BELLEVIEW

Case studies generate hypotheses that must be tested with other data. The case study and analyses of the staffing process led me to hypothesize that the staffings of Jenny, John, and the others were affected only in small part by the matching of the children's characteristics with some definition of learning disabilities. The definitions are so vague and the evidence so equivocal that staffing committees respond as much to the social and legal context as to the characteristics of the children. Jenny was learning disabled, if she was, only by the loosest of criteria. Yet she was staffed as such because her teacher could not cope with her. John was eventually staffed because his parents desired it. Although his characteristics matched no conventional definition of learning disabilities he was staffed as such because of the open-endedness of the law and the school district's fear that his parents would take legal action to secure the service they desired.

Combined with the availability of programs and the richness of special education resources, the pattern just described produced over-identification of learning disabilities in Belleview school district. The legal mandate for due process, bureaucratic regulations, and expanded ranks of professional evaluators created a staffing process that was unwieldy, costly, and with little benefit to the children.

The hypotheses generated by the case study and its analysis are subjected to verification and generalization in Part III. These hypotheses about the staffing process were supported by the results of survey research conducted in Colorado. Other evidence is pieced together in Chapter Eleven to indicate the nationwide picture of the staffing process.

CHAPTER TEN

THE COLORADO PCD STUDY

Alarmed by the growth in the numbers of pupils identified as learning disabled (Colorado refers to learning disabilities as Perceptual/Communicative Disorders or PCD), the state legislature authorized a study of identification practices. Contracted to the Laboratory of Educational Research, University of Colorado and directed by Dr. Lorrie Shepard, this study was controversial from its inception to long after its submission. Neither the Colorado Department of Education nor the majority of special education directors wanted the study conducted. There was considerable trepidation about its anticipated results.

According to the proposal for the study, answers to the following questions were sought. How many pupils are referred, evaluated, staffed and placed as PCD? Do the rates of prevalence

177

differ among districts or across time? What are the demographic and clinical characteristics of the children identified? What tests are used in the identification? How much weight is given to test results and do the tests have adequate reliability and validity? How is professional judgment used in identification? What are the costs of identification in staff and pupil time? What are the interventions used for pupils identified as PCD? How long do children with different learning disabilities remain classified as PCD?

A survey was conducted in which the population consisted of the files of all pupils identified as PCD for the most recent year. A sampling frame for this population was made available by the Colorado Department of Education. The sampling design was a two stage cluster sample design, with the primary sampling unit being the school district and the districts stratified by size. From the representative sample of districts selected, a probability sample of 1000 files of PCD pupils was chosen (3.8% of the population). With this design it was possible to specify the probability of each member of the population to be selected in the sample and to specify the error in generalizing from the sample data to the characteristics of the population.

Quantitative coding of 790 of the case files was performed to assess the characteristics of the sampled pupils. The information obtained from the files was as follows: demographic characteristics, referral information, previous history in special education, report of the staffing conference, the stated basis for handicapping condition, tests administered as part of identification, intelligence and achievement test scores, evidence of perceptual or processing disorders, indication of behavior or medical problems, and criteria used when and if the pupil left or completed the program. The reliability and validity of the coding were assessed and judged to be adequate. To gain better understanding of the characteristics of pupils identified as PCD, qualitative analysis was performed on the remaining 200 cases. Patterns and hypotheses emerged from this analysis to test against those obtained in the quantitative analysis.

Surveys of school personnel were conducted using the sampling design already described. School principals, psychologists, PCD teachers, speech specialists, and social workers were sent questionnaires. Returns exceeded 80 percent. Among the topics on the questionnaire were definitions of PCD used by the specialists as well

178

as beliefs about official definitions, the uses of various tests and clinical judgment in identification, and beliefs about the adequacy of various methods, the influence of parents and professionals on the process of identification, the validity, utility, and cost of identification, time spent in identification, opinions about funding policies, and criteria used to judge whether a pupil should be dismissed from the PCD program. A copy of two of the questionnaires used in this survey is included in Appendix D.

An analysis of documents from the Colorado and federal government revealed that there were no substantial differences between the Colorado definition of Perceptual Communicative Disorder and the federal definition of Specific Learning Disability. According to this analysis a central element in the definitions and selection criteria is that a child's "true potential is much higher than he is able to demonstrate on achievement measures because of interference from the disability" (p. 34). The underlying cause of this discrepancy is "believed to be some breakdown in the basic psychological or learning processes" (p. 35). The third element is an exclusionary clause; i.e., that other potential "causes" of the observed discrepancy--mental retardation, vision or hearing handicaps, emotional disorder or cultural disadvantage--must be ruled out in order for the staffing team to identify a pupil as PCD or learning disabled.

In the survey of professionals, a large majority of the respondents subscribed to the discrepancy and processing elements of the PCD definition.* The response to the exclusionary clause was more variable. For example, low achievement that is the result of linguistic differences is supposed to disqualify a child from PCD or LD status. But when asked whether "linguistically different children should be identified as PCD," some professionals disagreed, many were neutral, and from 12-24 percent agreed. These latter ones considered linguistic difference "as supporting evidence *for* the determination of PCD handicap" (p. 48, original emphasis).

---

*Although they agreed with the discrepancy definition, over half of the respondents did not know how to determine the magnitude of the discrepancy that is needed to be "significant."

Prevalence. Analysis of Colorado Department of Education documents revealed that the percentage of PCD had increased steadily over the years, from 2.1 percent in 1973-74 to 5.1 percent in 1979-80. The 1980 figures for Colorado exceeded the national average. The percentage of PCD in the population of the handicapped also increased. Those identified as PCD accounted for 22.4 percent of all handicapped in Colorado in 1973-74. The comparable figure for 1979-80 was 46.7 percent. There was substantial variability in percent PCD within the state among the districts. The district with the lowest rate of PCD in the total pupil population had 2.11 percent identified as PCD; the highest rate was 8.56 percent. Among the districts, there was a strong relationship between the percent identified as PCD and the percentage in other handicapping conditions. That is, those districts that had identified many pupils as PCD also tended to be those with high rates of emotional disturbed, speech and language handicaps, and handicaps in general.

"The variability among units and across years in the percent identified as PCD can be interpreted in one of two ways. Either there are true differences in the rates at which the psychological characteristic actually exists between (District X and District Y) or the differences are due to local policies and practices that systematically and arbitrarily produce varying rates of identification per se (not the characteristic per se). That is, some staffing committees may be overly strict and others overly lax, thus artificially creating this variability" (p. 57).

Assessment. The typical PCD case file contained a record of six or seven formal tests administered as part of identification. Additional tests not included in that average were given to plan instruction and evaluate progress. The average of six or seven covered a large range, however. Almost one-fourth of the files showed that these pupils were identified and placed without *any* standardized achievement tests. Eleven percent of the files showed that no test of intelligence was given. Twenty-five percent had three or more intelligence tests. Twenty-two percent had three or more achievement tests. Five percent had no tests of any kind. Thirty percent of the sample had nine of more formal tests given. Except for the one-quarter of the pupils identified as PCD who had insufficient testing, the PCD population had been tested repeatedly and redundantly.

Based on the surveys of professionals and case files, we listed the 19 tests used most often to identify PCD. The technical adequacy of these tests was evaluated using criteria published jointly by the American Psychological Association, American Educational Research Association and National Council on Measurement in Education. Published reviews of these tests were also employed to arrive at "grades" attached to each test. For example, the Wechsler Intelligence Scale for Children (WISC-R) was given an "A" grade while the Detroit Tests of Learning Aptitude was graded "F," based on their respective reliabilities and validities. The typical battery of tests and their grades given to them are printed in Table 5. Only six of these 19 most-used tests have grades of B or A, that is, have adequate technical qualities to allow valid identification of PCD.

The specialists who do the identifying were apparently unaware of the failings of the tests they use. In the survey, as many believed the Detroit Tests of Learning Aptitude was reliable and valid as believed the WISC-R was reliable and valid.

The results of the chapter on assessment were summarized as follows (p. 91):

"The current investment in PCD assessment is enormous and unwarranted in the light of the poor psychometric properties of most tests commonly used. There was multiple and excessive testing of some PCD children while more than one-third of the PCD pupils had not one valid IQ test. Although highly valid and reliable achievement tests are available, they are used less frequently than those other tests that are rated in the professional literature as technically inadequate. Measures of various processing abilities are consistently judged inadequate in the professional literature, yet many professionals not only use them in PCD identification but erronously believe the tests to be adequate.

"Unreliable tests, inappropriate use of subtest based diagnosis, and unconfirmed hypotheses generated by clinical judgment all contribute to misidentification of PCD in Colorado pupils."

TABLE 5

Evaluation of Typical Tests Administered to PCD Pupils in Colorado
as Part of Their Initial Assessment and Staffing

Tests	Used by more than 40% of:	Grade (Indicating Technical Adequacy)
Intelligence Tests		
Detroit Tests of Learning Aptitude	PCD; S/L	F
Peabody Picture Vocabulary Test	PCD; S/L	F as a measure of intelligence
		C as a measure of receptive vocabulary
Slosson Intelligence Test		C
WISC-R	PCD; Psych.	A
Achievement Tests		
KeyMath Diagnostic Arithmetic Test	PCD	A for instructional planning
		C for diagnosis of PCD
Peabody Individual Achievement Tests	PCD	B
Wide Range Achievement Test	PCD; Psych.	C
Woodcock Reading Mastery Tests	PCD	A -
Personality Tests		
Draw-A-Person	Psych.	C for clinical hypothesis formation
Sentence Completion	Psych.	D for placement decsions
Perceptual and Processing Tests		
Beery Developmental Test of Visual-Motor Integration	PCD; Psych.	C
Bender (Visual-Motor) Gestalt Test	Psych.	D
Spencer Memory for Sentences Test	S/L	D
Wepman Auditory Discrimition Test	S/L	C
Speech and Language Tests		
Boehm Test of Basic Concepts	S/L	B for instructional planning
		D for diagnosis of PCD
Carrow Tests for Auditory Comprehension of Language	S/L	C
Goldman-Firstoe Test of Articultion	S/L	B
Illinois Test of Psycholinguistic Abilities	S/L	F

From Shepard, <u>et al.</u>, 1981, p. 80.

Staffing. In order to identify a pupil as PCD, a school goes through four steps known collectively as the "staffing process." These are referral, assessment, staffing conference and placement.

Colorado Department of Education data for the academic year 1978-79 were cited to show that, of the 42, 195 pupils referred for any handicapping condition, 78 percent (32,792) were assessed. Of those assessed, 80 percent (26,088) were staffed. Of those staffed, 83 percent were placed and received services. thus, slightly more than half of those originally referred were eventually placed. We speculated that one of two things happened to the remainder: either their problems were alleviated or improved spontaneously before the next phase in the staffing process took place; or they were judged (by preliminary assessments or in mini-staffing) to be ineligible for services. Each step is governed by extensive federal and state regulations; actual practice seemed to conform with the regulations.

The staffing conference represents the culmination of the PCD identification process. It is the meeting of clinicians, educators and parents to discuss the results of the assessment, decide whether the pupil is handicapped, and what his services and program will be. The conference plays an important role in insuring due process, for the parents are thereby informed of their child's rights, and how the clinicians perceive him, and are given a voice in the decisions made. State and federal regulations specify what people should attend this conference, how reports are to be made and records kept as well as how its members should proceed to a decision.

According to the survey of case files the average number of people at a staffing conference was seven. Two percent of the cases had only one or two persons present, fewer than the minimum number required by the regulations. On the other extreme, 22 percent of the cases had nine or more persons present. Most of these were professional people employed by the school districts. The number and types of persons attending are listed in Table 6. The number of written reports submitted varied form none (11 percent of the cases) to eight. The average number of written reports was 3.7. Adequate records of the staffing decision had been kept for only about half the cases.

TABLE 6

Types of Individuals Submitting Written Reports

and Attending Staffings of PCD Pupils

Type of Individual	% of PCD Cases With Report Submitted	% of PCD Cases Attendance at Staffing
Regular Classroom Teacher	7%	58%
Special Education Teacher	66%	76%
Social Worker	48%	54%
School Psychologist	70%	71%
Private Specialist	2%	1%
Physician	1%	0%
Nurse	51%	54%
Principal	0%	58%
Parent	1%	48%
Speech/Language Specialist	44%	43%
Chairman	1%	39%
Others	3%	49%

From Shepard et al, 1981, p. 97.

Although the amount of time spent in staffing conferences was considerable (averaging about 45 minutes per conference),
the majority of specialists surveyed seemed satisfied. They reported
that current staffing procedures were thorough enough to insure
valid decisions and due process but not wasteful of staff time. One-
third of the respondents felt the procedures were so thorough as to
be wasteful. Between two-thirds and three-quarters of the respondents agreed that parents were intimidated by the presence of so
many professional people at the staffing conference.

Colorado school districts are generally in compliance
with extensive rules and regulations governing the staffing process.

Costs. Using the data from the survey of PCD case files
and the surveys of specialists, it was possible to compute estimates
for the amount of time spent by professionals in all stages of staffing. Using these estimates and state-wide averages of salaries of
the various professional groups, the cost for staffing a typical PCD
pupil was computed. This figure was $525 per year, per child, ex-
clusive of administrative overhead costs. Put into perspective, this
cost is almost as much as the cost of educating a pupil in the usual
PCD setting: the resource room.

CHARACTERISTICS OF PCD PUPILS IN COLORADO

From the representative sample of files of pupils already
identified as PCD, characteristics were described and compared
with stated definitions. To what extent, we asked, is there congru-
ence between the characteristics listed in legal and professional
definitions and the characteristics of children actually served under
the auspicies of these definition.

The answer was unequivocal. No more than 50 percent
of those identified as PCD in Colorado actually matched the definitions of the disorder. This conclusion was reached, according to Dr.
Shepard, by methods designed to give every benefit of the doubt as
to the validity of the current practives of identification. Table 7
was extracted from the report to show the actual characteristics of
the sample identified as PCD. By the most liberal criterion, 41
percent of the sample matched stated definitions of PCD. Ten
percent were not PCD but had other handicaps, such as hearing

TABLE 7

Quantitative Identification of Subgroups in the Colorado
PCD Population Presented in Major Categories

Other Handicaps	Estimated Pop. %		
EMR	2.6%		
Emotionally Disturbed	7.5%	Other Behavior Problems	
Hearing Handicapped	.2%	Hyperactivity	2.0%
	10.3%	Minor Behavior	
		Problems	3.7%
			5.7%

Learning Disabilities (true PCD)			
Strict Significant Discrepancy	20.5	Other Learning Problems	
High Quality Processing Deficit	4.7	Language Interference	6.6%
Brain Injured	.6	Slow Learners	11.4%
		Below Grade Level	6.1%
			24.1
Weak Sign Discrep. and Verbal/			
Performance Discrep.	3.6		
Weak Sign Discrep. and Med.		Other	
Qual. Proc.	1.1	Poor Assessment	6.4%
Medium Qual. Processing	6.6	(No IQ and no	
Deficit and Verbal/Performance		Ach. Tests)	
Discrep.		Miscellaneous	10.6%
Medium Quality Processing		(including normal)	
Deficit only	3.5		17.0
	40.6		

Shepard, et al., 1981, p. 129.

186

handicaps, emotional disorders, or mental retardation. Six percent had "other behavioral problems," including hyperactivity, which is not part of the PCD definition. Twenty-five percent had "other learning problems" but no signs of learning disabilities. Some of the children in this group were not achieving up to their potential because they came from homes where English was not the primary language spoken. Their education suffered, but not because of a perceptual processing failure. Others were merely behind their classmates in school but their levels of achievement were parallel to their intellectual abilities. All of the characteristics in this category fall outside the stated legal and professional definitions of learning disabilities.

These figures came from a careful coding of 790 representative PCD case files. Trained coders read the files and recorded the test scores from intelligence, achievement and perceptual-motor tests as well as the judgments of clinicians as to medical, emotional, behavior or perceptual problems. Statistical analyses were applied to these data to determine, for example, the extent of discrepancy between the pupils' intelligence and achievement, or between their age-and grade-level of achievement. The figures in Table 7 were then determined by use of a computerized sorting analysis. If a pupil's case showed discrepancy between his achievement and intelligence tests scores that was more than what one would expect by chance (p is less than .05) then that case was categorized as "strict significant discrepancy - true - PCD." Of the cases remaining after the above group was sorted out, if a pupils case showed no significant discrepancy between his intelligence and achievement but psycho-motor test scores showing a processing deficit, that case was categorized as "High quality processing deficit--true PCD." This sorting process continued until only the "Miscellaneous" category remained.

To gain better conceptual understanding of the characteristics of the PCD sample, we used qualitative analysis as well. Two hundred randomly selected case files from the original probability sample of 1000 were carefully read by the principal researchers. Using techniques proposed by Glaser and Strauss (1967), the researchers derived catgories and their properties from parts of the data, defining and testing the catgories on the rest.

Use of categories allows raw data to be organized in meaningful abstractions, themes, or features. Taken together the set of categories should explain the data as a whole. In the PCD study, the categories were significance of the discrepancy, marginality of placements, consistency, pupil cluster, and need for special education. The properties of the categories and findings following from them are described below.

1) Statistical significance of the discrepancy--the standard error of the difference between general intelligence and educational achievement was computed to determine if each case file met the operational definition of perceptual/communicative disorder. The significance of differences among subtests that clinicians used to interpret variability of separate intellectual and perceptual abilities was also computed or estimated. This calculation followed the recommendations of Salvia and Ysseldyke (1981).

Sixteen percent had insufficient data to calculate the significance of the discrepancy. Of all the cases, 39 percent had discrepancies that were statistically significant by the criterion employed (p is less than .05). Forty-five pecent of all the cases had no significant differences between any ability and any achievement measure.

2) Marginality of Placement--the researchers assessed, based on the significance of the ability/achievement discrepancy, the history of the case, and the patterns of ability test scores, whether the child's problem was severe or mild, if the problem was so pronounced that no subjectivity or inference at all was involved in the placement decision, or it was a toss-up to determine whether the child should be placed. If the pupil's symptoms were mild, if the clinical signs of his disability were equivocal, and if his need for help from special education was not obvious, he was counted as amarginal placement. Out of the cases studies, 35 percent were categorized as marginal placements.

3) Consistency. In all but the smallest districts, the child considered for placement in PCD programs had been evaluated by three, four, five, or even more professionals. Frequently, the same charactistics evaluated by one professional had been

evaluated by others. Thus one frequently sees separate tests of intelligence given by the psychologists, the special education diagnostician, and the speech-language specialist. Auditory processing also had been evaluated by separate tests given by each of these professional groups. The pupil's medical development had been evaluated by both social worker and nurse, and his emotional adjustment evaluated by both social worker and psychologist. No one would expect complete agreement among these different clinical appraisals. However, some consistency is expected; for example, separate assessments of intellectual potential should yield about the same results, identification of specific strengths and weaknesses ought to converge and not conflict. If a child's weakness is in reading, more than one test of reading achievement ought to reflect that fact.

Operating under these assumptions, we judged the consistency of evidence across clinicians and tests. Of the cases studied, the clinical evidence of 68 percent was judged to be of poor consistency. The remaining cases had good consistency; that is, the tests and clinicians presented evidence that converged on a coherent picture of the child's problems and characteristics.

4) Pupil Cluster. The typology of symptoms and characteristics was developed and the cases were classified by type. Their test results, histories, and reported symptoms were studied carefully and judged to fall into one of the following clusters.

a) Operational LD -- The official definition of learning disabilities is achievement significantly below ability. Pupils are excluded from this definition if their ability-achievement discrepancy can be explained by language, emotional, or cultural disability. Of the cases studied 21 percent fell into this cluster.

b) Clinical LD -- According to the professional literature, children with learning disabilities may not have a significant discrepancy between their ability and achievement either because they have compensated for their specific disability through their stronger, intact abilities or because their psycho-

189

logical processing disability depressed not only their achievement scores but their ability test scores. Children in this cluster, therefore, had no significant discrepancies between ability and achievement, but did have convincing evidence of a processing disorder that was consistent across tests, clinicians, and time. Five percent of the cases fell into this cluster.

c) <u>Slow Learner</u> -- Profiles of the learning disabled tend to contain both significantly high and low scores on separate abilities. Slow learners, in contrast, have all their separate abilities approximately the same and lower than those of children their own age. This is not considered to be a handicap by official or professional definitions. Of all the files of children placed as PCD and sampled for qualitative analysis, 13 percent were classified as slow learners. An additional 1 percent was classified as mentally retarded, having an IQ of less than 75 and no evidence of processing disorders.

d) <u>Emotionally-Disturbed</u> -- Twenty-two percent of all the PCD cases studied in the qualitative analysis were judged to be emotionally disturbed rather than learning disabled. That is, the evidence about their processing disabilities was weak or nonexistent. Some were victims of child abuse or severe family problems. They were said to be highly anxious or deeply withdrawn, abusive, hyperactive, or emotionally unstable. In some cases the parents or professionals resisted the label emotionally disturbed and opted for PCD as the preferred label or treatment. In other cases programs for the emotionally disturbed were not available in the district. In still other cases the professionals appeared to believe that these children actually were PCD and indeed some of the children had significant ability achievement discrepancies. However, the weight of evidence for these cases made it more reasonable to attribute the discrepancy to the emotional problem than to a perceptual or learning disorder. Regardless, a sizable share of PCD cases seemed to fall into this class.

e) <u>Language Problem</u> -- Twelve percent of the children represented in the PCD files were of the following type. They were of Hispanic or Indian descent. Some non-English native language was spoken in their homes. Their verbal abilities were significantly lower than their performance or quantitative abilities. They were evaluated by school clinicians to be PCD because of their low achievement, differences between language and non-language achievement, and difference between their scores on the verbal and performance score on the Wecshler Intelligence Scale. This latter characteristic was mistakenly judged as a marker of perceptual disorder when it probably marked language interference and signaled the need for intensive training in English or some other language program.

f) <u>Hearing, Vision, or Health</u> -- Some children have been categorized as PCD when their primary problem related to visual or hearing acuity or they have epilepsy or a physically based motor problem. Seven percent of the files in the qualitative analysis fell into this cluster.

g) <u>Miscellaneous</u> -- Twenty percent of the cases did not fall into the above clusters. For example, 8 percent had no discernable handicaps or problems at all and no characteristics that allow us to typify them. Perhaps they were simply children who were the lowest in classes or schools of above average children. Some looked more like underachievers (3 percent) than like children with handicaps. Some seemed to be slower to develop than children of their own age, but were not outside the normal distribution of developmental rates (5 percent). And some had problems that appeared to be attributed more to teaching problems, the classroom situation, or teacher-pupil conflicts than to any psychological characteristics of the children themselves (4 percent).

5) Need for Special Education. All of the children whose cases were chronicled in the PCD files had been judged by school committees to need help from special education. Yet it was readily apparent that some pupils had been more in need than othes. Some had all their achievement scores years behind their classmates while others were only a month behind in spelling. Some needed only a little more flexibility on the part of their classroom teacher. Some, perhaps, needed only to change from open-space to a self-contained class. Some needed only to have their parents' expectations become more realistic. The researchers judged whether each child needed help from special education. Sixty percent needed this help. Eighteen percent needed no help beyond that which a classroom teacher ought to be able to give. Twenty-two percent were judged to need a kind of help different from that which is typically available in PCD programs--psychotherapy, intensive English, tutorial help in basic skills. Emotionally disturbed children and children with second language problems do not need process training nor sensory-motor integration therapy. All children who are behind their classmates do not need diagnosis, nor handicapping labels, but simple remedial help.

In addition to the categories defined above, the qualitative analysis of cases yielded some hypotheses about how PCD identification works. For example, implicit definitions for learning disabilities are more important than official or professional ones. The most prominent implicit defining characteristic is "the child whose achievement is behind his classmates." The child who is behind is likely to be staffed and placed as PCD even though he doesn't meet the official criteria.

Although many children need extra help, many more children are identified as PCD than show any true symptoms of that handicap.

Instructional failure, teacher problems, and the like are rarely suggested as the explanation for a child's poor performance. The problem is always located "in the child" according to the PCD files.

Deficiencies in the reliability and validity of tests, the validity of subtest-based diagnosis, or the adequacy of clinical judgment are never considered as an explanation for observed patterns of a child's performance and characteristics.

The complexity of a district's identification and staffing process seems to be a function of its resources. Richer, more sophisticated districts are more likely to involve more types of professionals (occupational therapists, adaptive physical educators, etc.). The validity of decision-making does not necessarily increase with greater numbers of professionals. But the cost certainly does.

The qualitative and quantitative analyses were used as alternative methods of studying the same phenomenon. The analyses were not independent of each other in that the formation of clusters of characteristics was done jointly. The case files in the two analyses were randomly equivalent. But the actual coding of the two sets of cases was done by different individuals. The analysis of sample percentages that fell into different clusters was done separately (by computer in the quantitative analysis). Only after both analyses were completed were the findings compared and the differences between them interpreted. Thus the triangulation procedures recommended by Webb, Campbell, Schwartz, and Secrest (1966) were used as a means of converging on a valid inference using multiple measures.

The proposition that emerged from both the quantitative and the qualitative analysis was this: only a fraction of the population of pupils identified as PCD in Colorado have characteristics listed in the official or professional definitions of learning disabilities. The remainder of this population exhibited a variety of other characteristics. The numerical value of that fraction differed somewhat between the quantitative and qualitative analysis, a difference accounted for in the following paragraphs (p. 136-138).

"There were several highly consistent findings from the two analyses. The proportion of the qualitative analysis sample with 'operational' definition of learning disabilities (achievement significantly below ability) almost exactly equalled the proportion of the quantitative analysis sample labeled "strict significant discrepancy". The "clinical LD" cluster in the qualitative analysis differed only by sampling error from the "high quality processing deficit". The "slow learner" cluster in the qualitative analysis included those who were similarly defined in the quantitative analysis plus those considered EMR. The sum of percentages of the two clusters equals the proportion of slow learners in the qualitative analysis. The incidence of hearing, vision, health, and brain injury was so low in the population that discrepancies in the two samples can be attributed to sampling error. In the qualitative analysis, cases with inadequate assessment data were ruled out of the clusters. This constituted 5 percent of the qualitative sample, marginally consistent with the quantitative sample.

"The major sources of disagreement between the two methods were in the emotionally disturbed, language problem and miscellaneous clusters. Information on ethnicity or native language was missing from most of the cases but could be inferred by close examination of case histories. The close examination was more possible in the qualitative analysis than in the quantitative analysis. Language problems became a salient category only very late in this study, after we had discovered a set of children with Spanish surnames, depressed verbal abilities and language achievement, equivocal evidence of processing disorders, and histories of unsuccessful years spent in PCD programs. All these variables were considered jointly in the qualitative analysis, and the language problems cluster took precedence over other possible designations.

"Information on emotional disturbance is very difficult to quantify, although it is readily apparent and persuasive in the narrative histories of PCD children. Data on processing disorders are already in numerical form and sometimes carry more weight than they deserve. Coders of the quantitative sample were extremely conservative in interpreting the presence of emotional disturbance. They decided on operational criteria for coding which gave the benefit of the doubt to clinicians' interpretations of marginal evidence of processing disorders. In this respect, the coders were behaving in a fashion similar to staffing committees, who seem reluctant to deal with emotional disturbance. Readers of the qualitative sample showed no such hesitation, but placed cases in that cluster whenever the data indicating psychological maladjustment were more persuasive than the data on processing disorders.

The miscellaneous category in the qualitative analysis included normal children, children who were behind grade level but showed no real evidence of learning disabilities, those whose problems were "environmental" (as defined in the quantitative analysis), and many cases that no doubt would fall into the categories medium or weak discrepancy or processing deficit categories. It should be noted again that these latter categories were defined by extremely weak and unreliable indicators and give staffing committees great benefit of the doubt as to what characteristics validly constitute a learning disability. The qualitative analysis was not nearly so generous in this respect, so that many children with marginal evidence of PCD were classified as "miscellaneous."

CASE HISTORIES

Ten case histories, taken from the 200 files involved in the qualitative analysis, were written to acquaint the reader with the people behind the statistics. Obscured by the correlations, averages, and percentages listed in this report are living children and professionals faced with demands, motives, histories, and constraints of today's schools. Neither statistics nor narration can bring these individuals to life, yet they should not be lost sight of entirely. Included in this section are ten case histories of children who have been placed in programs for Perceptual/Communicative Disorders (PCD) in Colorado. They are a subset of the probability sample of such cases selected to illustrate the typical range of cases.

For the reader to interpret the material in the case histories, it is necessary to know in common sense terms the meaning of the clinical and statistical concepts as well as the assumptions used in the evaluation of a child suspected to suffer from a perceptual-communicative disorder (PCD).

Implicit in the evaluation files is the assumption of clinicians (those professionals who evaluate children referred to them) that intellectual functioning is the sum of a general intellectual ability plus a number of separate abilities. These separate abilities include memory, language, reasoning, perception--visual, haptic and auditory--and the cognitive integration or processing of perceptions; e.g., visual input with motor output. Clincians expect a child's intellect to grow at the same rate in all of these respects. When the development of one ability is substantially at odds with the development of the rest of that child's abilities or inconsistent with his age, there is cause for alarm; suspicion arises that a disability of some sort exists. For example, if a child can reason very well and can remember words he hears but cannot learn words he sees on flashcards, the clinician might suspect that he is deficient in visual-perceptual ability, and thus have a learning disability.

Thus unevenness of the growth of abilities is typically judged either by observing the child's performance in the classroom or by administering batteries of tests. In evaluating a child for PCD many tests (or subtests or complex multi-trait tests) are given, each of which purports to measure either general intelligence or one or more of the separate intellectual or perceptual abilities. The idea is to look for discrepant scores on one or more of the tests (or subtests), with a low score on one test of an ability signaling a specific learning disorder.

When tests are used, however, the technology and standards of psychological testing must be considered. Psychometricians (experts in the theory and mathematics of testing) require that the difference between any two of a person's test scores be large enough to rule out randomness--or chance--as an explanation for the difference. If the difference is numerically large enough-- said to be "reliable," "significant" or "beyond chance"--then one can make statements such as "Marilyn's memory is reliably worse than her language ability" or her "auditory perception is stronger than her visual perception." The simplest case of this "significance testing" is determining whether a child's achievement test scores are reliably lower than his general intelligence scores. This determination is embedded in the cirteria for eligibility for PCD programs in Colorado and federal law.

Once the difference between two scores of separate intellectual abilities is determined to be greater than chance, a clinician may infer that the difference is due to some underlying neurological or perceptual disorder. Judging the validity of this inference rests on three conditions. First, a body of scientific evidence should link the symptom (the difference between two tested abilities) with the disorder. Second, several different clinicians evaluating the same child should be able to confirm the pattern of tested abilities.* Third, other possible causes of the observed symptom should be ruled out. For example, a highly anxious child might not be able to recite many digits in a digit span test and the resulting low score would therefore be due to an emotional problem rather than a deficiency in short-term memory. Or a child of average intelligence might have quite low reading achievement scores because he was absent a great deal or changed schools so that he lacked an opportunity to learn to read like other children of the same age.

The ten case histories that follow are real cases. They contain the essential details abstracted from ten special education files studied in the qualitative analysis. They also include sections of analysis in which we interpret the case and classify it according to the categories derived from the qualitiative analysis. These are statistical significance of discrepancy, consistency, marginality of placement, necessity for special education, and cluster (implicit definition). These categories are explained earlier in this chapter.

Mike

Described by the school psychologist as "obviously a very bright boy who should be doing much better in his classwork," Mike was referred by his second grade

---

*The Bender Visual Motor Gestalt Test and the Beery Test of Visual Motor Integration purport to measure the same ability and are frequently administered by the school psychologist and the PCD specialist, respectively. This condition of validity specifies that when a child's Bender score is significantly low, his Beery score should also be low.

teacher and placed in the program for perceptual-communicative disorders.

In evaluating Mike's health, the school nurse found no medical indicators of a handicap. The speech-language specialist found no auditory or language problems. The psychologist found indications of a learning disability in the numerical discrepancy between Mike's general intellectual ability and two of the subtests that make up the intelligence test. The Wechsler Intelligence Scale for Children (WISC-R) yields an estimate of general intellectual ability as a composite of several subtests. Clinicians frequently interpret the pattern of WISC-R subtests as indicative of separate intellectual and perceptual abilities. The subtests fall into a verbal group or a performance group and separate IQ scores are usually computed for each of these groups. Mike's overall IQ score was 108, a score higher than 73 percent of the general population (73rd percentile). The two low subtest scores measured short term memory and eye-hand coordination. Further evidence for learning disabilities was discovered in the form of reading achievement scores that were significantly lower than what one would expect based on his general intelligence. His reading grade equivalent score on the Wide Range Achievement Test was 2.2, or the level of achievement associated with the average child in the second month of the second grade. This score was lower than his actual grade placement of 2.7.* His spelling and arithmetic scores were within expectancy and at his actual grade level. Mike's performance on the Bender Visual Motor Gestalt test (Bender) led the psychologist to suspect that Mike had "from moderate to severe visual perception disabilities."

The special education teacher found similar results on achievement tests—adequate performance in spelling

---

*The significance of the discrepancy relates to the difference between IQ and achievement and not the number of months separating grade placement and grade equivalent achievement test score.

and arithmetic and significantly low performance in reading. The Beery Test of Visual-Motor Integration (VMI) confirmed the results of the Bender. The Illinois Test of Psycholinguistic Abilities yielded no variation that the teacher could call significant, yet she interpreted weaknesses in auditory and visual memory as well as "grammatic closure." Like the other clinicians and Mike's classroom teacher, she noted that Mike was constantly in motion and failed to pay attention to the task at hand. The social worker described some mild forms of misbehavior and poor motivation on Mike's part. She described his family as "close-knit," with two sisters already in the PCD program.

The reason given for this placement was that a significant discrepancy existed between Mike's estimated intellectual potential and actual level of performance due to perceptual processing disorders. The discrepancy was statistically significant by our calculations, and the clinical pattern of test scores and behavior resembled what the professional literature identified as a learning disability; that is, adequate potential for learning but impaired learning, erratic performance across time or different subjects, highly variable scores on tests that measure special intellectual or perceptual abilities, and persistent, pervasive inattentiveness, distractibility, and frustration in school. Although the clinicians were not altogether consistent with one another (auditory problems were found by the psychologist and special education teacher but not the speech language specialist) there was sufficient overlap to be confident that all of Mike's intellectual and perceptual abilities were not developing at the same rate. Alternative explanations could not reasonably account for the observed pattern. For example, there was no evidence of Mike's lack of opportunity to learn, no interference from a second language, his psychological adjustment seemed to be adequate, and no teaching problems were mentioned.

Kristen

By the third grade Kristen had been referred, evaluated, and staffed four times. During first and second grade she was placed in a program of speech correction. Based on the school's regular program of screening tests, she was found to be deficient both in articulation abilities and receptive and expressive language. At the end of the second grade she was referred for possible placement in the PCD program because her performance was below grade level in all subjects and she was said to have difficulty in following directions. At that time the staffing committee found no evidence for a perceptual or communicative disorder and instead recommended that she repeat grade two.

Kristen's parents moved her to a different school rather than have her be retained. In the new school, third grade, she was referred again for special education staffing. On the referral form her teacher wrote the following: "She has auditory discrimination difficulties. Her visual memory and comprehension is poor. She seems to have more ability than she projects. She is insecure and unsure of herself" (sic).

In the subsequent evaluation (by that time she was in the fourth grade) the psychologist found that Kristen's general intellectual ability was in the "dull-normal" range (IQ approximately 82, the 12th percentile), having "extreme difficulties with short term memory, absorbing knowledge from her environment, using abstract reasoning for problem solving, and non-verbal concept formation." On the Bender-Visual Motor Gestalt Test (a test that measures visual-motor perceptual abilities by having the child copy designs), Kristen functioned similar to a seven year-old child. According to the psychologist, "While she is functioning approximately three years below her chronological age, she did not display those types of errors normally associated with serious perceptual problems. Instead they represent a development delay in this area."

Neither the social worker nor the nurse found evidence of a learning disability or emotional problem in their evaluations of Kristen. The speech-language specialist found deficiencies in auditory memory, reasoning, abstraction, comprehension, and expressive language.

The educational diagnostician gave Kristen tests of educational achievement and found her reading and math at the 4.2 and 4.4 grade levels, respectively. She was at that time in the sixth month of the fourth grade. These scores were interpreted as "definite academic deficiencies" and over-estimates of Kristen's day-to-day classroom work. All the clinicians agreed with the decision to place Kristen in the PCD program based on the discrepancy between her potential and performance, and her perceptual deficiencies.

Although Kristen was achieving below her grade level, a closer look shows that this achievement was actually *above* what one would predict from her general intellectual abilities. If any clinical term can be used to describe Kristen, it is "slow learner," a person whose general and separate, special intellectual and perceptual abilities are all approximately the same, below the average of the general population, but not so low as to be considered "retarded." In an urban or a poor rural school district, Kristen would probably not have attracted any attention. In some school districts, however, where the average socio-economic level and pupil intellectual level are high, children like Kristen look discrepant from the norm and become candidates for special education. Kristen's teacher was familiar with the argot of learning disabilities, and the clinicians accepted her construction of Kristen's problems as perceptual. No confirmation of this construction was forthcoming from the clinical evaluations.

Sean

According to the school social worker, Sean was referred by his kindergarten teacher because of poor auditory and visual memory and general immaturity. In spite of the fact that he had already repeated kindergarten he would not listen to or follow directions and was not developing learning readiness skills. The social worker, nurse, and speech-language specialist noted his behavior problems (bad temper and short attention span) and stuttering.

The psychologist was also aware of these problems. She administered the Wechsler Pre-school and Primary Test of Intelligence (WPPSI) and found Sean's intellectual abilities "at the upper end of the borderline range" (IQ approximately 78, the 7th percentile) but with significant differences between verbal and non-verbal portions and wide divergence among the subtests. For example, there were average scores on subtests that measure word knowledge, abstract reasoning and "visual interpretation of social situations," but very low scores on auditory memory, visual spatial orientation, assembly of abstract designs and visual-motor integration. This divergence of scores measuring separate abilities suggested serious learning disability, according to the psychologist. The results of the Bender-Visual Motor Gestalt Test, confirming some of the scores on the WPPSI, showed deficiency in visual-motor perception. Achievement testing on the Wide Range Achievement Tests placed Sean at the third month of kindergarten in reading and at the sixth month of kindergarten in arithmetic. His grade placement was the second month of kindergarten, but he had already been retained for a second year in that grade.

Tested by the special education teacher, Sean was labeled "high risk" by virtue of his score on the Evanston Early Identification Test, and deficient in auditory perception based on the Illinois Test of Psycholinguistic Ability, and the Wepman Auditory Discrimination Test. The Beery test of Visual-Motor Integration yielded scores that were equivalent to the typical youngster aged four and a half years. Based on an average score on the Peabody Picture Vocabulary Test, the special education teacher judged that Sean had good potential for learning but limited perceptual processing abilities.

The speech-language specialist found no auditory problems, but because of Sean's stuttering and deficiencies in receptive and expressive language, recommended speech therapy.

The staffing team placed Sean based on an "estimated discrepancy between potential and performance." However, the actual discrepancy was not statistically significant. Based on his rather low general intelligence score, Sean was performing at or above what one would expect. Results of the Bender and of the VMI could also be interpreted as those of a "slow learner." Nevertheless, the clinical pattern of perceptual disorder resembles what the professional literature defines as learning disabled. This was particularly true in the disparity between his vocabulary and abstract reasoning on the one hand, and his auditory perception and verbal expression on the other. Although it is difficult to unravel the effects of the low general intelligence from the effects of perceptual disabilities, in this case the benefit of the doubt must be given to confirm the judgment of the staffing team that Sean was learning disabled and needed the help of special education.

Marie

On Marie's "Individualized Educational Program" (IEP) under the heading "Basis for Determination of Handicap" the staffing committee wrote the following: "There is a significant processing disorder which results in at least a 30% discrepancy between assessed intellectual ability and current achievement levels, and there are persistent physical complaints related to stress and/or anxiety." This summary seems not to reflect much of the material in Marie's file. The most salient feature of the file is the number of statements made about her physical and mental health.

Two years before the staffing Marie was diagnosed as epileptic. Before that time there were no academic or behavioral problems at all, according to school records and her mother's report. After two years of petit mal seizures and medication, she was referred for staffing by her seventh-grade teacher. The words from the social worker's evaluation were as follows: disruptive behavior ... conflict between Marie and teacher ... low skills in math and reading, inability to follow directions ... wetting herself when under stress ... low maturity ... parents divorced ... poor self esteem ... resistive to authority, in psychotherapy.

The school psychologist relied on the intelligence test given by a private clinic, which placed Marie's intellectual level in the "low normal" region. He gave her the Wide Range Achievement Test which yielded reading and math achievement scores at the level of a beginning fifth grader. This was two years behind her grade placement. The Bender-Visual Motor Gestalt Test" was poorly executed and gives evidence of difficulty with visual-motor integration."

The speech-language specialist found Marie's language to be appropriate to her age, but her auditory memory was weak. The latter judgment was also made by the special education teacher who gave Marie the Detroit Tests of Learning Aptitude. This teacher reported that the test results could have been due either to inattentiveness or to learning disabilities. Further achievement testing was done, placing Marie in the third grade level proficiency in math and in the fourth grade in reading.

The staffing team placed Marie in the PCD resource room for two periods a day plus consultation with the specialist in emotional disturbance. Her primary instructional goal was to work on basic skills.

Marie's educational and psychological test scores are markedly inconsistent from clinician to clinician. Even the lowest of her achievement tests (very different scores were obtained by the psychologist and the special education teacher) was not *significantly* lower than her general intellectual ability. Two clinicians found deficiencies in auditory abilities, but one of them questioned whether this low test score was not due to emotional problems. Epilepsy, eneuresis and the medication therefore seem to have produced severe problems of mental health for Marie, a condition which can deflate not only classroom performance but performance on tests as well. The hypothesis that the test discrepancies are due to learning disabilities seems to be much less justified. Certainly Marie needed both academic and emotional therapy; probably no perceptual disorder was involved. The staffing committee appeared to use the PCD program as a readily available instructional resource for anyone who needed it, rather than a program for children with perceptual or communicative disorders.

Juan

Juan's first grade teacher referred him for special education staffing because of inattentiveness, distractibility and what she called "difficulty with visual-motor skills." What she meant by the latter, in concrete terms, was that his handwriting was bad. This referral led to a complete evaluation by five different professionals. The social worker interviewed Juan's mother whose judgment of Juan was that he had no emotional, behavioral, or family problems. Concurring in this evaluation, the social worker recommended no "social work intervention." Also interviewed by the nurse, Juan's mother related his medical history, which revealed no medical problems. There was mention that two febrile seizures had occurred when Juan was 18 months old, but left unstated was the meaning ascribed to them.

The psychological evaluation covered four different tests spread over two days. From his performance on an intelligence test, the school psychologist inferred that Juan's cognitive functioning was in the high average range (IQ about 119, the 90th percentile) and found no evidence of differences in traits revealed in the pattern of subtest scores. No emotional problems were revealed on the projective test of personality. The psychologist found that Juan's visual-motor integration as measured by the Bender Visual Motor Gestalt Test (Bender) to be within the average range, but his human figure drawing "does suggest some lag in visual-motor development."

Several educational achievement tests were given by the special education teacher, and these unequivocally showed reading, math, and spelling achievement at a level commensurate with the average child beginning the *second* grade; that is three months ahead of his actual grade placement. Several perceptual tests were also administered. The Frostig Developmental Test of Visual Perception (DTVP) showed Juan's abilities considerably better than his age mates while his motor speed subtest on the Detroit Test of Learning Aptitude was slightly behind. The Beery Test of Visual Motor Integration (VMI) indicated a moderate lag in development.

Based on the judgments of the staffing team that Juan had a perceptual problem, he was placed in the Resource Room for remediation of a Perceptual/Communicative Disorder. His goals included a better record of completing academic tasks, ability to work independently, and improvement of visual-motor integration skills. Concerning the latter goal, Juan was supposed to "be able to correctly form and place upper and lower case letters of the alphabet on first grade lined writing paper ... accurately show a sentence from the chalkboard with correct spacing (and) show an improvement in his ability to copy designs."

Juan was reevaluated at the end of the year and retained for a second year in the resource room.

There was no statistically significant discrepancy between Juan's potential and performance and no reliable evidence showing a perceptual disorder. The evaluation team relied on the teacher's definition of Juan's "problem" and test scores that weakly supported an inference of perceptual disorder even when the pattern of these scores was not reliable. They ignored test scores that would have disconfirmed this inference. For example, they relied on a slightly low score on the VMI in making their decision but ignored the average score on the Bender, which measures a similar ability. There was little consistency among the evaluators and the records fail to indicate whether or how they resolved or even noted this inconsistency. There is little in Juan's file to show that he has any handicap or that he needs help of any sort.

When Johnny was in kindergarten he was evaluated for placement in the PCD program, but was not placed in it despite the findings and recommendations of the school staffing committee. The psychologist gave the Stanford Binet intelligence test which yielded an estimate of Johnny's intelligence in the "lower end of the dull normal range" (IQ about 80, 9th percentile) with little divergence of subtest scores of separate abilities. In spite of this relatively even pattern of separate abilities and Bender Visual Motor Gestalt Test scores appropriate to Johnny's age, the psychologist referred to him as a learning disabled youngster and recommended the PCD program to develop his auditory perception and language skills. The special education teacher found his achievement to be within acceptable limits, his Beery Test of Visual-Motor Integration age score to be near his chronological age and no significant weaknesses on the Illinois Test of Psycholinguistic Abilities. The classroom teacher stated that he missed school often, didn't respond to the teacher and did little or no work. The committee recommended the PCD program citing a "significant discrepancy between estimated intellectual potential and actual level of functioning due to deficits in auditory memory." This decision was over-ruled by the district special education staff, however, when it was determined that Johnny's achievement was what one would expect of someone with his level of intellectual ability. Therefore no handicap existed, they said, and Johnny should be helped in the regular classroom.

A year later Johnny was reevaluated, and this reason was given, "We are going to try again to get Special Education to take him for help." His intellectual abilities were not retested. The speech-language specialist noted that some Spanish was spoken in the home: "Although he understands Spanish he doesn't speak much." She found that his receptive and expressive language was somewhat behind his age level, auditory memory was normal but auditory discrimination was weak. The special education teacher found no significant deviations on the perceptual tests she gave, but serious problems in reading skills and ability to follow directions given orally. She noted that he did not participate in class activities, did not respond to adults, and annoyed other children in class.

On the basis of this information and the judgment by the committee that "a significant discrepancy exists between potential and performance," Johnny was placed in the resource room for 90 minutes daily. He was given help in reading, math, language and auditory training.

One year later, Johnny was referred again for evaluation, because he was making no progress in the PCD program. This time the psychologist gave him the Wechsler Intelligence Scale for Children (WISC-R) which measures general intellectual ability in two components-- verbal and performance. When measured with the performance component, Johnny's intellectual ability was in the average range (IQ about 90-110) but his verbal intellectual ability was in the borderline range (IQ about 60-80) although his auditory memory and abstract reasoning were average. He was weak in vocabulary, general information, and mentally solving arithmetic problems presented orally. The psychologist recommended Johnny's continuation in the PCD program based on "difficulty in the auditory area: vocabulary, nominal recall, and understanding longer complex sentences and directions."

Johnny met neither the operational criteria for PCD specified in the Colorado law (achievement significantly below intellectual potential) nor the clinical patterns suggested in the literature on learning disabilities (reliable variability in separate perceptual abilities or school performance). The original assessments suggested that Johnny might be a slow learner--someone whose general and special abilities are all low and about the same and whose school achievement is at the level suggested by his intellectual abilities. Evidence on perceptual weaknesses was inconsistent from clinician to clinician.

The later evaluations provide another hypothesis. When Johnny's intellectual abilities were estimated with non-verbal measures, he appeared to be of average intelligence. But all tasks involving language, whether intelligence tests, reading achievement tests, or reading in the classroom, revealed poor performance. Some psychologists interpret a significant difference between WISC verbal and performance scores as indicative of a learning disability. Nevertheless, the more plausible hypothesis is that Johnny suffered in language-related activities from some condition related to his Spanish language heritage and home. This may be language interference or some other social or linguistic condition yet to be discovered. It is unlikely that "process training," which predominates in many PCD programs, would help him. Bilingual-bicultural education may the answer. Intensive English may be the answer. The current state of knowledge does not yield definitive solutions to this problem.

Karen

"Why isn't Karen performing in the classroom?" This was the plaintive question written by the teacher on the school district form under "Reason for Referral." "She is bright," but "classroom progress doesn't seem to be as great as it should." She is "not able to put things down on paper." She is a "procrastinator in spelling." "Although she is a good reader, her written work is poor." She "has a short attention span . . . it is hard for her to stick to tasks." Thus the evaluation for special education. The teacher wrote the Karen "is having a difficult time adjusting to school this year." Her performance has been low and the resulting psychological pressure is mounting.

The psychologist concurred in the teacher's assessment. He noted that she was frustrated by her academic failures, had begun to avoid her work, cried easily when she encountered failures and the resulting teasing from her classmates. Having an older sister who is successful at school had made her feel even worse. The psychologist gave Karen a test of general intelligence and confirmed that she was bright (IQ about 125, 95th percentile). Her reading achievement was within the range predicted by her general intelligence. Her arithmetic and spelling were significantly below what would be predicted, however. The psychologist found no evidence of perceptual disorders. The social worker also found that Karen's emotional problems were the result and not the cause of her learning problems.

The special education teacher recorded the erratic history of Karen's achievement test scores, varying from the 80th percentile in kindergarten to the 50th percentile in fourth grade. Her daily work in the classroom, particularly her written work had always been a problem. Based on the results of a half dozen tests, the special education teacher pieced together a complicated picture of Karen's educational performance. Her reading comprehension was good. She could work arithmetic problems in her head but failed on every task that required using paper and pencils to record answers or write sentences. Karen "does not know her math facts and must use her fingers to count . . . she starts out to do a subtraction problem, then in the middle begins to add." No perceptual problems were discovered on the various tests. The speech-language specialist determined from four other tests that Karen exhibited "average to above average auditory perceptual skills and receptive/expressive language abilities."

The clinicians were in accord that Karen had a learning disability evidenced in her "inconsistent rate of learning, persistent academic problems, inability to learn in a group situation . . . problems with written language and math concepts." She was placed in the resource room and also given emotional help from the social worker. Her goals and activities in the resource room were specifically directed toward remediating. her academic problems.

Karen's academic performance was significantly worse than her general intellectual ability in two areas. Although a specific disability was not diagnosed, the clinical pattern of erratic classroom performance and failure in written work was persuasive. One must always speculate about whether the obvious emotional problems are the result or the cause of the learning problems but in this case the chronology of evidence supports the former connection.

Karen needed the help of the PCD program and profited from it. By the eighth grade her achievement test scores had been raised to the level predicted by her general intelligence. She was retained for another year, however (this being for the academic year 1980-81) so that the need for further help from the PCD program was problematic.

Jim

The staffing responsible for Jim's current placement in PCD occurred when he was repeating the third grade. Counting kindergarten, he had been in three different schools in five years and his handicap had been redefined four times. He was originally staffed and placed in speech therapy while in kindergarten. Although the basis for the decision was his stuttering, the clinicians noticed emotional and family problems. While in first grade, Jim was evaluated and placed in the PCD program based on average intelligence tests scores and scattered tests and subtest scores on the Illinois Test of Psycholinguistic Abilities, the Detroit Test of Learning Aptitude and the Wepman Auditory Discrimination Test. The special education teacher defined his problem as "perceptual" and his resource room program involved training those perceptual processing abilities that were considered weak. After one year in the PCD program he was evaluated as being in "severe need" although his Wide Range Achievement Test scores were 1.4, 1.7, and 2.4 (very nearly equivalent to his grade placement). When he moved into a different district, he was automatically placed into the PCD program. But reevaluation resulted in the clinical judgment that severe emotional and family conflicts were at the root of Jim's academic problems. The speech-language teacher found him to be working at grade level in language arts and math and about a year behind in reading, this being influenced by auditory processing difficulties. The psychologist and social worker recommended psychotherapy. Words used to describe Jim included . . . social inappropriateness . . . anxiety . . . rage . . . manipulation . . . defy authority . . . self-derogation and derogation of others . . . poor self-concept . . . inattention of father and powerlessness of mother.

After receiving therapy for a time, Jim and his parents moved again and he was evaluated and placed again in the PCD program. The speech-language specialist found auditory difficulties. The psychologist found no perceptual problems and recommended psychotherapy. The special education teacher found no evidence of perceptual problems but very poor academic performance (the Wide Range Achievement Test grade equivalent scores were 1.4 for reading and 2.2 for arithmetic).

Besides his academic goals ("Jim will master his reading vocabulary with 90% accuracy"), Jim's current objectives in the PCD program, inexplicably, include the following "improve eye-hand coordination," "improve posture both standing and walking" (e.g., "When walking Jim will hold body in proper verticle alignment, using a smooth heel-toe gait and relaxed alternative arm swing observed 70% of the time"), "improve in balance skills," and "improve the level of physical fitness."

By the third grade Jim's achievement was reliably lower than his intellectual ability. The evidence that suggests Jim's handicap as emotional is much more compelling than any of the conflicting evidence about perceptual or processing problems. The most striking thing about this case, however, is that the nature of Jim's problem was redefined each time he changed schools. With each redefinition the program of remediation changed as well, varying from "rage reduction" to "posture improvement."

Scott was originally referred for special education staffing while ten years old and in the fourth grade. His teacher noted that he could not keep up with the class in reading and was having problems "putting letters together."

The psychologist administered the Wechsler Intelligence Scale for Children (WISC-R) and found Scott's IQ to be 100, right at the average of the general population. There was a difference between his verbal and performance-assessed intelligence, with the verbal IQ much lower. On the advice of the teacher, the psychologist administered the Jordan Left-Right Reversal Test and found Scott's score to be more like a typical seven year-old. This test indicated a lack of ability to recognize when letters or numbers are printed correctly. The Wide Range Achievement Test showed that Scott was performing in reading similar to the average child at the end of the third grade and in arithmetic like the average child beginning the third grade. His grade placement at that time was the third month of the fourth grade. The special education teacher gave the Developmental Test of Visual-Motor Integration and found Scott's visual perception similar to the average seven year-old. The decision to place Scott in the PCD program to remediate his visual perception and academic problems was unanimous.

In the resource room Scott worked on the Frostig materials to correct his visual perception problems. By the end of fourth grade, all of his objectives had been met so that he was discontinued from the PCD program.

In the sixth grade he was tested again as part of a re-evaluation of all former special education students. The psychologist was the only person to evaluate him. The WISC-R scores were the same as recorded two years earlier, with weaknesses again noted in the verbal area. Visual perception, however, was now interpreted as a strength (no doubt the result of his experience with the Frostig materials). His achievement was at the appropriate grade level in reading, about a year below in math and two years below (equivalent to a beginning fourth grader) in spelling. The latter score confirmed the report of Scott's teacher who said he had extreme difficulty writing down his responses, often reversed letters and numbers, and failed to express his full amount of knowledge.

The staffing committee agreed that he should be placed in the PCD program based on the difficulties with oral and written expression.

Scott had average ability and achievement significantly lower than what one would expect. Thus he qualified for the PCD program by virtue of the operational definition specified in state guidelines. The evidence of perceptual problems was reliable and consistent across clinicians and tests. He needed help, received the kind of treatment indicated in the evaluations, and profited from it. The team of clinicians did not belabor the process of evaluation, gave only those tests that were suggested by the referral problem, and emphasized the concrete details of what Scott could and could not do.

Rudy

Rudy is a Spanish-surnamed boy who was evaluated and placed in the PCD program while in the third grade and remains there three years later. No reason was given for his referral because he transferred in from another school district in which he had also been in the PCD program. Besides the resource room he had been and continued in speech therapy and bilingual-bicultural education.

The psychologist noted that English was the language spoken in the home although Rudy's father spoke some Spanish. The test of general intelligence given by the psychologist yielded an IQ of approximately 90, but pronounced differences were found between the verbal and performance parts of the test. The verbal score was in the low average range (about 88, the 21st percentile) while the performance score was in the upper part of the average range (IQ about 105, the 63rd percentile). According to the psychologist, this difference indicated a serious learning disability. He was weak in auditory memory and arithmetic reasoning. On the Wide Range Achievement Test, Rudy was reading at the upper first grade level, and his arithmetic skills were at the beginning second grade level. His performance on the Bender Visual Motor Gestalt Test showed no "significant lags in visual-motor perception skills." The psychologist recommended that Rudy remain in the PCD program based on his "serious learning disability" and be given the program called Auditory Discrimination in Depth to deal with his auditory problem.

The achievement tests given by the special education teacher showed rather a different picture than those given by the psychologist. The Woodcock-Johnson reading test placed Rudy at the middle of the second grade, and the Key Math test showed his math achievement to be right at grade level. The Beery Test of Visual-Motor Integration (VMI) showed that Rudy's visual-motor perception was equivalent to that of a child one year older than he. His auditory discrimination scores on the Wepman Auditory Discrimination Test were appropriate for his age level. The special education teacher interpreted the results this way, "he has made a lot of accommodations in the fine motor areas but the visual perceptual area from observation during testing needs much work."

The speech-language specialist did not test for auditory perception, but found Rudy's receptive language abilities below par and therefore recommended speech correction. No clinician mentioned any behavior problems. All recommended placement in the PCD program for remediation of his perceptual problems. The staffing summary read, "There is a significant discrepancy between estimated intellectual potential and actual level of performance manifested in disorders in math, reading, and language due to auditory and visual processing."

After three years in the program Rudy was still reading and spelling at a level equivalent to a beginning third grader. His math achievement was equivalent to the average child beginning the fifth grade.

Looking across the test scores and judgments of the clinicians and the progress over the three years one must suspect that Rudy was misplaced in the PCD program. First, there was no statistically significant discrepancy between his general intelligence (as measured by the full intelligence test) and his performance on tests of education achievement. Second, there was no credible evidence for the existence of a perceptual disorder. The various clinicians were extremely inconsistent in their scores and interpretations. Although many psychologists interpret a discrepancy between the verbal and performance sections of the WISC-R as indicative of a learning disability, many alternative explanations can be posed. Third, the PCD program based as it was on remediating perceptual disorders, failed to help Rudy in language skills. Rudy is bright enough, when intelligence is measured in ways unrelated to the English language but deficient in all tasks (both those on tests and those in the classroom) requiring use of the English language. Perhaps it is reasonable to hypothesize that, rather than a perceptual disability, Rudy's problems have some connection with language interference or some other cause related to his Spanish language background. The tragedy is that bilingual-bicultural education also failed to help him.

BELLEVIEW COMPARED TO COLORADO

Belleview is clearly not unique among Colorado school districts. Its rate of identifying the learning disabled is higher than the rate for the state as a whole. The costs Belleview incurs in identifying the learning disabled are greater, a reflection of the larger number of professionals involved and tests given. Like in other rich districts, a child in Belleview might be identified as PCD simply because the average potential in Belleview is so high that an IQ of 100 looks low by comparison. Yet the existing differences between Belleview and the rest of Colorado are those of degree rather than kind. One can see the same ritualistic procedures operating, the same tests of dubious validity used, the same implicit personal definitions over-riding the legal and professional ones, the same "mistakes" made in identification, the same desire to help children rather than compulsively match children to definitions, the same tendency to expand the rolls until resources are exhausted, the same growing bureaucracy.

CHAPTER ELEVEN

NOT JUST A COLORADO PROBLEM

The PCD study concluded that Colorado educators use legally correct procedures to decide who is learning disabled. They use explicit selection criteria that are the same as those prescribed nationally. The tests and diagnostic procedures are nationally available, not unique to this state, yet their technical adequacy is suspect. Since the passage of state and federal laws for educating the handicapped, professionals involved with staffing have grown in number and variety. Regulations are exacting, and educators struggle to comply.

For whatever reasons, the number of children identified as learning disabled has burgeoned, now accounting for half of all the handicapped. In this respect Colorado is like the nation as a whole. Many of those identified do not have characteristics that conform to the explicit definition and selection criteria. They have other handicaps or learning needs that lead some person in their environment to define them as problems in need of extra help. To obtain this assistance, the child must go through the elaborate, federally regulated and costly staffing procedures and be declared handicapped. In most states, a child who has not been declared handicapped by means of the staffing process is not eligible for help from special education.

The PCD study provided descriptive data from a statistically representative samply of the population of children identified as learning disabled through the staffing process in Colorado. It did not explain the pattern it revealed; no survey can. To find the explanation requires piecing together evidence from several sources, as I tried to do in Part II. At best this process yields hypotheses, suggestions for futher study.

Nor did the PCD study reveal the national pattern of staffing the learning disabled. The kind of nationally representative study needed to address this objective does not now exist (nor is it likely to be funded as the federal commitment to educational research vanishes). Studies being conducted by SRI, International of Palo Alto show how districts are complying with federal regulations concerning the handicapped. Another study in progress conducted by Applied Management Sciences of Baltimore will provide nationally representative data on definitions, tests, and selection criteria employed by educators relative to all handicapping conditions. Both studies should be available in 1983.

Even with the finished works before us, we will not have the basis for statistical generalization of data presented here. We must rely on conceptual analyses of perceived similarities and differences between the cases studied directly (Belleview and Colorado) and some hypothetical population of interest. We must look for confirming and disconfirming evidence to show that the over-identification and misidentification of learning disabilities is, as a critic of the PCD study stated "not just a Colorado problem".

In *Reforming Special Education* (1979), Richard Weatherley reported the results of research he conducted in three school districts in the Boston metropolitan area. The research methods consisted of indepth observation, interview, document analysis and surveys, all with the goal of understanding the staffing process (although he did not use that term). The facts of the assessment and decision making process revealed in this study directly parallel those of Belleview and Colorado as a whole.

The Core Evaluation consisted of extensive testing by professionals from doctors to learning disabilities specialists operating from a medical or deficit model and overlooking environmental explanations. "Such an approach focuses attention almost exclusively on the child and encourages a search for the 'cause' of his or her problem in an examination of the child's history. The solution then depends on application of the appropriate 'treatment'" (p.67)

The staffing conference in schools studied by Weatherley mirrors that of Colorado. The legislative forms were carefully followed, yet parental involvement was more apparent than real. A long list of test scores was recited and parents given the "hard-sell". The use of jargon provided "an aura of science" and "serves to assure the dominance of specialists over others" (p. 54). The meeting "serves as an almost ritualistic certification of the child's status—of having 'special needs'—and a recitation to the parent of decisions already made by school officials" (p. 51).

Weatherley blamed excessive special education regulations for increasing and changing the nature of the work loads of school personnel. "Time previously spent working with children was now allocated to paperwork and meetings. . . School personnel put forth extraordinary effort to comply with the new demands. However, there was simply no way that everything required could be done with the resources available. Their behavior does not so much reflect negatively on school personnel as it demonstrates how new demands are accommodated into the work structure of people who must consistently find ways of conserving resources and asserting priorities to meet the demands of their jobs." (pp. 49-51)

The heavy demands for comprehensiveness in evaluation and programming exceeded the resources available to pay for them, thus creating "strong pressures for mass processing" (p. 50) which is incompatible with the requirement that each child be treated individually.

The results of the staffing process, as detailed by Weatherley, were that wealthier individuals and schools were better able to take advantage of the special education laws and reimbursement formulas than minorities or poor.

The percentage of handicapped served by a district related directly to district wealth. "Schools will maximize resources under PL 94-142 by identifying and conducting education plan meetings for as many children as possible up to the 12 percent of enrollment ceiling, but serving them as cheaply as they can." (p. 144)

Weatherley concluded that the poor, ethnic minorities and more seriously handicapped may be disadvantaged as the limited financial resources are drained off in the service of the wealthy who are better able to make public bureaucracies work for them.

The Colorado problem is a Massachusetts problem. Staffing Belleview in 1978 was like that of richer districts Weatherley studied, with one major difference. Resources in Belleview were not constrained in 1978. Earlier resources were still adequate to provide comprehensive, individualized staffing and programming to as many suspected children as parents and teachers could identify. No rationing or mass processing was then necessary, though by 1982 this had changed.

THE YSSELDYKE STUDIES

The Insitute for Research on Learning Disabilities (IRLD) directed by James E. Ysseldyke, has conducted important research revealing how Minnesota educators identify learning disabilities. Multiple research methods were used in this research serial: surveys of assessment and decision-making practices, case studies, observation, and analysis of videotapes of actual staffing conferences, computer simulation of decision-making in which variables were experimentally controlled, and expost facto studies comparing pupils labeled LD with comparably performing but unlabeled peers. The findings of these studies were congruent with each other, despite their different methods.

The IRLD conducted observational studies of staffing conferences (Ysseldyke, Algozzine, and Thurlow, 1980), many of the results of which parallel studies in Belleview and Colorado. From analysis of videotapes of these meetings they concluded that:

"The purpose of the meeting was seldom stated by team members and there almost never was a statement of the decision(s) to be reached*. . . More time was spent in meetings describing needs than in generating alternative solutions to problems. . . The roles of team members were never clearly defined . . . Parents were never asked their understanding of the purpose of the meeting nor their expectations regarding the meeting. . . Parental input was requested occasionally during meetings, usually in verification of an observed problem. In only 27% of the meetings was language at a level that we believed parents could understand . . . Decisions were made in 88% of the meetings, yet we were unable to ascertain who made the decision or the specific nature of the decision . . . Regular classroom teachers participated very little in team meetings. . . Participants were satisfied with the meetings' outcomes, believed the team approach is an effective way to make decisions about students, and felt they were an important part of the meetings. . . Over 65% of the participants did not feel their view of the child had changed significantly as a result of the meeting" (Ysseldyke et al, 1980, pp. 6-8).

In the computer simulation study (Ysseldyke, Algozzine, Regan, Potter, Richey and Thurlow, 1980) professionals (e.g. school psychologists, special educators) were asked to consider assessment data and make judgments about a hypothetical pupil involved in staffing. They had available and could choose from data produced by 49 and tests and scales having been selected as a result of earlier surveys of assessment practices. The subjects' choices of data sources were recorded along with requests for technical information on the tests and scales. The sex, socioeconomic status, and type of referral statement for the hypothetical student were varied experimentally to see what factors influenced the judgment of the subjects. These judgments were their decisions about the eligibility of

*This finding was not true of Belleview.

222

the student for special services, diagnosis, prognosis, preferred placement, and perception regarding what sources of data had influenced their decisions. Although the subjects were told that the student had been referred for special education staffing, all sources of data showed the child to be *normal*, not disabled. Some conclusions from this study follow.

The majority of the professionals initially chose technically adequate instruments for use in their decision making. After good first and second choices, however, the instruments they chose were inadequate psychometrically. Those who had prior competence in technical features of tests chose better quality tests. Few of the professionals requested the available technical information about the tests they chose. Thus, the study corroborates our findings in Colorado.

The decisions made by these professionals also indicate how, like in Colorado, staffing committees decide that normal children are learning disabled.

"Fifty-one percent of the decision makers declared the normal child eligible for special education services. . . very likely to be LD. . . Almost two-thirds of the participants felt that the child would have difficulty in reading. . . Regular class with resource teacher consultation and part-time resource room were the most frequently recommended educational settings. . . Scores on achievement tests and intelligence measures and the disparity between the two were viewed as most influential. . . Professionals' estimates for various handicaps were far in excess of actual incidence figures" (Ysseldyke, et al, 1980, pp. 9-11).

Ysseldyke, Algozzine, Shinn, and McGue (1979) titled the report of their *expost facto* study "Similarities and Differences between Underachievers and Students Labeled Learning Disabled: Identical Twins With Different Mothers" *Nomen est omen*. The researchers selected 50 fourth grade children who had been staffed as learning disabled. From the same school districts they selected 49 fourth-graders who matched the learning disabled sample in level of achievement but had not been labeled disabled. Both groups were administered a battery of 49 tests or subtests commonly used in the identification of learning disabilities. "Percentage of overlap" was computed, as well as discriminate function analysis, to determine if the two groups could be differentiated by these measures. The researchers found that, "Percentage of overlap between the two groups ranged from 82 to 100, with a median overlap of approximately 96 percent... Clearly, using this method of contrast, membership in two supposedly discrete groups could not be differentiated" (Ysseldyke, et al., 1979, p. 9).

The next step was to compare the measured characteristics of both groups to the federal eligibility criteria. They employed three standards for judging the severity of ability-achievement discrepancy, a one standard deviation, one and one-half standard deviation and two standard deviation criteria. Only three of the 99 pupils met the two standard deviation criterion (97 percent were misclassified). Forty percent were misclassified under the other criteria.

The researchers concluded that, "this investigation indicates either serious confusion regarding definition or a failure on the part of decision makers to adhere to and decide in accord with an accepted definition" (Ysseldyke, et al., 1979, p. 12). They quoted Rains, Kitsuse, Duster, and Friedson (1975):

"A study of individuals who are classified, categorized, and differentiated in a common population is not likely by itself to yield an understanding of 'the problem' or a basis for assessing the relative value of programs of remediation or treatment. Quite literally, it is the process of differentiation that has created and defined 'the problem' and assigned it to those identified as 'having it'" (p. 91).

Christenson, Graden, Potter, Taylor, Yanowitz, and Ysseldyke (1981) summed up the IRLD studies, but could have spoken for Colorado.

"The reason for referral was very influential in the decision-making process... We believe that the referral statement sets in motion the search for pathology... The search for a problem within the child... a search for confirming evidence... There was heavy emphasis on testing in the assessment/decision-making process. The tests used were often technically inadequate. When educators looked at psychometric data, their identification of learning disabled students was no better than chance. Psychometric differentiation between low achieving and learning disabled students was not found. The more tests given, the more likely the child was to be called LD. Most of the time in team meetings was spent in presenting data rather than generating alternatives for programming. Parents and regular classroom teachers participated the least in team decision making. Data presented in team meetings generally did not relate to the final decision made" (Christenson, et al., 1981, p. 22).

One of these authors, a school psychologist, responded to the conclusions with the frustration of one who must balance the demands of public policy, the limitations of her discipline and the needs of the children referred to her.

"After reading the IRLD results I thought to myself, 'Why am I letting all the researchers make me feel guilty when everyone else I work with is praising me, in spite of, or maybe because of, my often irrational decision-making practices?'

"The parents I work with, for example, respond almost cheerfully when I tell them of their childs' newly discovered 'Learning Disability'. Many are relieved to hear that some 'expert' is finally agreeing that their child has a legitimate, socially-accepted problem. At last, they are not labeled as 'bad parents' who have neglected to provide a stimulating learning environment for their child. In addition, I am offering parents a possible alternative to the frequently demanding and demeaning regular classroom teacher--a trained learning disabilities specialist who is certain to understand and help with the 'problem'.

"The students I work with are also happy when informed of their disability. No longer are they being told they are crazy, lazy, or both. In fact, the same assignment that was criticized on Monday as being incomplete and inadequate, on Tuesday, is praised for its effort and achievement in light of the student's newly labeled handicap. . .

"The regular teachers in my school are also pleased with me for absolving them of their responsibility for these non-achieving students and for taking the identified problem child off their hands. My learning disability teachers are grateful to me for justifying their program and allowing them to teach remedial reading to rather pleasant, benign children. . .

225

"Members of the Association of Parents of Children with Learning Disabilities are pleased with me for identifying more potential members to march and demonstrate before the legislature in demand of more funds to serve the needs of handicapped children. Our State (Utah) Office of Education, once assured that all the required signatures are in their proper places, is happy that I am working in compliance with PL 94-142, thereby ensuring our State its share of federal funds" (Christenson, et al., 1981, pp. 33-34).

Abandoning her ironic tone, the author maintained that school psychologists have closed their eyes to the problems of defining and diagnosing learning disabilities. They have done so with the honorable motive of obtaining remedial education for pupils in need of it. Yet, she warned, trying to do too much for those marginally in need may result in insufficient resources and commitment for the "truly disabled". Her remarks provide additional support for the generality of findings and conclusions reported here.

In this book I have tried to describe how some educators decide who is learning disabled and to account for their decision-making. In so doing, I have identified a problem facing educators. It is my belief that there are individuals who, for some neurological reason, see b's where there are d's, or who are blind to numerals on a page or who fail to record the spoken word in their memories. Despite much ideology to the contrary, we must use the word "belief" because science has given us few facts. We know that the available definitions do not allow us to draw one boundary (or several smaller boundaries) that would allow us to say "this pattern characterizes learning disabilities; this pattern does not." And we know that even people with years of experience cannot discriminate reliably the learning disabled from the non-disabled. Yet law and public policy demand that educators define and serve the undefinable and undiagnosable. Educators look for help from psychology, yet despite its many strengths, it is not equal to this task. Not only is its psychometric technology inadequate, its theories direct us to look for the problem in the child rather than in the classroom or the home, or in ourselves.

The psychological ambiguities permit the intrusion of social forces into decision-making. The community of professionals expands and benefits as the rolls of identified cases of learning disabilities expand. Bureaucracies expand and gain influence. Schools can both explain their failures and keep them enrolled. Teachers benefit from smaller and more homogeneous classes. Children can move into less competitive learning environments and benefit from remedial instruction. Middle class parents can account for their children's lack of success.

A great deal is riding on that staffing conference.

APPENDICES

APPENDIX A

METHODOLOGY AND METHODS

There is a methodological message in the works of Ernest R. House and Arthur E. Wise* for anyone studying a problem such as the identification of the learning disabled: viz., those who advocate centralized programs to reform education and those who preach positivist social science find common cause. The positivist view of science is that the researcher can reduce human phenomena to a few variables, call one the independent and one the dependent, control the rest through randomization, and bingo, out come context-free empirical generalizations. Push these independent-dependent variable relationships one step further and they become the inputs and outputs of a systems analysis model. From there they become tools for imposing a general solution on an intransigent problem. Then, the assumption goes, one needs only to stand back and watch the dependent variable-outputs change, and the problem is solved.

The problem in this case was the failure of many public schools to educate the blind, deaf, crippled, and mentally-ill. The solution, imposed everywhere by Federal law, included FAPE, LRE, Due Process, Fair Evaluation, Child Find, and money. But everything that House said about Follow-Through and Wise said about educational productivity programs applies to this problem. General solutions are based on a science of education that does not exist. Federally imposed programs, no matter how well-conceived, are inevitably modified by local circumstances. Positivist research and evaluation models designed to study these programs overlook these local circumstances and therefore are bound to fail. They always have.

The foregoing expresses my belief about the methods appropriate for studying this research problem--not all problems, but this one. To understand the phenomenon, the researcher must observe it directly and question the people involved with it, study its antecendent, consequences and correlates in the context in which it exits.

*House, E. 1979 and 1980; and Wise, A.E., 1979.

229

This is the belief on which naturalistic inquiry is based (cf. Denzin, 1971; Smith, 1979). The researcher defines the case, any "bounded system," and studies the phenomenon within that case. He studies first-hand and at length, without intervening in the natural flow of events. He becomes close enough to the people affecting and affected by the phenomenon to understand it from their points of view, believing that contextual and personal meanings modify the phenomenon from place to place. From an extensive record of careful observations and interviews, he formulates descriptions of the phenomenon and its case, and then interprets or explains them for the absent reader.

In naturalistic inquiry, the researcher is the instrument, not some observation schedule or questionnaire. Control is achieved through the researcher's self-criticism and self-analysis and extends to careful checking of the validity of data and inferences through local and empirical analysis.

The methods I used in this study were aimed at the ideal just described. Three months were spent negotiating access to the site and studying documents on what the identification practices were designed to be. Six months were spent full-time in direct observation of staffing conferences, meetings, and other relevant interactions, indepth interviews with clinicians, teachers, parents, school and government officials, and others, and analysis of documents such as files of pupils identified as learning disabled. Two months were spent analyzing the data and writing the preliminary report for the district. Twelve months were spent on other projects with a small amount of time for reading and thinking about the problem as well as absorbing the reactions of the district to the preliminary report. The Colorado PCD study (methods of which are described in Chapter 10) took six months and revived my interest in this project. I finished with a full three months of analysis and writing.

The observation methods used were similar to those described by Light (1980). I used no mechanical recording device and no structured observation schedule, but recorded conversations as close to verbatim as possible, then recovering context, body language, and asides as soon as the meetings were over. This was not as difficult as unstructured observation of a classroom, for example, because in most meetings and staffing conferences, people speak in orderly sequences. Many interviews were informal; that is, consisting of questions asked in passing, at the beginning or end of staffing conferences, or over the telephone. I conducted formal interviews much as I have conducted sessions of psychotherapy, with non-directive methods, following where the interviewee leads in his story, but with a mental agenda of issues and possible questions or probes. Many interviews were tape recorded.

Document collection and analysis were straightforward—the district provided me with complete files of pupils' data and histories, laws, rules and regulations, and the like.

Analysis of data followed loosely the prescriptions described by Glaser and Strauss (1967) as the constant comparative method. The entire record of data was combed and a set of categories emerged. Data were sorted into categories, some of which fell apart or merged with others as the analysis proceded. The purpose of any data analysis is to reduce the quantity of data without loosing its essential features, to move from description to interpretation. Therefore, my goal was to select a set of categories or themes that best interpreted or explained the phenomenon as I understood it. The next step was to define the properties of the categories, ending eventually with a propositional statement or hypotheses for each one. Although this was not meant to be a hypotheses-testing study, I attempted some preliminary confirmation of the propositional statements by searching through the data for disconfirming instances. I looked for data that might have been confirmed by alternative methods or alternative sources (e.g., interviews vs. observation, informant A vs. informant B, informant vs. document). I will describe how this set of procedures worked for the proposition 'Implicit definitions are pre-eminent over official definitions.'

According to official Belleview school district documents, (see p. 13), the learning disabled are those with (a) a discrepancy between potential and achievement, (b) caused by a perceptual disorder, and (c) where other possible causes of the discrepancy are ruled out by virtue of the professional judgment of the staffing team, or (d) those judged to be learning disabled by the staffing team. Although (a) is clear, (b) through (d) are ambiguous. This ambiguity was acknowledged by all at the beginning of the study and recognized as an area of difficulty by some school people. For my part I assumed that even with a clear definition, mistakes in diagnosis occur, and I expected them to be like Type I errors, the rate of false positives in a normal distribution. The first staffing conference was unsettling. The various teachers and clinicians recited the litany of test scores and observations that were to become so familiar. Nowhere in that litany was any reference made to the official definition nor information given that the characteristics of the boy involved matched the characteristics of that definition. In spite of this, there was clear consensus of everyone connected with the school that this boy needed help and was therefore eligible for the resource room program for the learning disabled. His achievement was a full grade level below his peers, the lowest in his class; and if he was not to be placed in the resource room, he would have to repeat his grade. The staffing chairman (emissary of the district special education office) tried to impose the official definition. In fact his achievement was *not* significantly below his potential. Then there was enormous pressure brought to bear on the chairman. The boy's mother cried, fearing that he was destined for a life of failure if he was not helped now. The social worker claimed to be a "child advocate" and strongly suggested that the boy's need for help should take precedence over bureaucratic regulations, and so on.

Because I feared the power of first impressions in any clinical study, the events of this staffing conference were a burden on me and I took special care to look for data that might show it to be atypical. About half of the next 26 staffing conferences I observed dealt with pupils whose characteristics matched those of the official definition. Even for this group, the official definition was given only lip service, or was mentioned only by the staffing chairman. What really counted was the fact that the children needed more help than a teacher could give and were behind their peers. The pattern that emerged was that what constituted the need for help was variable from school to school and consistent within a school. This was partially confirmed by comparing the characteristics of children staffed at Aspen and Poplar, the teachers taking much more responsibility for children marginally in need at the latter school. In this way the notion of "implicit definitions" was adopted.

For the many children identified but not matching the official definition, a variety of ploys were used to hold to the local implicit definitions and finesse the official one. Outside experts were brought in to attest to the child's needs for services. Data were twisted in some cases using age norms instead of grade norms to "establish" a significant discrepancy (see page 13), professional judgment of disability was invoked to outweigh the negative evidence of tests, the parents pressured school officials to provide services, and so on.

These were the patterns that were present in the record of data based on both observations and documents. They matched information provided by informants, many of whom (e.g., school psychologists, special education teachers) were not even aware of what the official definition was.

There was no accountability from the school to the district or from the district to the state concerning whether a particular child identified as learning disabled actually matched the official definition. This fact was discerned in an observation of a site-visit of Belleview's special education program by members of the Colorado Department of Education and confirmed by interviewing a state official. This lack of accountability creates a vacuum and makes the implicit definitions more powerful.

An obvious disconfirming instance existed in the data. That was the case of John (page 51). His achievement was not significantly below his potential, but his mother insisted that he was behind and needed help. She brought in an outside expert to attest to John's needs. Although the teachers and clinicians agreed that he needed extra help, they held to the official definition of learning disabilities and agreed only to provide therapy by the speech language specialist. This ordinarily would have sunk my hypothesis, but for an event that took place nine months after John's staffing conference. At that time, John's mother insisted he be reevaluated, took her case to the district special education director, and although John still did not match the official definition, he was declared learning disabled and placed in the resource room. Thus my hypothesis was spared.

The results of the Colorado PCD study further confirmed and extended the hypothesis. Only about half of the identified population of learning disabled actually matched the official definition. Yet almost 80 percent were judged to be in need of some help beyond that which a good teacher can provide.

The role taken by a researcher in naturalistic inquiry is often more important than the methods used in collecting and analyzing data (Williams, 1981). Thus a word about my role deserves a place here. In the continuum of research roles from pure participant to pure observer (Gold, 1958), I was more observer than participant. First, I had no official role in the Belleview school district. Second, I am more comfortable as an outsider looking in, being as unobtrusive as possible, not taking part in the action. As a result the perspective I took was as an outsider. The reader should be aware that this is only one of the possible perspectives from which this research could have been done. One can image the problem as seen through the eyes of a teacher of the learning disabled or from an affected parent. No doubt the final product would have been quite different. My justification for the role and perspective I took is that a parent would not have had the access to information that I had. A teacher would have an interest or stake in the outcome.

The reader should know that this study originated as a commissioned study, an evaluation that the school district wanted me to undertake. My consent to doing the study was conditional on their permission to let me do a case study with no hypotheses and with a role and methods of my own choosing. Thus I was able for the most part to avoid the evaluator's usual role as judge. I could promise confidentiality and offered control over the information to any parent, teacher, or clinician who provided it. Thus any data that might be associated with the individual who gave them were shown to him or her before the report was submitted. In no case was information suppressed as a result of this clearance policy, but having it probably gave me access to data that I would not otherwise have had.

Following the submission of the report, the evaluation office of the school district organized several committees to react to it. Their reactions became part of the data record for this project. To my knowledge, no action was taken by the school district as a result of the report. This is a fate common to many evaluation reports, and was not unexpected. Someone within the district, however, gave a copy to a state legislator, who used it to push for a state-wide evaluation of identification practices. Finding that the tests used are not technically adequate, that many of those identified as learning disabled are not, and that the whole procedure is unjustifiably expensive has not made me popular with the special education community. Some of them have even implied that I do not have the best interests of the handicapped at heart. Declaring that this is untrue will not convince them. My justification is that the researcher has the obligation to be neither sadistic nor altruistic toward those she is studying. Though some methodologists (cf. Becker, 1967) deny that such ethical neutrality is possible for the researcher, it is this stance I attempt to maintain.

Because in naturalistic inquiry, the researcher is the instrument, I will describe something about the instrument employed here. I am not learning disabled nor do I have a child who is or has been considered such. I am not an expert in the field of learning disabilities. This fact will lower my credibility in some eyes and enhance it in others. There are no formal connections between myself and any school district, government agency, or professional association connected with learning disabilities. I am a research methodologist and secondarily a psychologist. My approach to this problem was an intellectual one. My motivation to do the study had less to do with its substance than its method. I did it because I wanted to do a case study, and this problem afforded the opportunity. So eager was I to do a case study -- to improve my interviewing, observation, and analysis skills and to produce a report -- that I donated my time for six months and lived off my savings (the district paid me $4000 over one year's time). Therefore my stake in the outcomes of this study was minimal. I believe neither that special education is an unqualified benefit nor that labeling is inherently harmful. The empirical evidence is equivocal on both points.

Nor did I have an interest in promoting the methodology of naturalistic inquiry over other methods. After ten years of performing research and evaluation under grants and contracts, I have used virtually every technique. The research method should suit the problem. I prefer doing naturalistic methods, this being more related to personality quirks than ideological commitments. Certain research conclusions are associated with my name (research shows that psychotherapy is effective, that psychotherapists are not sex-biased, that class-size and achievement are related). But these are only tangentially related to the present work.

It would be difficult to tag me with a political label, the only exception to this being my frequently stated observation that planned, centralized government has worked poorly. No doubt this belief both affected and was reinforced by this project. If the data had shown otherwise, I would have believed the data.

My worst failing in this study, besides imperfect skills, sensitivity and memory, was that for a time I became emotionally involved with Jenny. Although we never met, my own feelings of helplessness and alienation were aroused by the people involved with her staffing. They meant well, but they were caught up in all the forces I later attempted to understand and explain. Her placement in special education seemed to hinge on a crushing bureaucratic mechanism that, once started, produced an inevitable outcome. She was a frustrating little girl, no doubt, but a misunderstood and falsely labeled one.

What researchers of human beings must inevitably face is the projection of their own needs and fantasies on their subjects. George Devereux (1967) spoke of this countertransference as both the principal source of misapprehension and the principal source of truth. When properly interpreted and understood, the feelings and reactions of the researcher can be an accurate gauge of the feelings and experience of those he studies. Through the help of my friends and colleagues, I believe that my reactions to Jenny revealed rather than twisted the truth about her experience. The reader will have to make his own judgment.

APPENDIX B

BELLEVIEW STAFFING FORMS

BELLEVIEW STAFFING FORMS

BELLEVIEW PUBLIC SCHOOLS
Form A: Request for Special Education Referral

REASON FOR REFFERAL FOR SPECIAL STUDY AND CONCLUSIONS, IF ANY, BASED ON REVIEW OF THE
CHILD'S SCHOOL REDORDS, i.e., PRELIMINARY ASSESSMENT   (Please be specific)

PERSONNEL TO CONDUCT SPECIAL STUDY: The following personnel, as deemed appropriate,
will be included in the assessment for the special study: Educational Specialist,
Reading Specialist, Psychologist, Social Worker, Nurse, Speech/Language Specialst,
Adaptive Physical Education Specialist, and Vision or Hearing Specialist.

The results of the special study may be used to determine whether or not the student
is eligible for special education services.

Principal_____

PARENT CONSENT

PART B

I have been provided the opportunity for a face-to-face conference with school personnel
in a language in which I am fluent, prior to assessment of my child and hereby agree that
special study be made to assist in education planning for my son/daughter. I understand
that it will be conducted by the professional persons indicated above and that an
interpretation of the results will be available to me upon its completion. I understand
that any reports of the special study will become a part of my son's/daughter's school
record and may be reviewed by me.

I have read and understand the contents on the reverse side of my rights as a parent and
of the procedure available for the resolution of any differences that I might have with
school personnel concerning the determination of the most appropriate program available
to meet my child's educational needs.

Date_____   Parent's Signature_____

See OVER for procedure to resolve differences statement

DISTRIBUTION: *White-Sp.Ed. Office; Yellow-Principal; Pink-Parent; Blue-Support Personnel*

Special Education' Form A Revised 7/78

BELLEVIEW PUBLIC SCHOOLS

REQUEST FOR SPECIAL EDUCATION STAFFING   Date referred:_____

(Staffing will be arranged by Special Education Office)   Referred by:_____

STUDENT'S NAME_____ D.O.B._____ School:_____

Referred for staffing in: P/CD   E/BD   SLIC   HEARING   VISION
(circle)   PHYS.HNCP.   SPEECH   LANGUAGE

STUDENT INFORMATION (PLEASE BE SPECIFIC)

1. a. Listening skills and following directions_____
    _____
    b. Verbal language skills _____
    c. TEST DATA:

		GRADE LEVEL EQUIV.	GRADE LEVEL
TEST	DATE_____	Stand. Test	Teacher Est.
TOTAL READING PERFORMANCE			
WORD ATTACK		_____	_____
COMPREHENSION		_____	_____
TOTAL MATH PERFORMANCE			
COMPUTATION		_____	_____
CONCEPTS		_____	_____
APPLICATION		_____	_____

    d. WRITTEN LANGUAGE SKILLS
    e. SPELLING
    f. SELF-CONCEPT
    g. CLASSROOM BEHAVIOR/PEER RELATIONSHIPS _____
    _____
    _____
    h. ATTENDANCE_____
    i. VISION/HEARING_____
    j. PHYSICAL IMPAIRMENTS_____
    k. OTHER_____

2. STRENGTHS_____

3. STEPS TAKEN TO ASSIST CHILD IN CLASSROOM
    a._____   c._____
    b._____   d._____

4. EVALUATION AND/OR ASSISTANCE PROVIDED TO STUDENT BY OUTSIDE AGENCY (PLEASE FORWARD
    COPY OF RECORDS TO SPECIAL EDUCATION OFFICE.)_____

5. The following people participated in the educational planning conference:
    PRINCIPAL_____   EDUCATIONAL SPECIALIST_____
    PARENT_____   READING SPECIALIST_____
    TEACHER_____   NURSE_____
    PSYCHOLOGIST_____   SPEECH/LANGUAGE SPECIALIST_____
    SOCIAL WORKER_____   ADAPTIVE P.E. SPECIALIST_____
    OTHER_____   OTHER_____

This is to confirm that the parent has been notified of the submission of this form to the
Special Education office, and that a Special Education staffing will be called.

_____   _____
        Date   Principal's Signature

DISTRIBUTION: WHITE - Principal; Green - Sp. Ed. Office

INDIVIDUALIZED EDUCATIONAL PROGRAM

ASSESSMENT SUMMARY FOR _____

School _____

Grade _____ (Last) _____ D.O.B. _____ (First) _____ C.A. _____ (Middle) _____ Date of Staffing _____

Area Assessed	MEASUREMENT				Test Scores	Present Levels of Performance
	Method	Date	Assessor			
LANGUAGE (Oral)						
SPEECH PRODUCTION						
READING						
MATHEMATICS						
HANDWRITING Manuscript Cursive						
WRITTEN LANGUAGE						
SPELLING						

DISTRIBUTION: WHITE–SP. ED.; YELLOW– PARENT; BLUE– SP. ED. TEACHER

FORM C-3

INDIVIDUALIZED EDUCATIONAL PROGRAM

CONTINUED ASSESSMENT SUMMARY FOR _____ (Last) _____ (First) _____ (Middle) _____ D.O.B. _____

Area Assessed	Method	MEASUREMENT Date	Assessor	Test Scores	Present Levels of Performance
PERCEPTION (Visual)					
GROSS MOTOR SKILLS					
SELF-CARE SKILLS					
PRE-VOCATIONAL SKILLS					
INTELLECTUAL FUNCTIONING					
OTHER					

SOCIAL ADAPTATION
Appropriate Behaviors _____

Other Behaviors _____

SOCIAL WORK SUMMARY _____

HEALTH REPORT _____

VISION: Deficit _____ Corrected _____ Normal _____ HEARING: Deficit _____ Corrected _____ Normal _____
DISTRIBUTION: White-Sp. Ed. Office; Yellow-Parent; Blue-Sp. Ed. Teacher

PLACEMENT STAFFING - RECOMMENDATIONS   INDIVIDUALIZED EDUCATIONAL PROGRAM FOR 19 _____ to 19 _____

FORM C-4a

_____
(Last)   (First)   (Middle)   D.O.B. _____ Grade _____

Identified Handicap

	Delivery System		Basis for Determination of Handicap:

Limited Intellectual Capacity   ___ S/C ___ Level ___ Resource
Perceptual/Communicative Disorders   ___ S/C ___ Level ___ Resource
Emotional/Behavioral Disorders   ___ S/C ___ Level ___ Resource
Speech/Language Disorders   ___ S/C ___ Level ___ Itinerant
Hearing Disorders   ___ S/C ___ Level ___ Itinerant
Vision   ___ S/C ___ Level ___ Itinerant
Physical Condition, Impairment or Illness ___ S/C ___ Level ___ Itinerant
Other   ___ S/C ___ Level

Recommended Schools: 1) _____ 2) _____
(The Director of Special Education, or his designee, shall determine the appropriate school placement)
Recommended Date of Entry: _____ Anticipated duration of program: _____
Description of extent to which student will be able to participate in regular educational program: _____

Support Services	Estimate of Pupil's Time	Comments	Review Date

RECOMMENDATIONS FOR INSTRUCTION

Motivational Techniques   Instructional Strategies   Comments :
Physical Environment   Materials

Placement in Special Education not appropriate
for these reasons: _____

Signatures of Staffing Committee Attending:

Parent/Guardian _____   Alternatives to Special Education Placement:
School Administrator or Designee _____   _____
Regular Classroom Teacher/Counselor _____
Special Education Teacher _____   I give my permission for my child to be placed
Psychologist _____   in the Special Education program indicated
Social Worker _____   above. I have read and understand the contents
Speech/Language Specialist _____   on the reverse side of my rights and of the
Nurse _____   due process procedures available.
Reading Specialist _____
Other _____   _____
                                Parent and/or Guardian   Date

DISTRIBUTION: White—Sp. Ed.; Yellow— Parent; Blue—Sp. Ed. Teacher

_____
Special Education Director/Designee Date

INDIVIDUALIZED EDUCATIONAL PROGRAM FOR 19___ to 19___

ANNUAL GOALS AND OBJECTIVES FOR _____ _____ _____
(Last)   (First)   (Middle)

ANNUAL GOALS: This learner will

	OBJECTIVE OUTCOME				
	PERFORMANCE	DECISION		EXPLANATION	

Obj. No.	Obj. met as stated	Progress Made	Observ. no progress	Carry over obj.	Carry over obj. Postpone	Drop Obj.	St. lacks pre-req. skills	Obj. too difficult	Other	Obj. inapprop.	Lacks Motivation
1											
2											
3											
4											
5											
6											

OBJECTIVE 1
This learner will _____ Date____
_____
From _____ to _____ by ____
as measured by _____

OBJECTIVE 2
This learner will _____ Date____
_____
From _____ to _____ by ____
as measured _____

OBJECTIVE 3
This learner will _____ Date____
_____
From _____ to _____ by ____
as measured _____

OBJECTIVE 4
This learner will _____ Date____
_____
From _____ to _____ by ____
as measured _____

OBJECTIVE 5
This learner will _____ Date____
_____
From _____ to _____ by ____
as measured _____

OBJECTIVE 6
This learner will _____ Date____
_____
From _____ to _____ by ____
as measured _____

IEP Planning or Review Meeting Participants Approval: Sp. Ed. Director or Designee_____ Other_____
DISTRIBUTION: White-Sp.Ed.; Yellow-Parent; Blue-Sp.Ed.Teacher

APPENDIX C

PERCEPTUAL TRAINING MATERIALS

APPENDIX C
PERCEPTUAL TRAINING MATERIALS

Auditory Perception Training Package

Among the boxes and files of materials on the resource room's shelf is a brightly patterned green and white box. This holds "Auditory Perception Training--Figure Ground" one program in a series of perceptual-motor and academic programs developed and marketed by Developmental Learning Materials, an Illinois corporation.

In the box are 10 audio cassette tapes, a teacher's guide and a set of spirit masters from which work sheets can be duplicated. The lessons are arranged in a series from Level I-Lesson I, progressing in difficulty to Level II-Lesson 6. Each tape is about five minutes long.

The manual defines Auditory Figure Ground as the "ability to screen out extraneous noises and concentrate on a particular stimulus." Under "uses," the manual states "This series can be utilized with students having minimal brain dysfunction, those identified as having auditory perception deficits and those in a developmental school readiness program, as well as regular primary classes. This series allows the flexibility of use in small groups with individuals or total classes." To do Level I-Lesson I requires the child to recognize colors (red, yellow, blue, green), directions (e.g., next to, around), and the shapes and figures that are arranged on the worksheet (house, chair, apple, tree, book, lamp, umbrella).

The cassette tape for Level I-Lesson I presents a main stimulus-voice that gives directions for completing the lesson, and background noise. The background noise for this initial lesson is slight--lower than an openspace school or a class that is individually paced, but louder than a self-contained class all reading. There is no voice of a teacher in the background nor can any words be discriminated. The stimulus voice is several times louder than the background noise. Here is a sample of dialogue from the main speaker (who has a rich, male radio-announcer voice).

246

Sonorous radio announcer voice:	"DLM Auditory Figure Ground - Level I" "To complete this lesson, you will need a box of crayons." "Listen. These are the sounds you might hear in a classroom. You must listen carefully in order to do what I tell you. Let's try to do some work while the children are takling. Listen carefully to what I am going to say. Look at your worksheet. Do what I tell you to." "Find the picture of the house . . . . Draw a red circle next to the picture of the house (12 sec.) Find the picture of the tree. Draw a yellow line around the picture of the tree. . . . .

With a blue crayon, write your name on the line. Write your first and last name. If you cannot write your last name, write the initial of your last name . . . . That's the end of this lesson. Did you listen well?"

Level II, Lesson 5 followed a similar format but was much more difficult. The stimulus voice giving directions was only marginally louder than the background distraction. Not only can you hear every word of this conversation, but the speakers are working (not very efficiently) on the same task, supplying the correct numbers in the series of five "space stations" on the worksheet. A sample of the interference is below:

Stimulus	Background
You must listen carefully in order to do your work. Let's try to do some work while we hear the persons talking. Listen carefully. Look at your work sheet. Do what you are told to do. I am an astronaut. Being an astronaut is an exciting job . . . Today I have a special job. Many of the men working in space need to be picked up and dropped off . . . Will you please keep track of the people we drop off and pick up at each of the space stations.	"Do you know that when I went home last night my father had brought home a new puppy. And it was the cutest puppy and you know what my mother said? The dog or me has to go. We all took a vote and . . .
	(Noises of other children doing the same lesson counting down the space ship lift-off . . .)
That's space station number 1. . . We're going to drop off 3 men and pick up 2 men and return to earth. How many men are returning to earch from this station? Write the number in the circle inside space station 1.	"This is probably one of the funest ones that we've had" How many? I don't know. He said leave some off and pick someone up. Why don't we write down . . . . 4! That sounds like a good number. Make it 5 - its how many men altogether. Four and five are six. Write that down. (sigh)
We're on our way to station 2.	

A COLORADO SURVEY OF ATTITUDES AND PRACTICES FOR IDENTIFYING PERCEPTUAL AND COMMUNICATIVE DISORDERS

A COLORADO SURVEY OF ATTITUDES AND PRACTICES FOR IDENTIFYING
PERCEPTUAL AND COMMUNICATIVE DISORDERS

Form A: PCD Teachers

Dear _____ :   Code # _____

    You are being asked to participate in a statewide study on the identification,
assessment, placement, and remediation of perceptual and communicative disordered
children in Colorado. The study was mandated by the Colorado Legislature and is
funded by the Colorado Department of Education. It is being conducted by faculty
and staff of the Laboratory of Educational Research, University of Colorado.

    Your district or BOCS is one of the 22 Special Education units selected at
random to be included. Your superintendent has been informed of our procedures
and permission to contact you directly has been obtained from the Director
of Special Education.

    Our purpose in sending you this questionnaire is to adequately describe the
perceptions of Colorado special education teachers about the PCD identification
process. Your name was selected at random from PCD teachers in the participating
districts. While participation is voluntary, we urgently need your response to
represent those of other teachers who were not chosen themselves.

    The following questionnaire should take about 45 minutes to complete. The
questions deal with procedures used in assessing and identifying PCD children.
If there are any questions that you would prefer not to answer, you may omit
them. Although you may not benefit directly from the study, it is hoped special
education will benefit, particularly if the study leads to improved definitions
of PCD and Department of Education guidelines for identifying such children.

    Your name should appear only on the first sheet. Your name will be removed
from the questionnaire and destroyed. Data will be analyzed only with your code
number and all information will be completely confidential. We need your name
only so that we can follow up on nonrespondents.

    Dr. Lorrie Shepard, the director of the study, will be glad to answer any
questions you might have. She may be contacted at 492-8108. Also the Director
of Special Education in your district or BOCS attended a workshop where the
purposes and procedures of the study were discussed.

    Questions concerning your rights as a subject may be directed to the
Human Research Committee at the Graduate School of the University of Colorado;
upon request you may obtain a copy of this Institution's General Assurance
from the Human Research Committee Secretary, Graduate School, University of
Colorado, Boulder, CO 80309.

    Please complete the questionnaire as soon as possible. The follow-up of
nonrespondents will begin in about two weeks. Mail the completed questionnaire
in the envelope provided directly to Dr. Shepard at the Laboratory of Educational
Research, University of Colorado, Boulder 80309.

    Thank you very much for your time and cooperation.

A COLORADO SURVEY OF ATTITUDES AND PRACTICES FOR IDENTIFYING PERCEPTUAL AND COMMUNICATIVE DISORDERS

Definition of Perceptual and Communicative Disorders

Do you agree or disagree with the following statements? Circle the number that best describes your opinion.

1 = Strongly Agree   2 = Agree   3 = Neutral or Undecided

4 = Disagree   5 = Strongly Disagree

1.* In my opinion, perceptual and communicative disorders are the result of neurological impairments.

Strongly Agree   1   2   3   4   5   Strongly Disagree

2.* A PCD child can be distinguished from a slow learner.

Strongly Agree   1   2   3   4   5   Strongly Disagree

3.* PCD is an administrative way whereby nonretarded children can receive the help they need.

Strongly Agree   1   2   3   4   5   Strongly Disagree

4.* Perceptual & communicative disorders result from an intrinsic disorder, whereas learning problems or learning difficulties result from environmental factors.

Strongly Agree   1   2   3   4   5   Strongly Disagree

5.* A formula (e.g. including factors such as mental age, achievement and age) can reasonably be used to determine if a perceptual or communicative disorder is present.

Strongly Agree   1   2   3   4   5   Strongly Disagree

6.* Existing assessment techniques are adequate for the diagnosis of PCD disorders.

Strongly Agree   1   2   3   4   5   Strongly Disagree

7. Classroom teachers sometimes refer a child for evaluation as PCD simply because the child is lowest in the class and not because he is disabled.

Strongly Agree   1   2   3   4   5   Strongly Disagree

8. The most important evidence that a child is PCD is that he is unable to function in the regular classroom.

Strongly Agree   1   2   3   4   5   Strongly Disagree

9. A child who is having academic problems but who is dominant in a language other than English should be excluded from PCD because linguistic differences probably explain the learning problems.

Strongly Agree   1   2   3   4   5   Strongly Disagree

10. A child who has been absent for more than 30 percent of the school days should not be identified as PCD since the missed instruction probably explains the severe deficit in achievement.

Strongly Agree   1   2   3   4   5   Strongly Disagree

11. The decision that a child is PCD is almost never influenced by whether or not there is a space for him or her in a resource room or self-contained class.

Strongly Agree   1   2   3   4   5   Strongly Disagree

12. In most cases when a staffing committee decides whether a child is PCD, they do not give enough consideration to whether classroom instruction might be what is causing his or her poor performance.

Strongly Agree   1   2   3   4   5   Strongly Disagree

13. PCD is something in the makeup of a child rather than the result of inappropriate instruction.

Strongly Agree   1   2   3   4   5   Strongly Disagree

*asterisked items were adapted from "a Survey of Attitudes Concerning Learning Disabilities" by S. A. Kirk, P. B. Berry, and G. M. Senf in the Journal of Learning Disabilities, 1979, 12, 239-245.

14. In many cases moving a child from one teacher to another or from an "open-space" to a "closed-space" classroom is enough to remedy a mild or moderate perceptual or communicative disorder.

Strongly Agree 1 2 3 4 5 Strongly Disagree

15. What people refer to as a PC disorder is really a condition that most children grow out of naturally.

Strongly Agree 1 2 3 4 5 Strongly Disagree

16. Many children are identified as PCD because they have behavioral or emotional problems rather than a neurological or perceptual problem that causes poor academic performance.

Strongly Agree 1 2 3 4 5 Strongly Disagree

17. Slow learners should be entitled to as much special education help as children who are diagnosed as having a perceptual or communicative handicap.

Strongly Agree 1 2 3 4 5 Strongly Disagree

18. The way the PCD identification and placement procedures now work results in few false designations of PCD, i.e. identifying a child as PCD who in reality has no handicap.

Strongly Agree 1 2 3 4 5 Strongly Disagree

19. The way the PCD identification and placement procedures now work results in few cases of overlooked diagnosis, i.e. failing to identify a child as PCD who in reality has such a handicap.

Strongly Agree 1 2 3 4 5 Strongly Disagree

20. Once the decision is made that a child has PCD, the PCD teacher is capable of designing an effective instructional program.

Strongly Agree 1 2 3 4 5 Strongly Disagree

21. In my opinion, many ethnic minority pupils who are perceptually-communicatively disordered are overlooked in the PCD identification and placement procedures of our district.

Strongly Agree 1 2 3 4 5 Strongly Disagree

22. Sometimes, the judgment of certain individuals is more important than test evidence in the identification and placement of pupils with PCD. In your opinion, do the following individuals have too much, too little, or the right amount of influence on the decision? (Check one blank in each row)

	Too Much	Too Little	Right Amount	Don't Know
1. Pupil's parents	_____	_____	_____	_____
2. School principal	_____	_____	_____	_____
3. Psychologist	_____	_____	_____	_____
4. Outside evaluators	_____	_____	_____	_____
5. Classroom teacher	_____	_____	_____	_____
6. District spec. educ. administrators	_____	_____	_____	_____
7. Special education teacher	_____	_____	_____	_____
8. Speech/Lang. specialist	_____	_____	_____	_____
9. Other_____	_____	_____	_____	_____
10. Other_____	_____	_____	_____	_____

23. Indicate in the table below the importance of each factor in determining whether a child has a perceptual or communicative disorder.

1 = Among the most critical factors. Its presence would cause me to _believe_ that the child _was_ PCD (positive indicator).

2 = Important factor. Its presence would cause me to _suspect_ that the child was PCD (positive indicator).

3 = Not an important factor. Its presence leads me neither to believe or not believe that the child is PCD.

4 = Important factor. The presence of this characteristic would lead me to _suspect_ that the child was _not_ PCD (negative indicator).

5 = Among the most critical factors. Its presence would cause me to believe that the child was _not_ PCD (negative indicator).

Factors Affecting Determination of Handicapping Category	Among most critical/ positive indicator	Important/ Positive	Not an important factor either positive or negative	Important/ Negative	Among most critical/ negative indicator
Average IQ	1	2	3	4	5
Verbal/performance discrepancy	1	2	3	4	5
Inadequate speech/language functioning	1	2	3	4	5
Achievement/ability discrepancy	1	2	3	4	5
Below grade-level achievement	1	2	3	4	5
Chronic problem that has not responded to remedial instruction	1	2	3	4	5
Lack of other sources of support in the environment	1	2	3	4	5
Inadequacy of teaching	1	2	3	4	5
Socio-economic disadvantage	1	2	3	4	5
Psychological process deficits	1	2	3	4	5
Physiological-neurological inequalities	1	2	3	4	5
Cultural deprivation	1	2	3	4	5
Linguistic differences	1	2	3	4	5
Minority group membership	1	2	3	4	5
Student is a girl	1	2	3	4	5
Inappropriate Emotional/Behavioral functioning	1	2	3	4	5
Distractibility	1	2	3	4	5
Poor self-help skills	1	2	3	4	5
Good social skills	1	2	3	4	5
Generally good physical health status	1	2	3	4	5
Lack of motor coordination	1	2	3	4	5
IQ between 80 and 85	1	2	3	4	5
Short attention span	1	2	3	4	5
Premature birth	1	2	3	4	5
Achievement good one day but bad the next.	1	2	3	4	5
Aggressiveness	1	2	3	4	5
Achievement adequate in some areas but poor in others.	1	2	3	4	5
Other (Specify)	1	2	3	4	5

Questions 24 and 25

We need to know your perception of the thoroughness and efficiency of the PCD identification process as it is currently implemented in your district. (Check one answer in each set of statements. The first set deals with accurate identification of PCD children; the second set deals with satisfying due process requirements. Due process refers to all those procedures that guarantee the rights of parents to understand each step in the identification process and provide their consent).

24. Set 1: Identification procedures are:

___ Not thorough enough to identify accurately a PCD child and wasteful of staff time.
___ Not thorough enough to identify accurately a PCD child but not wasteful of staff time.
___ About right in thoroughness and efficiency.
___ Thorough enough to identify accurately a PCD child and not wasteful of staff time.
___ Thorough enough but wasteful of staff time.

25. Set 2: Identification procedures are:

___ Not thorough enough to satisfy due process requirements and wasteful of staff time.
___ Not thorough enough to satisfy due process requirements but not wasteful of staff time.
___ About right in thoroughness and efficiency.
___ Thorough enough to satisfy due process requirements and not wasteful of staff time.
___ Thorough enough but wasteful of staff time.

26. Some parents have said that the presence of so many professional people at the staffing conference is intimidating. In your experience, have parents felt this intimidation?

Yes ___ No ___ Not sure ___

27. How far below grade level should a child be to be diagnosed as having a PC disorder? (For example, if you think a first grader must be at least 6 months below grade level to be considered PCD, check 0.5 years.)

	0.0 A PCD child does not have to be below grade level.	0.5	1.0	1.5	2.0	2.5
Years below grade level.						
at grade 1						
at grade 3						
at grade 6						
at grade 9						
at grade 12						

28. If a third grade child had a WISC-R IQ score of 90, in your opinion, how low should his or her reading grade equivalent score be (in October) to be a significant discrepancy?

1. 2.7 (35th percentile) or lower
2. 2.5 (28th percentile) or lower
3. 2.2 (21st percentile) or lower
4. 2.0 (12th percentile) or lower

Questions 29 - 32

On the following questions, please state your opinion about the identification of processing disorders (e.g., in memory, language, visual or auditory perception).

29. What percent of PCD children have no processing deficit but have some other evidence of a handicap? _____ %

30. What percent of PCD children have a processing deficit diagnosed by clinical observation rather than test scores? _____ %

31. What percent of PCD children have a processing deficit diagnosed because of wide scatter on a processing test? _____ %

32. What is the minimum difference between a child's scale scores and his average scale score which you would require on the Illinois Test of Psycholinguistic Abilities to identify a significant weakness? _____ points

33. Tests Used in Identifying Perceptual & Communicative Disorders

Consider the tests in all of the following categories. Please evaluate the reliability and validity of each measure you are familiar with, even if it is usually administered by some other specialist.

Frequency of Use

Think of all of the staffings & assessments you have participated in in the last 2 years which lead to a PCD placement (as well as those who were potentially PCD but were staffed and not placed). Indicate below in approximately what % of the cases you used the following tests.

Reliability & Validity

Please indicate below which tests have adequate reliability evidence and are valid for the purpose of identifying perceptual or communicative disorders. Of course, any test could be invalid if used inappropriately. But which tests have research evidence of their validity when used appropriately? Check the columns that apply:

1=Adequate 2=Inadequate 3=Don't know

	Never 0%	Rarely 1-15%	Some-times 16-50%	Often 51-85%	Nearly Always 86-100%	Reliability 1	2	3	Validity 1	2	3
Intelligence Tests											
Detroit Tests of Learning Aptitude											
Peabody Picture Vocabulary Test (PPVT)											
Slosson Intelligence Test for Children and Adults											
Stanford Binet Intelligence Scale											
WISC-R											
Woodcock-Johnson Psychoeducational Battery											
Achievement Tests											
Brigance Diagnostic Inventory of Basic Skills											
California Test of Basic Skills (CTBS)											
Diagnostic Reading Scales											
Durrel Analyses of Reading Difficulty											
Gates-MacGinitie Reading Tests											
Gates-McKillop Reading Diagnostic Tests											
Gillmore Oral Reading Test											
Gray Oral Reading Test											
Iowa Test of Basic Skills (ITBS)											
KeyMath Diagnostic Arithmetic Test											
Metropolitan Achievement Test											
Peabody Individual Achievement Tests (PIAT)											
Spache Diagnostic Reading Scales											
Sucher Allred Reading Placement Inventory											
Test of Reading Comprehension											
Test of Written Language											
Wide Range Achievement Test (WRAT)											
Woodcock Reading Mastery Tests											
Behavioral Recordings											
Frequency counting or event recordings											
Permanent products											
Adaptive Behavior Scales											
AAMD Adaptive Behavior Scale School Version											
Vineland Social Maturity Scale											

	Frequency of Use					Reliability & Validity					
						1=Adequate 2=Inadequate 3=Don't Know					
	Never 0%	Rarely 1-15%	Some-times 16-50%	Often 51-85%	Nearly Always 86-100%	Reliability 1	2	3	Validity 1	2	3

Personality Tests

	Never 0%	Rarely 1-15%	Some-times 16-50%	Often 51-85%	Nearly Always 86-100%	1	2	3	1	2	3
Draw-A-Person (Goodenough-Harris Drawing Test)											
Kinetic Family Drawing											
Piers-Harris Self-Concept Scale											
Sentence Completion											

Perceptual and Processing Tests

Beery Developmental Test of Visual-Motor Integration (VMI)											
Bender (Visual-Motor) Gestalt Test											
Frostig Developmental Test of Visual Perception											
Goldman-Fristoe-Woodcock Test of Auditory Discrimination (GFW)											
Lindamood Auditory Conceptualization Test											
Memory for Designs Test											
Motor-Free Visual Perception Test											
Purdue Perceptual-Motor Survey											
Spencer Memory for Sentences Test											
Wepman Auditory Discrimination Test (The Wepman)											

Speech and Language Tests

Boehm Test of Basic Concepts											
Carrow Tests for Auditory Comprehension of Language											
Fisher-Logemann Test of Articulation Competence											
Goldman-Fristoe Test of Articulation											
Illinois Test of Psycholinguistic Abilities (ITPA)											
Northwestern Syntax Screening Test											
Slingerland Screening Test for Identifying Children with Specific Language Disability											
Templin-Darley Tests of Articulation											
Test of Language Development											
Token Test											
Utah Test of Language Development											
Wiig											

Do you agree or disagree with the following statements? Circle the number that best describes your opinion.

34. Observation of a discrepancy in the classroom between potential and performance should be sufficient evidence of a PC disorder even if there is not a significant discrepancy on standardized tests.

Strongly Agree   1   2   3   4   5   Strongly Disagree

35. It is possible to make valid diagnoses of PC disorders from invalid tests if they are only used as stimuli to test clinical hypotheses.

Strongly Agree   1   2   3   4   5   Strongly Disagree

36. Tests results should be clearly secondary to clinical judgments in arriving at a PCD diagnosis.

Strongly Agree   1   2   3   4   5   Strongly Disagree

37. If you agree or strongly agree, describe what steps should be taken by professionals to ensure the validity of clinical judgments.

38. A "non-categorical" category should be created to meet the needs of children with mild handicaps who cannot be identified by the standard definition of PCD.

Strongly Agree   1   2   3   4   5   Strongly Disagree

39. Even if a scientifically verifiable handicap cannot be identified, there are many children for whom special education, is essential because their needs cannot be met in the regular classroom.

Strongly Agree   1   2   3   4   5   Strongly Disagree

Recommendations for changes in the state requirements or guidelines for the identification of PCD:

40. First, in order to improve the validity of the PCD identification process would you recommend that the requirements and guidelines be made:

_____ Stricter?   _____ Less strict?   _____ Be left unchanged?

41. Please give your specific suggestions for policy changes:

Allocation of Specialists' Time

42. Approximately how many assessments and staffings for the identification of handicapped children did you participate in during the 79-80 school year? _____

43. How many of these pupils were identified as PCD? _____

44. How many of these pupils had some PCD-like characteristics but were eventually not placed in PCD? _____

45. How many of these pupils had some other handicap or were considered for a handicapped placement other than PCD? _____

46. In your school, what is the approximate length in minutes of the average staffing meeting where placement decisions are made (excluding time spent on the IEP)?

Average length: _____ minutes

47. What was the length of the shortest meeting?_____mins.; the longest meeting?_____mins.

48. Consider all of the time you spent last year attending all <u>staffings</u>. Estimate what percent of time was spent in the following types of staffings:

_____ % was spent in staffings to determine handicapping condition and placement.
_____ % was spent in IEP or other staffing for instructional planning.
_____ % was spent in annual reviews.
_____ % other, specify_____.
100 % of total time spent in staffing.

49. Consider all of the time you spent last year in <u>screening, testing and assessment</u>. Estimate what percent of time was spent in the following types of assessment activities:

_____ % was spent in assessment to determine if a handicap existed and in preparing for placement staffings.
_____ % was spent in assessment for purposes of instructional planning.
_____ % was spent in assessment to measure pupil progress in special education placements.
_____ % other, specify_____.
100 % of total time spent in screening, testing and assessment.

Instructional Programs for PCD Pupils

Indicate whether you agree or disagree with the following statements:

50. Teaching such learning processes as attention, memory, and discrimination is a necessary part of teaching skills such as reading, writing, etc.

Strongly Agree   1   2   3   4   5   Strongly Disagree

51. One need not concern oneself with learning processes such as memory, attention, and discrimination if one uses a task analysis approach.

Strongly Agree   1   2   3   4   5   Strongly Disagree

52. Many PCD teachers conduct further assessments--<u>following the staffing or IEP decision</u>--to plan the instructional program for pupils newly identified as PCD. Do you use assessment devices for post-staffing planning?   Yes_____   No_____

53. If you answered yes to the above question, please list the 10 assessment devices which you most often use to <u>plan the instructional program</u> for pupils newly identified as PCD.

1_____   6_____

2_____   7_____

3_____   8_____

4_____   9_____

5_____   10_____

Questions 54 - 59

For the time when you are providing <u>direct</u> services to <u>PCD children</u>, estimate what percent of time you spend doing each of the following activities:

54. Repetition & drill on basic skills which are prerequisites for regular classroom (grade-level) work.   _____ %

55. One-to-one instruction or tutoring with regular classroom work.   _____ %

56. Direct training of psychological processes such as visual discrimination, auditory memory and attention.   _____ %

57. Process training using materials adapted from regular classroom work.   _____ %

58. Teaching appropriate behaviors; informal counseling aimed at improving self-concept; or behavior modification.   _____ %

59. Other. Please describe. _____
_____
_____

_____
100 % (Total time you spend in direct services to PCD students).

60. Is your assignment in   a self-contained classroom _____
                               a resource room _____? _____

61. What is your average case load, i.e., the number of students to whom you provide instructional services during a typical week? (Do not count consultation with regular classroom teacher or screening, assessment & staffing.)   _____ pupils

62. Many handicapped children may have a part-time placement in your classroom. At any one time during the school day or school year, what is the maximum number of students you ever have in your classroom at the same time?   _____ pupils

63. Estimate the <u>average</u> number of children that you have in your classroom at one time.   _____ pupils

64. Indicate how important the following factors are likely to be in your decision to recommend that a child be STAFFED OUT of PCD placement.

       1 = Among the most critical factors
       2 = Important, but not one of the most critical factors
       3 = Positive sign, but not sufficient by itself
       4 = Considered, but among the least important factors
       5 = Not considered

Factors Affecting Decision to Staff out of PCD	Among Most Critical	Important	Positive Sign	Among Least Important	Not Considered
Test results show that the child no longer has a significant discrepancy between ability & achievement.	1	2	3	4	5
Test results show that the child no longer has <u>any</u> discrepancy between ability and achievement.	1	2	3	4	5
Test results show that academic performance has been brought up to grade level.	1	2	3	4	5
In your judgment academic performance has been brought up to grade level.	1	2	3	4	5
Instructional goals set on the IEP have been attained.	1	2	3	4	5

Factors Affecting Decision to Staff out of PCD	Among Most Critical	Important	Positive Sign	Among Least Important	Not Considered
Test results show elimination of processing disorders which were present initially.	1	2	3	4	5
In your judgment, processing deficits have been sufficiently reduced so they no longer interfere with classroom performance.	1	2	3	4	5
Reduction of behavior problems such as inattention or hyperactivity.	1	2	3	4	5
Your judgment about ability to function in the regular classroom without further help.	1	2	3	4	5

Background Information of Respondent

65. Type of School:
    Elementary _____
    Middle _____
    Junior High _____
    High _____

66. In selecting you for this survey, we have identified you as a PCD teacher. Is this classification correct for the 1980-81 school year? Yes ____ No ____ If this classification is incorrect, please indicate your specialty.

    1. Speech and Language Specialist
    2. School Psychologist
    3. Social Worker
    4. Teacher
    5. Other _____

67. How many years have you held this kind of position? State the nearest whole number of years and count this year (80-81) as one year.

    Number of years: _____ in this district

    _____ in Colorado, other than in this district

    _____ outside of Colorado

    _____ Total number of years of experience in this kind of position

68. In addition to the years reported above, how many years of experience have you had in other educational positions?
    _____ years.

69. Please indicate below the academic degrees you have earned; and for each degree indicate the year the degree was earned and the institution (college or university) that awarded the degree.

Degree	Year	Institution
Bachelors	____	_____
Masters	____	_____
Specialist	____	_____
Doctorate	____	_____

70. What educational certificates do you hold?

	Colorado	Other State
Classroom teacher	_____	_____
Special education teacher	_____	_____
Other (Specify)	_____	_____

71. Please indicate which of the following have been most influential in helping you understand the characteristics of PCD pupils and in shaping your current assessment practices for the identification of PCD children.

Check those which apply and indicate year of participation:

	I participated in (✔)	I was strongly influenced by (✔)	Most recent year of Participation
College or University degree program			
More recent non-degree course work at a College or University			
District inservice			
Other workshops: Specify _____			
CDE site visit			
Reading in professional journals			
Regional or national professional meeting			
A colleague's informal advice or consultation			
Other (Specify) _____			

A COLORADO SURVEY OF ATTITUDES AND PRACTICES FOR IDENTIFYING
PERCEPTUAL AND COMMUNICATIVE DISORDERS

Form E: Principals

Dear _____ :   Code # _____

    You are being asked to participate in a statewide study on the identification,
assessment, placement, and remediation of perceptual and communicative disordered
children in Colorado. The study was mandated by the Colorado Legislature and is
funded by the Colorado Department of Education. It is being conducted by faculty
and staff of the Laboratory of Educational Research, University of Colorado.

    Your district or BOCS is one of the 22 Special Education units selected at
random to be included. Your superintendent has been informed of our procedures
and permission to contact you directly has been obtained from the Director
of Special Education.

    Our purpose in sending you this questionnaire is to adequately describe the
perceptions of Colorado principals about the PCD identification process. Your
name was selected at random from principals in the participating districts.
While participation is voluntary, we urgently need your response to represent
those of other principals who were not chosen themselves.

    The following questionnaire should take about 35 minutes to complete. The
questions deal with procedures used in assessing and identifying PCD children.
If there are any questions that you would prefer not to answer, you may omit
them. Although you may not benefit directly from the study, it is hoped that
special education will benefit, particularly if the study leads to improved
definitions of PCD and Department of Education guidelines for identifying such
children.

    Your name should appear only on the first sheet. Your name will be removed
from the questionnaire and destroyed. Data will be analyzed only with your
code number and all information will be completely confidential. We need your
name only so that we can follow up on nonrespondents.

    Dr. Lorrie Shepard, the director of the study, will be glad to answer any
questions you might have. She may be contacted at 492-8108. Also, the Director
of Special Education in your district or BOCS attended a workshop where the
purposes and procedures of the study were discussed.

    Questions concerning your rights as a subject may be directed to the
Human Research Committee at the Graduate School of the University of Colorado;
upon request you may obtain a copy of this Institution's General Assurance
from the Human Research Committee Secretary, Graduate School, University of
Colorado, Boulder, CO 80309.

    Please complete the questionnaire as soon as possible. The follow-up of
nonrespondents will begin in about two weeks. Mail the completed questionnaire
in the envelope provided directly to Dr. Shepard at the Laboratory of Educational
Research, University of Colorado, Boulder 80309.

    Thank you very much for your time and cooperation.

A COLORADO SURVEY OF ATTITUDES AND PRACTICES FOR IDENTIFYING
PERCEPTUAL AND COMMUNICATIVE DISORDERS

Definition of Perceptual and Communicative Disorders

Do you agree or disagree with the following statements? Circle the number that best describes your opinion.

1 = Strongly Agree   2 = Agree   3 = Neutral or Undecided

4 = Disagree   5 = Strongly Disagree

1.* A PCD child can be distinguished from a slow learner.	Strongly Agree	1 2 3 4 5				Strongly Disagree
2.* PCD is an administrative way whereby non-retarded children can receive the help they need.	Strongly Agree	1 2 3 4 5				Strongly Disagree
3. Classroom teachers sometimes refer a child for evaluation as PCD simply because the child is the lowest in the class and not because he is disabled.	Strongly Agree	1 2 3 4 5				Strongly Disagree
4. The most important evidence that a child is PCD is that he is unable to function in the regular classroom.	Strongly Agree	1 2 3 4 5				Strongly Disagree
5. A child who is having academic problems but who is dominant in a language other than English should be excluded from PCD because linguistic differences probably explain the learning problems.	Strongly Agree	1 2 3 4 5				Strongly Disagree
6. A child who has been absent for more than 30 percent of the school days should not be identified as PCD since the missed instruction probably explains the severe deficit in achievement.	Strongly Agree	1 2 3 4 5				Strongly Disagree
7. The decision that a child is PCD is almost never influenced by whether or not there is a space for him or her in a resource room or self-contained class.	Strongly Agree	1 2 3 4 5				Strongly Disagree
8. In most cases when a staffing committee decides whether a child is PCD, they do not give enough consideration to whether classroom instruction might be what is causing his or her poor performance.	Strongly Agree	1 2 3 4 5				Strongly Disagree
9. PCD is something in the makeup of a child rather than the result of inappropriate instruction.	Strongly Agree	1 2 3 4 5				Strongly Disagree
10. In many cases moving a child from one teacher to another or from an "open-space" to a "closed-space" classroom is enough to remedy a mild or moderate perceptual or communicative disorder.	Strongly Agree	1 2 3 4 5				Strongly Disagree
11. What people refer to as PC disorders is really a condition that most children grow out of naturally.	Strongly Agree	1 2 3 4 5				Strongly Disagree
12. Many children are identified as PCD because they have behavioral or emotional problems rather than a neurological or perceptual problem that causes poor academic performance.	Strongly Agree	1 2 3 4 5				Strongly Disagree
13. Slow learners should be entitled to as much special education help as children who are diagnosed as having a perceptual or communicative handicap.	Strongly Agree	1 2 3 4 5				Strongly Disagree

*asterisked items were adapted from "a Survey of Attitudes Concerning Learning Disabilities" by
S. A. Kirk, P. B. Berry, and G. M. Senf in the Journal of Learning Disabilities, 1979, 12, 239-245.

14. In some schools principals are using resource rooms to relieve some of the pressure of class size in regular classrooms.
Strongly Agree   1   2   3   4   5   Strongly Disagree

15. Between initial referral and final placement of a potentially PCD child, every possible alternative is considered and tried, therefore almost all pupils who are eventually staffed are confirmed to be PCD.
Strongly Agree   1   2   3   4   5   Strongly Disagree

16. In my school, the mini-staffing (or assessment) team is very effective in eliminating cases who are not truly PCD. Therefore, a very large percentage of those who reach a final staffing are confirmed as PCD.
Strongly Agree   1   2   3   4   5   Strongly Disagree

17. If the general education budget could pay for remedial education, there would not be the need to place so many children as PCD.
Strongly Agree   .1   2   3   4   5   Strongly Disagree

18. Regular classroom teachers, if effectively trained, could teach all but the most severe PCD children.
Strongly Agree   1   2   3   4   5   Strongly Disagree

19. The present identification and staffing procedures leave too little discretion for the school principal to deal with the educational needs of children with PCD.
Strongly Agree   1   2   3   4   5   Strongly Disagree

20. In my school there is good cooperation between the classroom teachers and the PCD teachers over the education of a PCD child.
Strongly Agree   1   2   3   4   5   Strongly Disagree

21. It is up to the professionals (PCD teachers, psychologists, speech-language specialists) to decide what tests to give and how much time to spend in evaluating a potentially PCD child.
Strongly Agree   1   2   3   4   5   Strongly Disagree

22. The way the PCD identification and placement procedures now work results in few false designations of PCD, i.e. identifying a child as PCD who in reality has no handicap.
Strongly Agree   1   2   3   4   5   Strongly Disagree

23. The way the PCD identification and placement procedures now work results in few cases of overlooked diagnosis, i.e. failing to identify a child as PCD who in reality has such a handicap.
Strongly Agree   1   2   3   4   5   Strongly Disagree

24. Once the decision is made that a child has PCD, the PCD teacher is capable of designing an effective instructional program.
Strongly Agree   1   2   3   4   5   Strongly Disagree

25. In my opinion, many ethnic minority pupils who are perceptually-communicatively disordered are overlooked in the PCD identification and placement procedures of our district.
Strongly Agree   1   2   3   4   5   Strongly Disagree

26. How far below grade level should a child be to be diagnosed as having a PC disorder? (For example, if you think a first grader must be at least 6 months below grade level to be considered PCD, check 0.5 years.)

Years below grade level

	0.0 A PCD child does not have to be below grade level.	0.5	1.0	1.5	2.0	2.5
at grade 1						
at grade 3						
at grade 6						
at grade 9						
at grade 12						

27. Sometimes, the judgment of certain individuals is more important than test evidence in the identification and placement of pupils with PCD. In your opinion, do the following individuals have too much, too little, or the right amount of influence on the decision?

Check one blank in each row

	Too Much	Too Little	Right Amount	Don't Know
1. Pupil's parents	___	___	___	___
2. School principal	___	___	___	___
3. Psychologist	___	___	___	___
4. Outside evaluators	___	___	___	___
5. Classroom teacher	___	___	___	___
6. District spec. educ. administrators	___	___	___	___
7. Special education teacher	___	___	___	___
8. Speech/Lang. Specialist	___	___	___	___
9. Other_____	___	___	___	___
10. Other_____	___	___	___	___

28. Some parents have said that the presence of so many professional people at the staffing conference is intimidating. In your experience, have parents felt this intimidation?

Yes ___ No ___ Not sure ___

29. In what percent of cases (which reach formal staffing) are parent desires and pressures strongly influential in the decision regarding PCD placement?   _____ %

Please break down this percent into those who advocate and those who resist PCD placement. For example, if 10% of the cases are strongly influenced by parent desires, and of these half advocate PCD placement and half resist it, report 5% and 5%.

_____ % advocate PCD placement

_____ % resist PCD placement

30. Overall, how would you rate the validity of the PCD identification process as it is implemented in your school? (Circle the number which best reflects the degree of validity.)

1	2	3	4	5	6
Extremely valid		Moderately valid		Completely invalid	I don't feel qualified to judge the validity of the identification procedures

31. Nationally, there has been a trend in recent years for Special Education to require a larger proportion of the total education budget because more handicapped children are being identified and served.

Would you say that this trend has also occurred in your school district?

Yes _____ No _____

32. In your school, is there a need for greater resources for Special Education (e.g., more specialist teachers, psychologists or social workers) than you currently have available?

Yes _____ No _____

33. Would you prefer to see more or less allocation to Special Education from the following sources?

	More	Less	Should stay the same
Federal	___	___	___
State	___	___	___
Local District	___	___	___

Questions 34 and 35

We need to know your perception of the thoroughness and efficiency of the PCD identification process as it is currently implemented in your district. (Check one answer in each set of statements. The first set deals with accurate identification of PCD children; the second set deals with satisfying due process requirements. Due process refers to all those procedures that guarantee the rights of parents to understand each step in the identification process and provide their consent).

34. Set 1: Identification procedures are:

___ Not thorough enough to identify accurately a PCD child and wasteful of staff time.
___ Not thorough enough to identify accurately a PCD child but not wasteful of staff time.
___ About right in thoroughness and efficiency.
___ Thorough enough to identify accurately a PCD child and not wasteful of staff time.
___ Thorough enough but wasteful of staff time.

35. Set 2: Identification procedures are:

___ Not thorough enough to satisfy due process requirements and wasteful of staff time.
___ Not thorough enough to satisfy due process requirements but not wasteful of staff time.
___ About right in thoroughness and efficiency.
___ Thorough enough to satisfy due process requirements and not wasteful of staff time.
___ Thorough enough but wasteful of staff time.

Recommendations for changes in the state requirements or guidelines for the identification of PCD:

36. First, in order to improve the validity of the PCD identification process would you recommend that the requirements and guidelines be made:

_____ Stricter?   _____ Less strict?   _____ Be left unchanged?

37. Please give your specific suggestions for policy changes:

38. In your school, what is the approximate length in minutes of the average staffing meeting where PCD placement decisions are made (excluding time spent on the IEP)?

Average length: ___ mins.

39. What is the length of the shortest meeting? ___ mins.; the longest meeting? ___ mins.

40. What proportion of your time (using 40 hours as an arbitrary base rate) do you spend in or preparing for staffing meetings for PCD children?

___ average # of hours out of 40/per week

41. What is the average number of pupils in regular classes in your school? ___

42. What is the average number of pupils served at any one time,

in self-contained Special Education classes in your school   ___

in resource rooms in your school?   ___

43. Indicate how important the following factors are likely to be in your decision to recommend that a child be STAFFED OUT of PCD placement.

1 = Among the most critical factors
2 = Important, but not one of the most critical factors
3 = Positive sign, but not sufficient by itself
4 = Considered, but among the least important factors
5 = Not considered

Factors Affecting Decision to Staff out of PCD	Among Most Critical	Important	Positive Sign	Among Least Important	Not Considered
Test results show that the child no longer has a significant discrepancy between ability & achievement.	1	2	3	4	5
Test results show that the child no longer has any discrepancy between ability and achievement.	1	2	3	4	5
Test results show that academic performance has been brought up to grade level.	1	2	3	4	5
In the teacher's judgment academic performance has been brought up to grade level.	1	2	3	4	5
Instructional goals set on the IEP have been attained.	1	2	3	4	5
Test results show elimination of processing disorders which were present initially.	1	2	3	4	5
In the teacher's judgment, processing deficits have been sufficiently reduced so they no longer interfere with classroom performance.	1	2	3	4	5
Reduction of behavior problems such as inattention or hyperactivity.	1	2	3	4	5
The teacher's judgment about ability to function in the regular classroom without further help.	1	2	3	4	5

<u>Background Information of Respondent</u>

44. Type of School: Elementary ____
Middle School ____
Junior High School ____
High School ____

45. In selecting you for this survey, we have identified you as a school principal. Is this classification correct for the 1980-81 school year? Yes ____ No ____ If this classification is incorrect, please indicate your current role.

46. How many years have you held this kind of position? State the nearest <u>whole</u> number of years and count this year (80-81) as one year.

Number of years: ____ in this district

____ in Colorado, other than in this district

____ outside of Colorado

____ Total number of years of experience in this kind of position

47. In addition to the years reported above, how many years of experience have you had in other educational positions?

____ years.

48. Please indicate below the academic degrees you have earned; and for each degree indicate the year the degree was earned and the institution (college or university) that awarded the degree.

<u>Degree</u>	<u>Year</u>	<u>Institution</u>
Bachelors	____	_____
Masters	____	_____
Specialist	____	_____
Doctorate	____	_____

REFERENCES

Abeson, A.; Burgdorf, R. L. Jr.; Casey, P. J.; Kunz, J. W.; and McNeil, W. Access to Opportunity. In N. Hobbs (Ed.), *Issues in the Classification of the Children, V. II.* San Francisco: Jossey-Bass, 1975.

Anastasi, Anne. *Differential Psychology.* New York: Macmillan, 1958.

Arnold, I. E. Is this Label Necessary? *Journal of School Health,* 1973, *23,* 510-514.

Arter, J. A. and Jenkins, J. R. Differential Diagnosis--Prescriptive Teaching: A Critical Appraisal. *Review of Educational Research,* 1979, *49,* 517-555.

Ayers, A. J. Deficits in Sensory Integration In Educationally Handicapped Children. *Journal of Learning Disabilities,* 1969, *2,* 160-168.

Ayers, A. J. Improving Academic Scores through Sensory Integration. *Journal of Learning Disabilities,* 1972, *5,* 338-342.

Becker, H. S. *Outsiders: Studies in the Sociology of Deviance.* Glencoe, Ill.: Free Press, 1963.

Becker, H. S. Whose Side are We On? *Social Problems,* 1967, *14,* 239-247.

Belmont, I. Perceptual Organization and Minimal Brain Dysfunction. In H. E. Rie and E. D. Rie (Eds.), *Handbook of Minimal Brain Dysfunction.* New York: John Wiley & Sons, 1980.

Belmont, L. Epidemiology. In H. E. Rie and E. D. Rie (Eds.), *Handbook of Minimal Brain Dysfunction.* New York: John Wiley & Sons, 1980.

Berry, M. F. *Language Disorders of Children.* New York: Appleton-Century-Crofts, 1969.

Blaschke, C. Case Study of the Implementation of P. L. 94-142 (Final Report). Washington, D. C.: Education Turnkey Systems, Inc., 1979. Cited in *To Assure the Free Appropriate Public Education of All Handicapped Children*, U.S. Department of Education, 1980.

Blatt, B. The Legal Rights of the Mentally Retarded. *Syracuse Law Review*, 1972, *23*, 991-993.

Blumer, H. Social Problems as Collective Behavior. *Social Problems*, 1971, *18*, 298-305.

Bryan, T. and Bryan, J. H. Learning Disorders. In H. E. Rie and E. D. Rie (Eds.), *Handbook of Minimal Brain Dysfunction.* New York: John Wiley & Sons, 1980.

Burt, R. A. Judicial Action to Aid the Retarded. In N. Hobbs (Ed.), *Issues in the Classification of Children, Vol. II.* San Francisco: Jossey-Bass, 1975.

Buss, W. G.; Kirp, D. L.; and Kuriloff, P. J. Exploring Procedural Modes of Special Classification. In N. Hobbs (Ed.), *Issues in the Classification of Children, Vol. II.* San Francisco: Jossey-Bass, 1975.

Cantwell, D. P. Drugs and Medical Intervention. In H. E. Rie and E. D. Rie (Eds.), *Handbook of Minimal Brain Dysfunctions.* New York: John Wiley & Sons, 1980.

Christenson, S.; Graden, J.; Potter, M.; Taylor, J.; Yanowitz, B.; and Ysseldyke, J.E. Current Research on Psychological Assessment and Decision-Making: Implications for Training and Practice. *Monograph No. 16.* Minneapolis: University of Minnesota Institute for Research on Learning Disabilities, 1981.

Clements, S. D. *Minimal Brain Dysfunction in Children—Terminology and Identification* (USPHS Publication No. 1415). Washington, D.C.: U.S. Government Printing Office, 1966.

Coles, G. S. The Learning-Disabilities Test Battery: Empirical and Social Issues. *Harvard Educational Review*, 1978, *48*, 313-340.

Craig, P. A. Counting Handicapped Children: A Federal Imperative. *Journal of Education Finance,* 1976, *1,* 318-333.

Craig, P. A., Kaskowitz, D. H., and Malgoire, M. A. Studies of Handicapped Students, Vol. II: Teacher Identification of Handicapped Pupils (ages 6-11) Compared with Identification Using Other Indicators. *SRI Research Report EPRC 4537-11.* Menlo Park, CA: SRI International, 1978.

Craig, P. A., and McEachron, N. B. The Development and Analysis of Base Line Data for the Estimation of Incidence in the Handicapped School Age Population. *Research Note 19.* Menlo Park, CA: SRI International, 1975.

Denzin, N. K. The Logic of Naturalistic Inquiry. *Social Forces,* 1971, *50,* 166-182.

Devereux, G. *From Anxiety to Method in the Behavioral Sciences.* The Hague, Netherlands: Mouton & Co., 1967.

Dreger, R. A Progress Report on a Factor Analytic Approach to Classification in Child Psychiatry. In J. Jenkins and J. Cole (Eds.), *Research Report No. 18.* Washington, D.C.: American Psychiatric Association, 1964.

"Estimating the Costs of Equity: The 'Resource-Cost Model'". *Institute for Research on Educational Finance and Governance,* 1981, *2,* 5-6.

Franks, D. J. Ethnic and Social Status Characteristics of Children in EMH and LD Classes. *Exceptional Children,* 1971, *37,* 537.

Friedson, E. *Professional Dominance: The Social Structure of Medical Care.* New York: Atherton, 1970.

Frostig, M. The Relationship of Diagnosis to Remediation in Learning Problems. *Learning Disabilities: Selected ACLD Papers.* Boston: Houghton Mifflin Company, 1975.

Geertz, C. *The Interpretation of Cultures.* New York: Basic Books, 1973.

Glaser, B. G. and Strauss, A. L. *The Discovery of Grounded Theory.* Chicago: Aldine, 1967.

Gofman, H. The Physician's Role in Early Diagnsois and Management of Learning Disabilities. In L. Tarnopol (Ed.), *Learning Disabilities.* Springfield, Ill: Charles C. Thomas, 1969.

Gold, R. L. Roles in Sociological Field Observations. *Social Forces,* 1958, *36,* 217-223.

Goldberg, L. R. Simple Models or Simple Processes? Some Research on Clinical Judgment. *American Psychologist,* 1968, *23,* 483-496.

Grossman, H. J. The Child, the Teacher and the Physician. In W. Cruickshank (Ed.), *The Teacher of Brain-Injured Children: A Discussion of the Basis for Competency.* Syracuse, N.Y.: Syracuse University Press, 1966.

Hammill, D. D. and Larsen, S. C. The Effectiveness of Psycholinguistic Training. *Exceptional Children,* 1974, *41,* 5-14.

Hobbs, N. *The Futures of Children.* San Francisco: Jossey-Bass, 1975.

House, E. R. *Evaluating With Validity.* Beverly Hills: SAGE, 1980.

House, E. R. The Objectivity, Fairness, and Justice of Federal Evaluation Policy as Reflected in the Follow Through Evaluation. *Educational Evaluation and Policy Analysis,* 1979, *1,* 28-42.

Kahneman, D. and Tversky, A. On the Psychology of Prediction. *Psychological Review,* 1973, *80,* 237-251.

Kakalik, J. S. Issues in the Cost and Finance of Special Education. In D. C. Berliner (Ed.), *Review of Research in Education, Vol. 7.* Washington, D. C.: American Educational Research Association, 1979.

Kanfer, F. and Phillips, J. *Learning Foundations of Behavior Therapy*, New York: John Wiley & Sons, 1970.

Kavale, K. A. Learning Disability and Cultural-Economic Disadvantage: The Case for A Relationship. *Learning Disabilities Quarterly*, 1980, 3, 97-112.

Kavale, K. and Mattson, P. D. "One Jumped Off the Balance Beam": Meta-Analysis of Perceptual-Motor Training. Riverside, CA: University of California School of Education, 1980 (offset).

Kephart, N. C. Perceptual-Motor Problems of Children. *Learning Disabilities: Selected ACLD Papers.* Boston: Houghton Mifflin Company, 1975.

Kessler, J. W. History of Minimal Brain Dysfunctions. In H. E. Rie and E. D. Rie (Eds.), *Handbook of Minimal Brain Dysfunction.* New York: John Wiley & Sons, 1980.

Kirk, S. A.; Berry, P. B.; and Senf, G. M. A Survey of Attitudes Concerning Learning Disabilities. *Journal of Learning Disabilities*, 1979, 12, 34-40.

Kirk, S. A. and McCarthy, J. M. *Learning Disabilities: Selected ACLD Papers.* Boston: Houghton Mifflin, 1975.

Kirp, D. L.; Kuriloff, P. J., and Buss, W. G. Legal Mandates and Organizational Change. In N. Hobbs (Ed.), *Issues in the Classification of Children, Vol. II*, San Francisco: Jossey-Bass, 1975.

Klaus, M. H. and Kennel, J. H. Mothers Separated from Their Newborn Infants. *Pediatric Clinic of North America*, 1970, 17, 1015-1037.

Landsdell, H. Theories of Brain Mechanisms in Minimal Brain Dysfunctions. In H. E. Rie and E. D. Rie (Eds.), *Handbook of Minimal Brain Dysfunction.* New York: John Wiley & Sons, 1980.

Lerer, R. J. An Open Letter to an Occupational Therapist. *Journal of Learning Disabilities*, 1981, 14, 3-4.

Lerner, J. W. *Children with Learning Disabilities* (Second Edition). Boston: Houghton Mifflin Company, 1976.

Levine, M. D.; Brooks, R.; and Shonkoff, J. P. *A Pediatric Approach to Learning Disorders.* New York: John Wiley & Sons, 1980.

Liaison Bulletin. A Publication of NASDSE, Inc., 1201 Sixteenth Street N.W., Suite 610 E, Washington, D. C. 20036, 1981, Vol. 7, #12, pp. 1-6.

Light, Donald, *Becoming Psychiatrists.* New York: W. W. Norton and Company, 1980.

Lortie, D. C. *Schoolteacher.* Chicago: University of Chicago Press, 1975.

Lumsden, J. Review--Illinios Test of Psycholinguistic Abilities. *The Eighth Mental Measurement Yearbook.* Highland Park, N.J.: The Gryphon Press, 1978.

Lynn, R. *Learning Disabilities: An Overview of Theories, Approaches, and Politics.* New York: The Free Press, 1979.

MacMillan, D. L. and Meyers, C. E. Educational Labeling of Handicapped Learners. In D. C. Berliner (Ed.), *Review of Research in Education,* Vol. 7. Washington, D. C.: American Educational Research Association, 1979.

McCarthy, J. J. and McCarthy, J. F. Learning Disabilities. Boston: Allyn and Bacon, Inc., 1969.

Meehl, P. *Clinical versus Statistical Prediction.* Minneapolis: University of Minnesota Press, 1954.

Meier, J. H. Prevalence and Characteristics of Learning Disabilities in Second Grade Children. *Journal of Learning Disabilities,* 1971, 4, 1-16.

Meldman, M. J.; Wellhausen, M.; and Jacobson, J. *Occupational Therapy Manual.* Springfield, Ill: Charles C. Thomas, 1969.

Mercer, J. R. *Labeling the Mentally Retarded.* Berkeley: University of California Press, 1973.

Mercer, J. R. Protection in Evaluation Procedures. *Developing Criteria for the Evaluation of Protection in Evaluation Procedures Provisions.* Philadelphia: Research for Better Schools, Inc., 1979.

Mercer, J. and Ysseldyke, J. E. Designing Diagnostic-Intervention Programs. In T. Oakland (Ed.), *Psychological and Educational Assessment of Minority Children.* New York: Brunner-Mazel, 1977.

Miller, G. A. The Magical Number Seven, Plus or Minus Two: Some Limits on Our Capacity for Processing Information. *Psychological Bulletin,* 1956, 63, 81-97.

Morra, L. G. Introduction. *Developing Criteria for the Evaluation of Individualized Education Program Provisions.* Philadelphia: Research for Better Schools, 1979.

Moynihan, D. P. State vs. Academe: Nationalizing the Universities. *Harper's,* 1980, 261, 31-40.

Myers, P. I. and Hammill, D. D. *Methods for Learning Disorders* (2nd Edition). New York: John Wiley & Sons, Inc., 1976.

Myklebust, H. R.; Killen, J.; and Bannochie, M. Learning Disabilities and Cognitive Processes. In H. R. Myklebust (Ed.), *Progress in Learning Disabilities, Vol. II,* New York: Grune and Stratton, 1971.

Newcomer, P. L. and Hammill, D. D. *Psycholinguistics in the Schools.* Columbus, Ohio: Charles E. Merrill Publishing, 1976.

Nystrom, R. O. and Staub, W. F. The Courts as Educational Policymakers. In C. P. Hooker (Ed.), *The Courts in Education: The Seventy-Seventh Yearbook of the National Society for the Study of Education.* Chicago: The University of Chicago Press, 1978.

Orton, S. T. *Reading, Writing, and Speech Problems in Children.* New York: Norton, 1937.

Paine, R. S.; Wherry, J. S.; and Quay, H. C. A Study of Minimal Cerebral Dysfunction." *Developmental Medicine and Child Neurology,* 1968, *10,* 505-520.

"Paralegal an Angel to State's Handicapped." *The Denver Post,* 1981.

Paternite, C. E.; Loney, J.; and Langhorne, J. E. Relationships Between Symptomatology and SES-related Factors in Hyperkinetic/MBD Boys. *American Journal of Orthopsychiatry,* 1976, *46,* 291-301.

Peterson, C. R. and Beach, L. R. Man as an Intuitive Statistician. *Psychological Bulletin,* 1967, *68,* 29-46.

Poulton, E. C. the New Psychophysics: Six Models for Magnitude Estimation. *Psychological Bulletin,* 1968, *69,* 1-19.

"Progress Toward a Free Appropriate Public Education. A Report to Congress on the Implementation of Public Law 94-142," U.S. Office of Education, January, 1979.

Pyecha, J. A Natinal Survey of Individualized Education Programs (IEPs) for Handicapped Children. Research Triangle Park, NC: Research Triangle Institute, 1979.

Rains, P. M.; Kitsuse, J. J.; Duster, T.; and Friedson, E. The Labeling Approach to Deviance. In N. Hobbs (Ed.), *Issues in the Classification of Children (Vol. 1),* San Francisco: Jossey-Bass, 1975.

Rebell, M. A. and Block, A. R. Educational Policy-Making and the Courts. *Final Report.* NIE Contract #400-77-0011, 1979.

Reed, H. C. B., Jr. Southern Calfornia Sensory Integration Tests. *The Eighth Mental Measurements Yearbook.* Highland Park, N.J.: Gryphon Press, 1978.

Rie, H. E. Definitional Problems. In H. E. Rie and E. D. Rie (Eds.), *Handbook of Minimal Brain Dysfunction.* New York: John Wiley & Sons, 1980.

Rodin, E.; Lucas, A.; and Simson, C. A Study of Behavior Disorders in Children by Means of General Purpose Computers. In K. Enslein (Ed.), *Proceedings of the 1963 Rochester Conference on Data Acquisition and Processing in Biology and Medicine* (Vol. 3). New York: Pergamon Press, 1963.

Routh, D. K. Developmental and Social Aspects of Hyperactivity. In C. K. Whalen and B. Henker (Eds.), *Hyperactive Children.* New York: Academic Press, 1980.

Routh, D. K., and Roberts, R. D. Minimal Brain Dysfunction in Children: Failure to Find Evidence for a Behavioral Syndrome. *Psychological Reports,* 1972, *31,* 307-314.

Rutter, M.; Tizard, J.; and Whitmore, K. *Education, Health, and Behavior.* London: Longman, 1970.

Ryan, W. *Blaming the Victim.* New York: Vintage, 1972.

Sadler, R. Intuitive Data Processing as a Potential Source of Bias in Naturalistic Evaluations, *Educational Evaluation and Policy Analysis,* 1981, *3,* 25-31.

Salvia, J. and Ysseldyke, J. E. *Assessment in Special and Remedial Education.* Boston: Houghton Mifflin, 1981.

Sarason, S. and Doris, J. Mainstreaming: Dilemmas, Opposition, Opportunities. In M. C. Reynolds (Ed.), *Futures of Education for Exceptional Children: Emerging Structures.* Reston, VA: Council for Exceptional Children, 1978.

Satz, P. and Fletcher, J. M. Minimal Brain Dysfunctions: An Appraisal of Research Concepts and Methods. In H. E. Rie and E. D. Rie (Eds.), *Handbook of Minimal Brain Dysfunction.* New York: John Wiley & Sons, 1980.

Schrag, P. and Divoky, D. *The Myth of the Hyperactive Child.* New York: Dell Publishing, A Laurel Edition, 1975.

Schumaker, J. B.; Warner, M. M.; Deshler, D. D.; and Alley, G. R. *An Epidemiological Study of Learning Disabled Adolescents in Secondary Schools: Details of the Methodology.* Lawrence, Kansas: Institute for Research in Learning Disabilities, University of Kansas, 1980 (offset).

Shepard, L. A. Validity of Tests Used to Diagnose Learning Disabilities. Unpublished paper. Boulder, CO: Laboratory of Educational Research, University of Colorado, 1979 (offset).

Shepard, L. A.; Smith, M. L.; Davis A.; Glass, G. V.; Riley, A.; and Vojir, C. *Evaluation of the Identification of Perceptual-Communicative Disorders in Colorado.* Boulder, CO: Laboratory of Educational Research, University of Colorado, 1981 (offset).

Sieben, R. L. Controversial Medical Treatment of Learning Disabilities. *Academic Therapy,* 1977, *13,* 133-147.

Silverman, L. J. and Metz, A. S. Numbers of Pupils with Specific Learning Disabilities in Local Public Schools in the United States: Spring 1970. In F. F. dela Cruz, B. H. Fox, and R. H. Roberts (Eds.), *Minimal Brain Dysfunction.* New York: New York Academy of Sciences, 1973.

Siqueland, E. R. Biological and Experimental Determinants of Exploration in Infancy. In L. F. Stone, H. T. Smith, and L. B. Murphy (Eds.), *The Competent Infant.* New York: Basic Books, 1973.

Smedslund, J. The Concept of Correlation in Adults. *Scandinavian Journal of Psychology,* 1963, *4,* 165-173.

Solkoff, N.; Yaffe, S.; Weintraub, D.; and Blase, B. Effects of Handling on the Subsequent Development of Premature Infants. *Developmental Psychology,* 1969, *1,* 765-768.

Smith, L. M. An Evolving Logic of Participant Observation, Educational Ethnography, and Other Case Studies. In Shulman, L. (Ed.), *Review of Research in Education*. Chicago: Peacock Press, 1979.

Stearns, M. S.; Green, D.; and David, J. L. Local Implementation of P.L. 94-142. (Draft Year 1 Report.) Menlo Park, CA: SRI International, 1979.

Stearns, M.; Norwood, C.; Kaskowitz, D. and Mitchell, S. Validation of State Counts of Handicapped Children, Vol. 2. Menlo Park, CA: SRI International, 1977.

Strauss, A. A. and Lehtinen, L. E. *Psychopathology and Education of the Brain-Injured Child,* 2 Vols., New York: Grune & Stratton, 1947.

Summers, D. A.; Taliaferro, J. D.; and Fletcher, D. J. Subjective vs. Objective Description of Judgment Policy. *Psychonomic Science,* 1970, *18,* 249-250.

"To Assure the Free Appropriate Education of All Handicapped Children," Second Annual Report to Congress on the Implementation of Public Law 94-142: The Education for All Handicapped Chidren Act. U.S. Department of Education, 1980.

Tversky, A. and Kahneman, D. Belief in the Law of Small Numbers. *Psychological Bulletin,* 1971, *76,* 105-110.

Tversky, A. and Kahneman, D. Judgment Under Uncertainty: Heuristics and Biases. *Science,* 1974, *185,* 1124-1131.

Unanswered Questions on Educating Handicapped Children in Local Public Schools. *HRD-81-43.* Washington, D.C.: U.S. General Accounting Office, 1981.

Valett, R. E. *The Remediation of Learning Disabilities: A Handbook of Psychoeducational Resource Programs.* Palo Alto, CA: Fearon Publishers, 1967.

Wason, P. C. On the Failure to Eliminate Hypotheses: A Second Look. In P. C. Wason and P. N. Johnson-Laird (Eds.), *Thinking and Reasoning*. Baltimore: Penguin Books, 1968.

Weatherley, R. A. *Reforming Special Education*. Cambridge, MA: The MIT Press, 1979.

Webb, E. J.; Campbell, D. T.; Schwartz, R. D. and Secrest L. *Unobtrusive Measures: Nonreactive Research in the Social Sciences*. Chicago: Rand-McNally, 1966.

Weiner, P. S. Development Language Disorders. In H. E. Rie and E. D. Rie (Eds.), *Handbook of Minimal Brain Dysfunction*. New York: John Wiley & Sons, 1980.

Werner, E. E. Environmental Interaction in Minimal Brain Dysfunctions. In H. E. Rie and E. D. Rie (Eds.), *Handbook of Minimal Brain Dysfunctions*. New York: John Wiley & Sons, 1980.

Werner, E. E.; Bierman, J. M.; and French, F. E. *The Children of Kauai: A Longitudinal Study from the Prenatal Period to Age Ten*. Honolulu: University Press of Hawaii, 1971.

Werner, E. E. and Smith, R. S. *Kauai's Children Come of Age*. Honolulu: University Press of Hawaii, 1977.

Werry, J. S. Studies on the Hyperactive Child, IV. An Emperical Analysis of the Minimum Brain Dysfunction Syndrome. *Archives of General Psychiatry*, 1968, *19*, 9-16.

Williams, D. *Understanding the Work of Naturalistic Researchers*, Unpublished doctoral disseratation, University of Colorado, 1980.

Wise, A. E. *Legislated Learning*. Berkeley: University of California Press, 1979.

Wolcott, H. F. *Teachers vs. Technocrats*. Eugene, Oregon: Center for Educational Policy and Management, 1977.

Ysseldyke, J. E. Current Issues in the Assessment of Learning Disabled Children and Some Proposed Approaches to Appropriate Use of Assessment Information. Paper presented at the Bureau of Education for the Handicapped Conference on Assessment in Learning Disabilities, Atlanta, May, 1977.

Ysseldyke, J. E. Implementing the "Protection in Evaluation Procedures" Provisions of 94-142. *Developing Criteria for the Evaluation of Protection in Evaluation Procedures Provisions.* Philadelphia: Research for Better Schools, Inc., 1979.

Ysseldyke, J. E.; Algozinne, B; Regan, R. R.; Potter, M.; Richey, L.; and Thurlow, M. Psychoeducational Assessment and Decision-Making: A Computer Simulated Investigation. *Research Report No. 32*, Minneapolis: University of Minnesota Institute for Research on Learning Disabilities, 1980.

Ysseldyke, J. E.; Algozzine, B.; Shinn, M.; and McGue, M. Similarities and Differences Between Underachievers and Students Labeled Learning Disabled: Identical Twins with Different Mothers. *Research Report No. 13.* Minneapolis: University of Minnesota Institute for Research on Learning Disabilities, 1979.

Ysseldyke, J. E.; Algozzine, B.; and Thurlow, M. A Naturalistic Investigation of Special Education Team Meetings. *Research Report No. 40,* Minneapolis: University of Minnesota Institute for Research on Learning Disabilities, 1980.

Zettel, J. J. and Abeson, A. The Right to a Free Appropriate Public Education. In C. P. Hooker (Ed.), *The Courts in Education: The Seventy-Seventh Yearbook of the National Society for the Study of Education.* Chicago: The University of Chicago Press, 1978.